IMAGES
of America

PLYMOUTH COUNTY

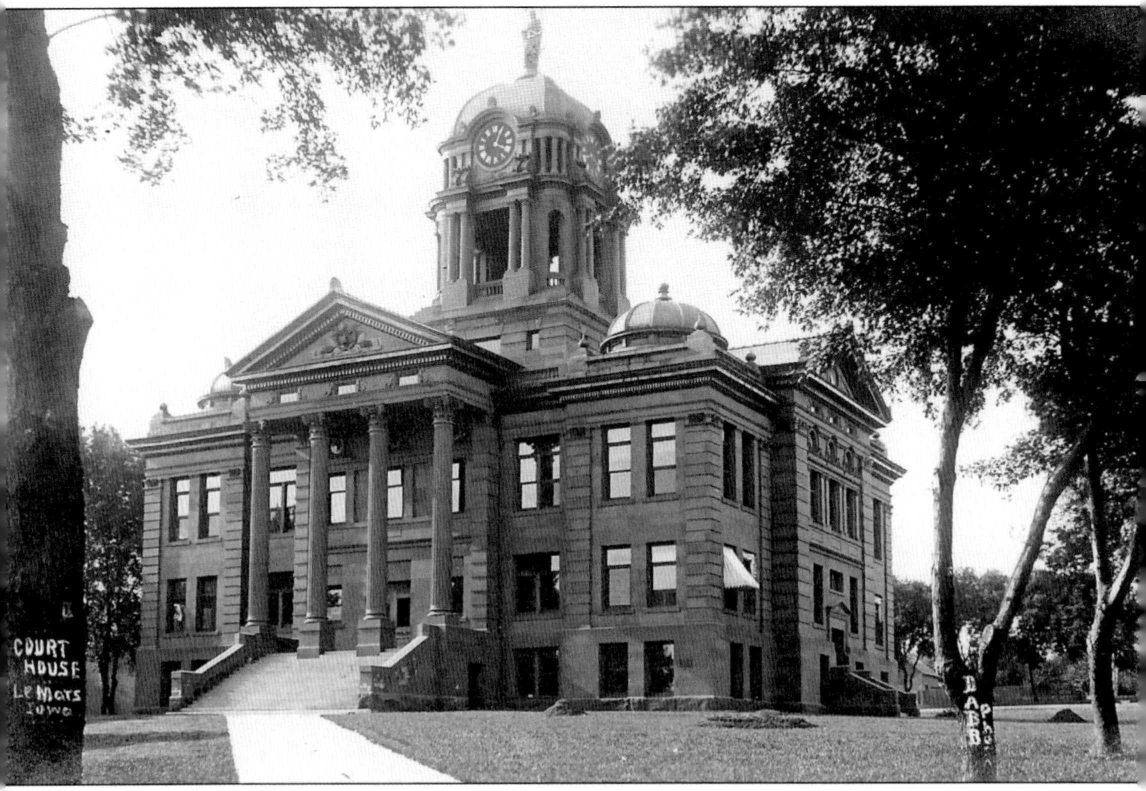

The Plymouth County Courthouse was built in 1901 and occupied in the summer of 1902. The new courthouse was constructed of red portage entry stone, which contained a deep rich red hue and lasting durability. The building was 76 by 98 feet in dimension, and its greatest height was 108 feet from the grade to the top of the tower. On the top of the tower was the female figure of Justice, standing 13 feet high. (Courtesy Plymouth County Historical Museum.)

On the cover: Please see page 61. (Courtesy Vernon and Karen Harrington.)

IMAGES
of America

PLYMOUTH COUNTY

Linda Ewin Ziemann

ARCADIA
PUBLISHING

ISBN 978-0-7385-6083-0

Published by Arcadia Publishing
Charleston, South Carolina

Printed in the United States of America

Library of Congress Control Number: 2009920611

For all general information contact Arcadia Publishing at:
Telephone 843-853-2070
Fax 843-853-0044
E-mail sales@arcadiapublishing.com
For customer service and orders:
Toll-Free 1-888-313-2665

Visit us on the Internet at www.arcadiapublishing.com

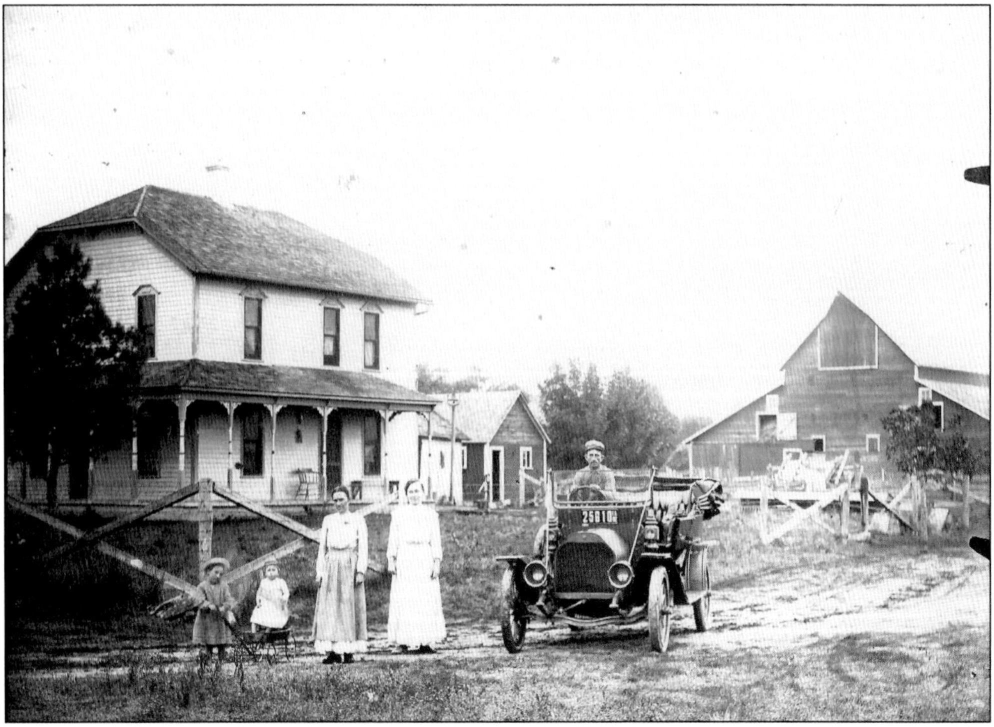

A Plymouth County farm family is standing directly in front of the two-story farmhouse. Proudly, the papa farmer sits in his open convertible car, while the two children and two adult females stand at attention for the picture. (Courtesy Plymouth County Historical Museum.)

Contents

ACKNOWLEDGMENTS

The idea of this Plymouth County pictorial history book project appeared to be an impossible task to accomplish sitting at my computer in my home in north Texas. I began making telephone calls and sending e-mails requesting advice and assistance. The book has become a reality because so many dear friends and dedicated folks have answered my call for help.

Huge thanks go to the Plymouth County Historical Museum in Le Mars, Iowa. Many of the vintage photographs were located in the archives at the museum during several visits that I made to Le Mars this year. I am indebted to the museum staff for allowing the loan of photographs for scanning. Thanks to my friend Mary Holub in Le Mars, for her diligence in scanning the pictures, and for keeping an eye peeled for good photographs as the months passed. She found pictures, scanned them, and placed them on a flash drive, and mailed it to me in Texas.

I am grateful also to Vernon and Karen Harrington of Plymouth County. They provided the original photograph to the publisher for scanning and use for the cover. The Brunsville Booster photograph was found in the personal Harrington collection.

One of my former classmates from the class of 1966 at Le Mars High School has also been diligent with wonderful ideas and photographs to consider. Tim Tone deserves more than honorable mention. Tim came through with another flash drive in the mail and fabulous images. Tim's sweet, 91-year-old mother, Dorothy Locer Tone, also provided some help with detail and identity.

There are many others who sent photographs and offered help. Their names will be in parentheses at the end of each caption on the pages of this book. I thank you one and all.

A special thanks, also, to my husband and family for seeing me through this book project process. My 84-year-old dad, who was raised in Plymouth County, endured my questions and always came through with answers.

God bless each of you as we look forward to the future and treasure the past! This book is dedicated to anyone who has ever called Plymouth County his or her home.

INTRODUCTION

Plymouth County is one of the largest counties in Iowa. There are three main river valleys (Little Sioux, Big Sioux, and the Floyd River) that flow through the county. Imagine observing this county in the early years. It was mile after mile of long prairie grass blowing in a pattern that resembled ocean waves. Trees were scarce until farmers began planting them for windbreaks. The early pioneers made this observation, "if you stared long enough at the open prairie, it would stare back at you!"

The first white settlers arrived in 1856 and began the work to establish the communities of Westfield and Melbourne in that same year. The first settlers were from Germany, Luxembourg, and Ireland. The state legislature designated the region as a county. The new county was formed from a part of Woodbury and called Plymouth. The bordering counties were the same in the early days as they are today, with Woodbury County on the south, Cherokee County to the east, Sioux County to the north, and the Big Sioux River on the west. In 1859, Melbourne was chosen as the county seat.

The town of Le Mars was founded in 1869, when the railroad construction reached Le Mars from Sioux City on October 1, 1869. The town name was derived from the first initials of five women who visited the site with a railroad official. The new railroad bypassed Melbourne. The county seat was moved to Le Mars in 1872. The citizens of Le Mars called it "the gateway" to the northwest. Le Mars began thriving as a trade and cultural center of its day. It was truly a gateway to the richest farmlands in the country.

This Plymouth County book portrays a broad overview of the story of the county in early photographs. The history of this county began with early settlers who pioneered and persevered decade after decade, making their living from the soil. Life on the new land and prairie did not come without a price. Sacrifices had to be made. The early settlers forged ahead and endured the struggles so that they and the next generations would have a better life.

Many families lost so much, including the crops to grasshoppers, prairie fires, disasters striking their farms, and the loss of children to disease. Buried today under the Plymouth County sod are many who never had a good start to life, others died young of uncontrollable disease, even others died in adulthood after hard work and little substance to continue.

It is documented that in 1860 the first religious congregation was formed in Plymouth County. People gathered together in homes, forming the first United Evangelical Church at Melbourne. That trend continued in the years ahead. Many other church congregations sprang up throughout the county. Those churches were filled with people who turned to God, thanking him for the good times and trusting him for the ability to withstand the hard struggles of early farm life.

Many different denominations are now represented in present-day Plymouth County. Faith in God has been the cornerstone of survival since the early log cabin days. God has always been supreme, and God will continue to be the hope for the future.

This pictorial history book is a story of the county told in the pictures that have been submitted. As you turn the pages ahead, you will be viewing a broad cross-section of photographs. Over 200 pictures were submitted for consideration. These pictures were categorized and divided into chapters for the sake of content. Not every facet of the county history is addressed in the photographs. Other gifted county historians have already done an excellent job of telling the Plymouth County history in other published and nonpublished writings. Those are excellent sources for detail. This book is intended to be just a sampling of the county history in photographs, stretching from the early prairie to present-day Plymouth County.

The last chapter contains randomly submitted photographs of county people through the years. There are wonderful pictures of early people and beautiful children, representing all our ancestors and the life they lived in Plymouth County. Perhaps you will catch a glimpse of an ancestor or someone from a family that you knew in an earlier time.

One

PRAIRIE PIONEERS AND THE COMING OF THE RAILROAD

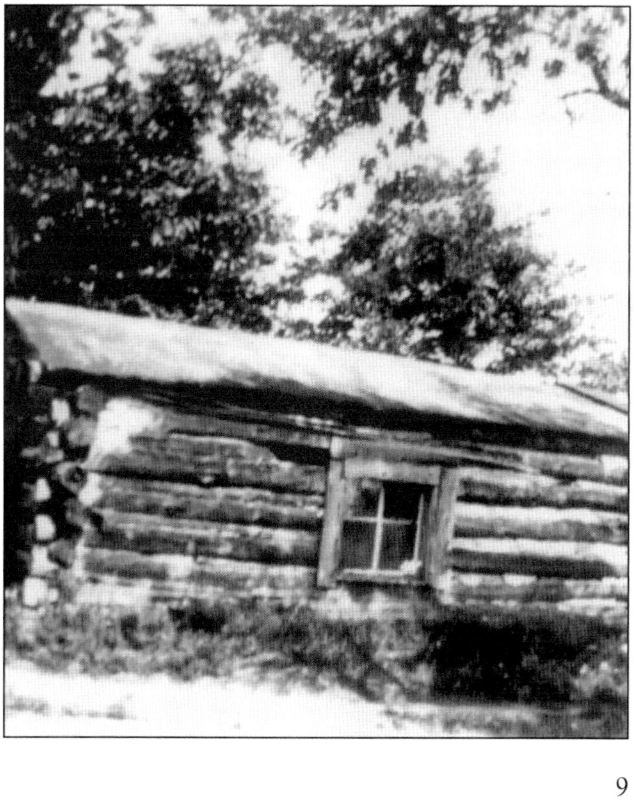

The Winter family log cabin was constructed in 1856, located on the bank of a creek in Plymouth Township. Dietrich Winter Sr. was part of the first band of white permanent settlers in 1856. At the time of their settlement, Plymouth County was part of Woodbury County. A group of 28 settlers originally from Germany settled in the Floyd River valley, at the early settlement known as Melbourne. Because of their success, the first Plymouth County seat was located in Melbourne until 1872. (Courtesy Justin Herbst.)

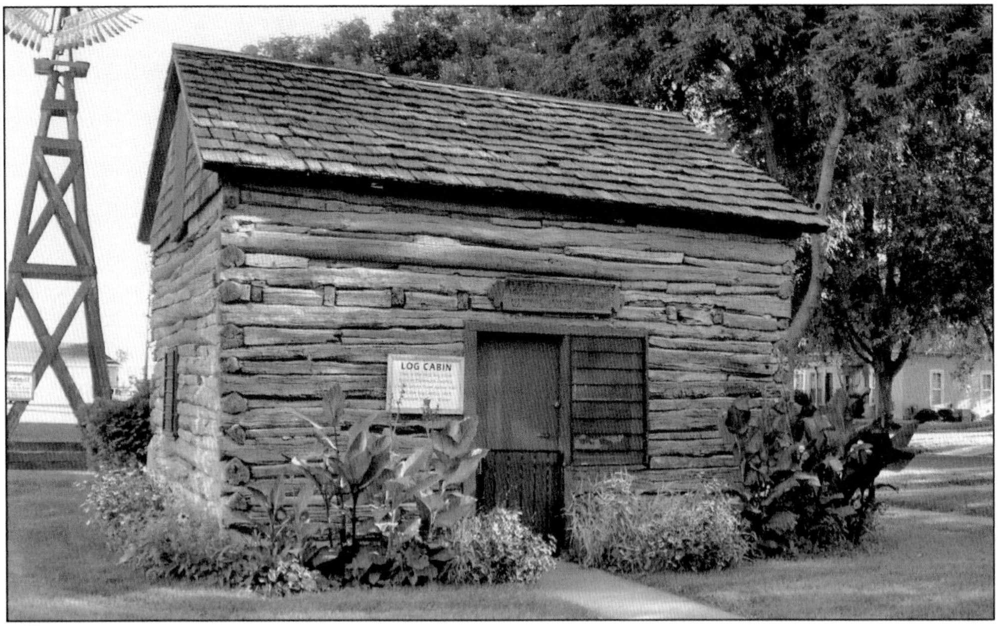

The early farmers of Plymouth County, for the most part, bypassed the sod house stage of settlement and built log cabins. The log cabin in this photograph is on exhibit at the Plymouth County Historical Museum in Le Mars. This is the first log cabin built in the newly formed Plymouth County, constructed from native oak and elm logs about 1865. The cabin was donated to the museum by O. L. Webber in 1966. (Courtesy Linda Ewin Ziemann.)

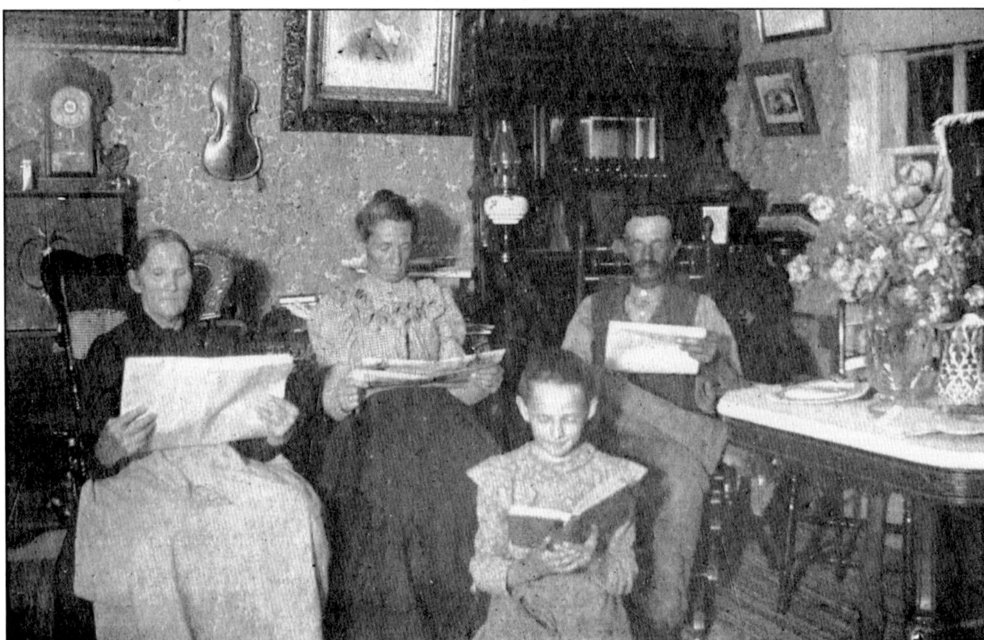

This is a 1901 photograph of the Fred Hancer farm home, built in 1876, located near Merrill, Washington Township. The family members are, from left to right, Eda Ann Boyd House (wife of Henry Harrison House and mother of Emma Hancer), Emma Catherine (House) Hancer, and Fred Hancer. Hazel, the youngest, is at center front. (Courtesy Justin Herbst.)

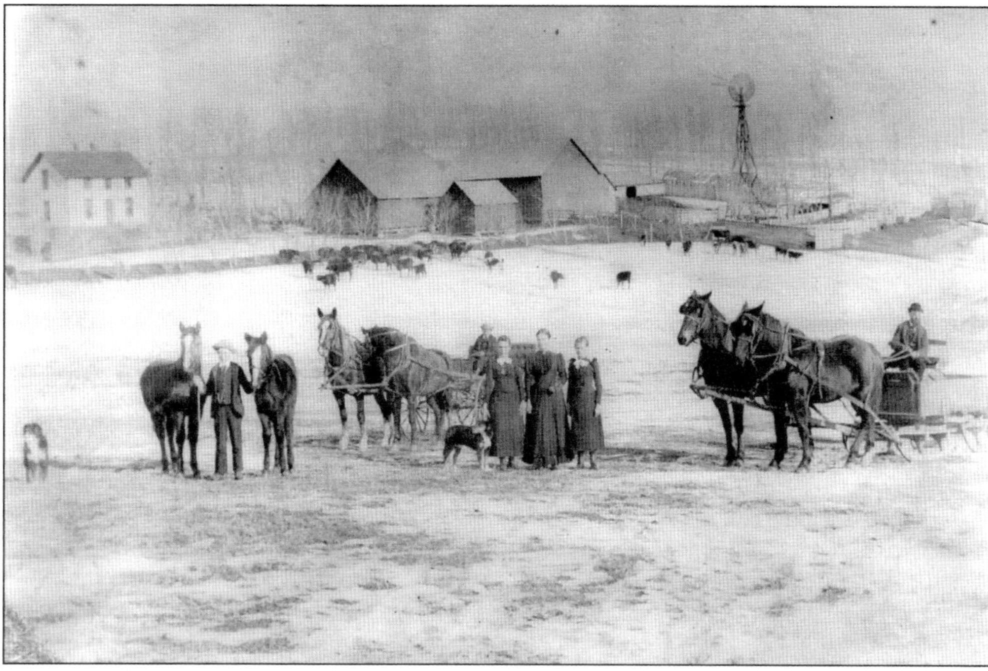

August Herbst homesteaded this farm beginning on October 3, 1876. The farm, located west of Merrill in Plymouth Township, still remains in the family today. Pictured from left to right are unidentified, Caroline (Herbst) Dahms, their mother Barbara Weinhardt Herbst, Minnie (Herbst) Howes, and their father August Herbst Sr. August (Guss) Herbst Jr. is in the buggy. (Courtesy Justin Herbst.)

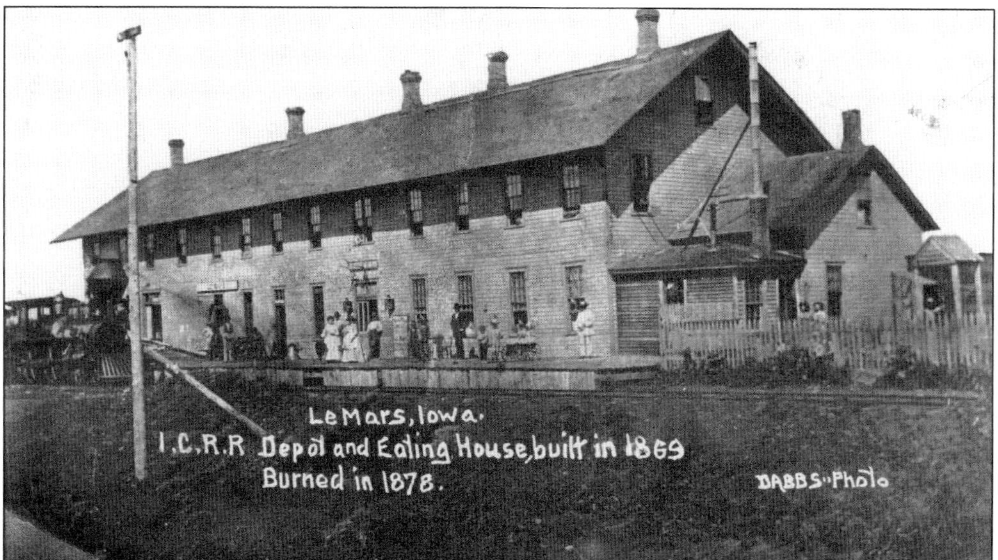

In 1877, Le Mars was served by at least four passenger trains every day. The center of activity was the Illinois Central Railroad depot and eating house, which was built in 1869. The depot was complete with hotel rooms and a restaurant. Unfortunately, the building and contents were destroyed by fire in 1878. A new station building was constructed in its place. (Courtesy Plymouth County Historical Museum.)

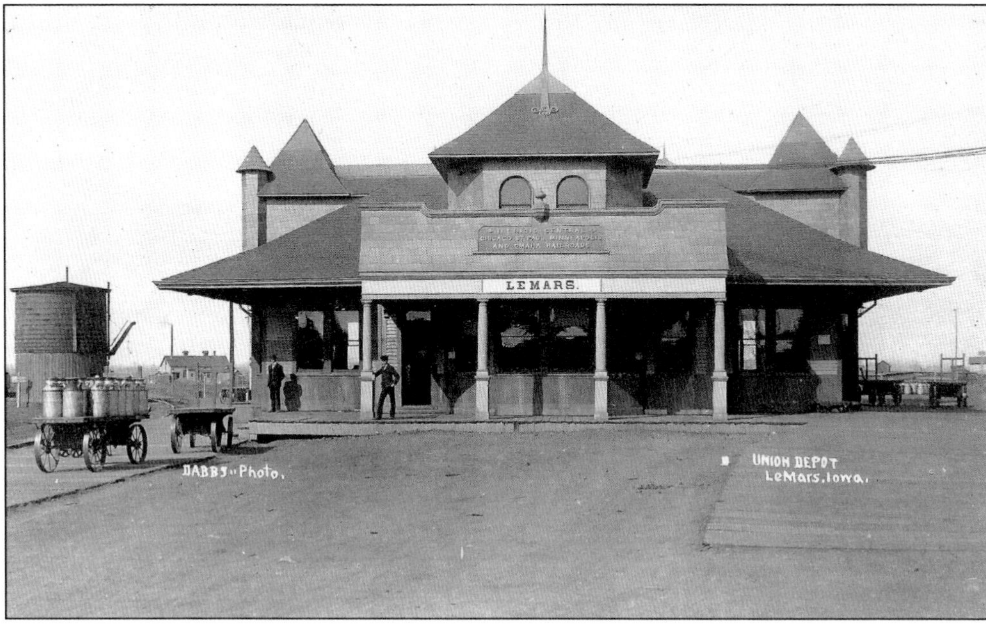

The new Le Mars Union Depot served the Illinois Central Railroad and the Chicago, St. Paul, Minneapolis and Omaha Railway. Built of Victorian design with a slate roof in 1895, it featured both men's and women's waiting rooms, which were heated with big pot-bellied stoves. The union depot was torn down in 1952 and replaced with a small, cement block building. (Courtesy Plymouth County Historical Museum.)

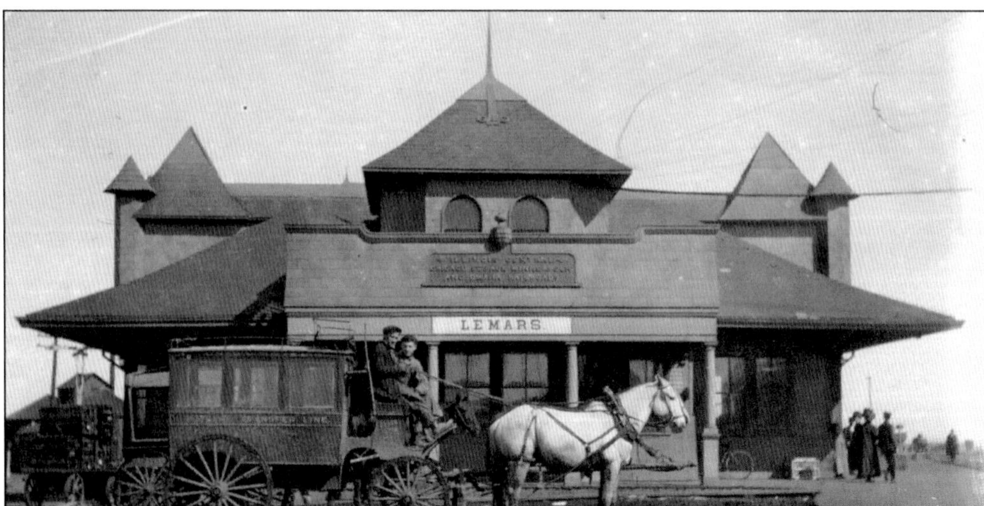

Barney Miller drove the Butler's Transfer Line horse-drawn bus from the Union Hotel to the Le Mars Union Depot to pick up passengers and traveling salesmen and their wares arriving by train. Miller also drove the U.S. mail from the post office to the depot. (Courtesy Plymouth County Historical Museum.)

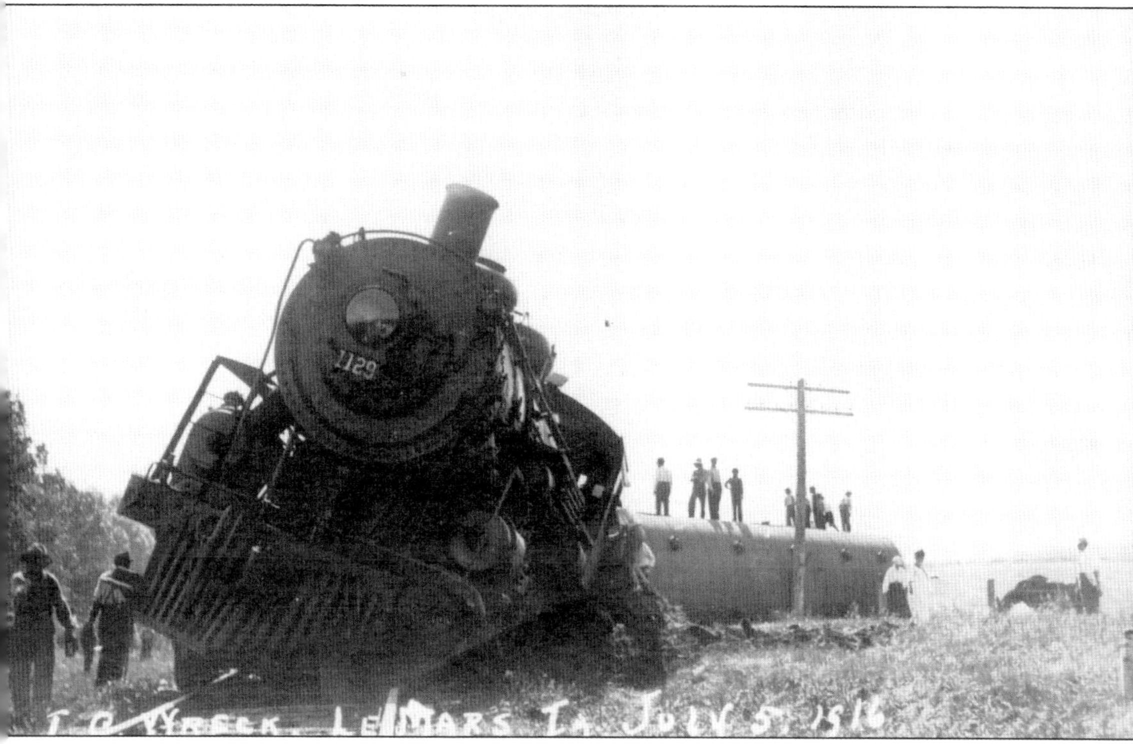

The *Le Mars Globe-Post* of July 13, 1916, reported the news story about the train wreck shown in this photograph. The incident was determined to be one of the worst railroad wrecks that ever occurred in Plymouth County, happening on Wednesday morning, July 12, 1916, between Le Mars and Oyens. The Illinois Central Flyer known as the Chicago Limited No. 611, westbound, was derailed. Rotten ties were determined to be the cause of the accident. A considerable amount of credit was given to the engineer and firemen for their nerve in sticking to their engine until the train had been stopped. The passengers were also commended for the minimum amount of excitement shown. (Courtesy Plymouth County Historical Museum.)

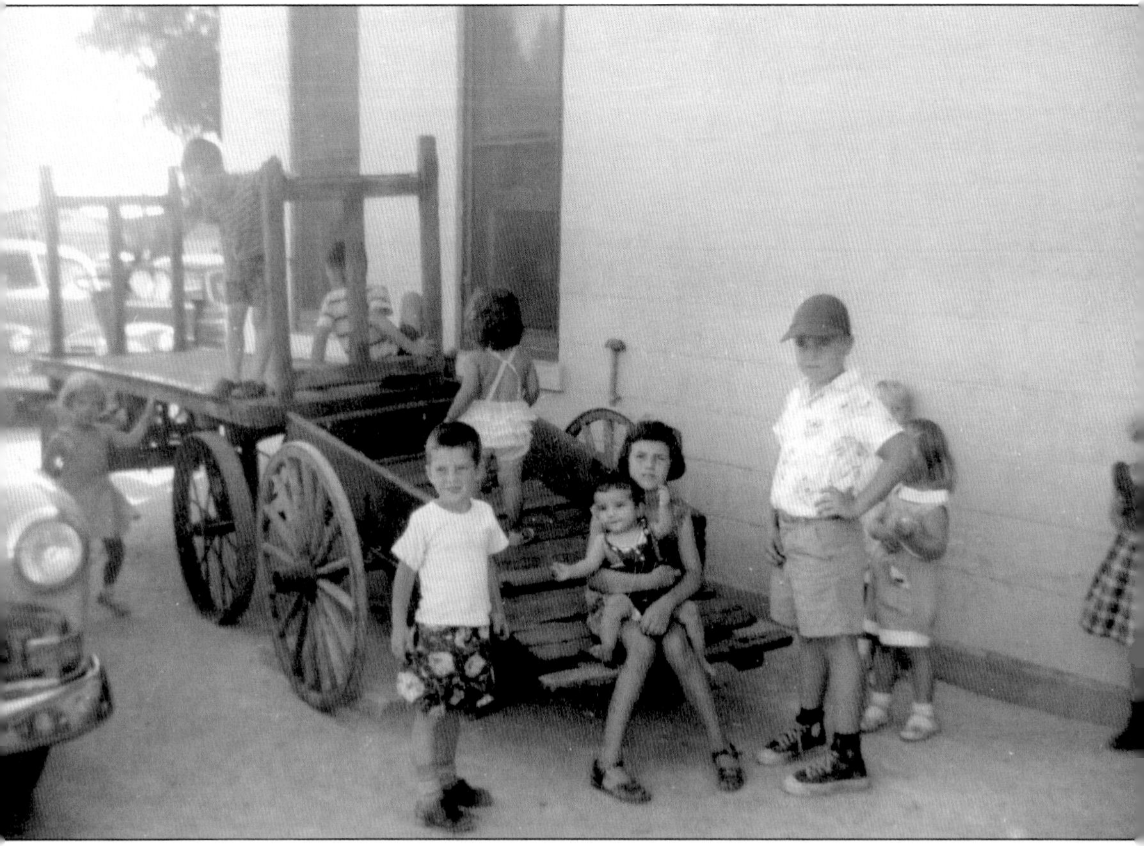

In the summer of 1956, while waiting on the passenger train at the Le Mars depot, this group of 11 young cousins played on the old wooden baggage cart left over from the early-20th-century depot. These are the grandchildren of Charles and Gladys Ewin of Seney. Three of the children and their mother, Frances Ewin Bos, were bound for San Antonio, Texas, from Le Mars via passenger train. This trip was the conclusion of a week of vacation spent in Plymouth County visiting relatives and friends. (Courtesy Linda Ewin Ziemann.)

Two

COUNTY GOVERNMENT AND BUSINESS VENTURES

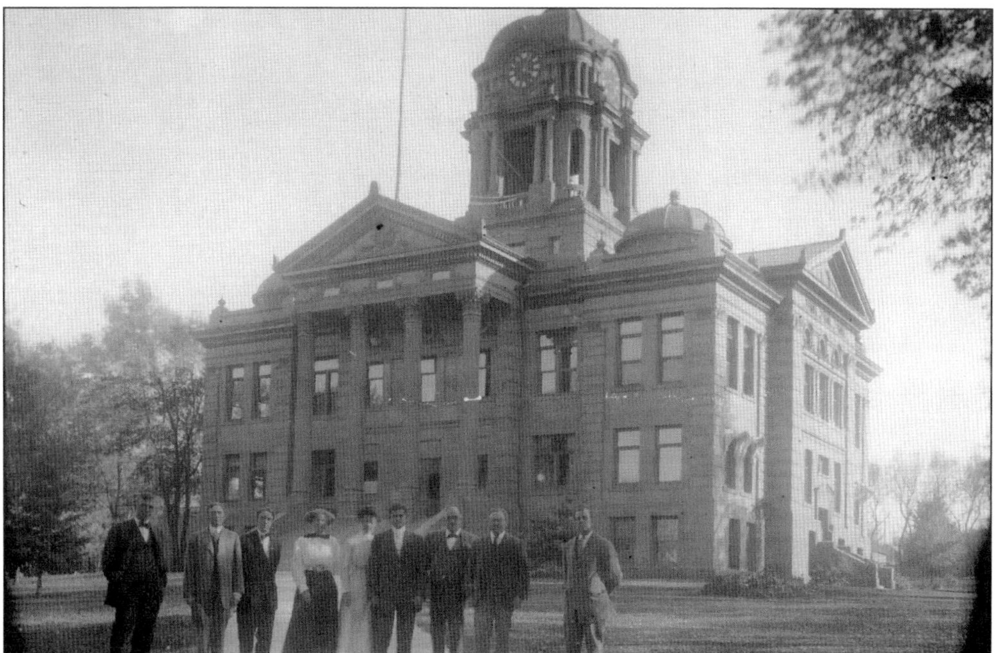

The Plymouth County Courthouse in Le Mars in 2009 is the same building that was completed in 1902, minus the bell tower and the Justice statue. The May 6, 1902, edition of the *Le Mars Sentinel* published a detailed article about the construction of the new courthouse building. The courthouse today still has a spiral iron staircase leading into the basement, where old records are stored. (Courtesy Plymouth County Historical Museum.)

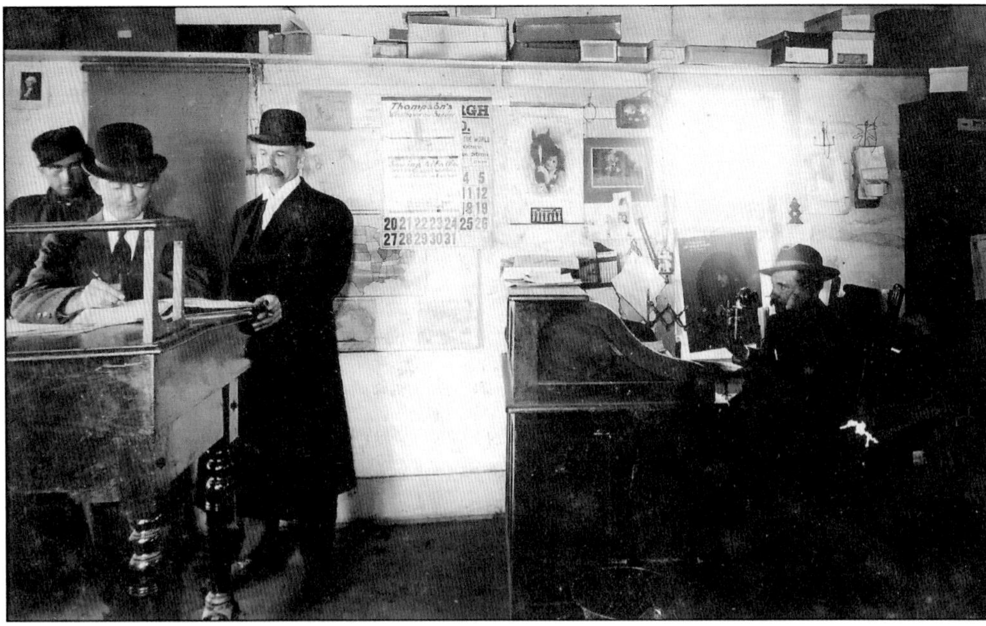

This photograph is an inside look at an office inside the Plymouth County Courthouse. One man appears to be signing a ledger, while two other men watch him. Another man at the desk on the right side is talking on a candlestick telephone. The small calendar on the wall reads January 1909. None of the men in the photograph are identified. (Courtesy Plymouth County Historical Museum.)

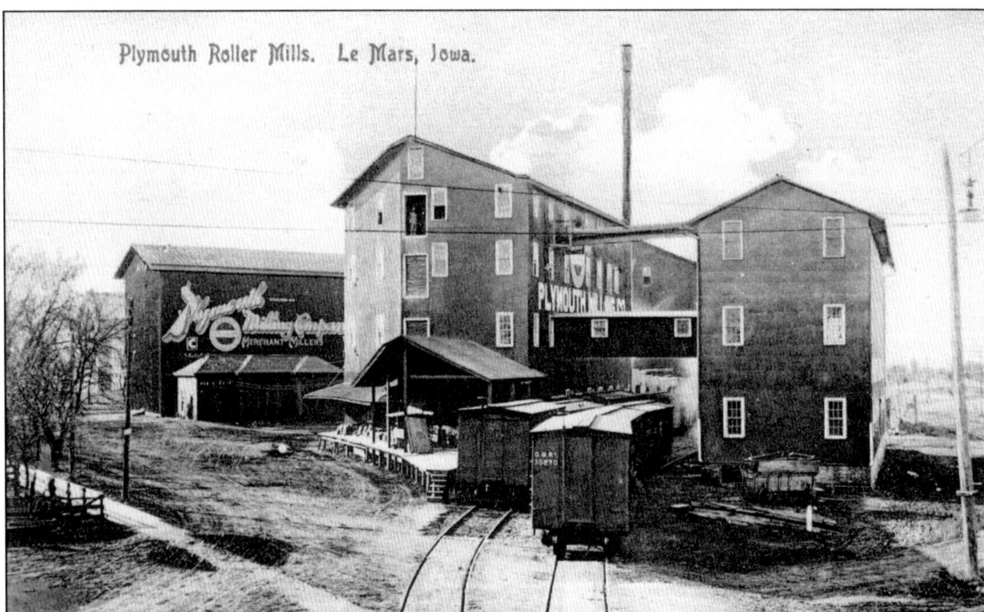

Plymouth Milling Company was established in 1878 and was one of the largest in the state of Iowa. The Plymouth Roller Mills was located on Eagle Street between Fourth and Fifth Streets. The 1897 city directory listed the mill with a capacity of 700 barrels of flour, 200 barrels of cornmeal, and 8 cars of feed. F. W. Burns was listed as president and C. A. Wernli as secretary of the company. (Courtesy Plymouth County Historical Museum.)

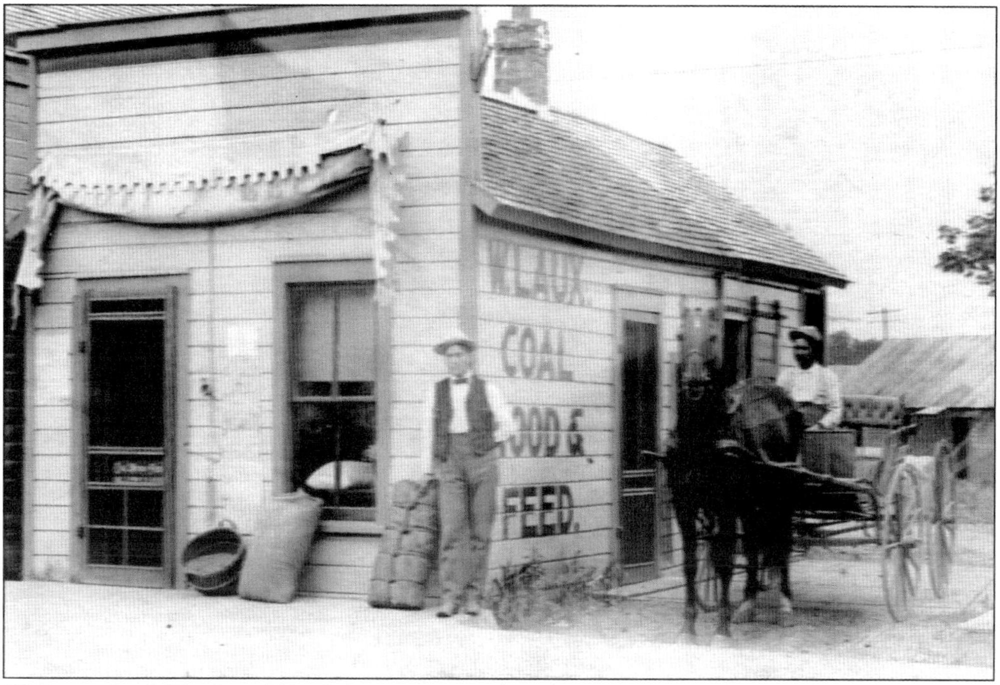

W. Laux Coal, Food and Feed Company was listed in the Plymouth County 1897 directory at 905 Main Street in Le Mars. This August 1903 photograph identifies one of the men as Russell L. Laux. (Courtesy Plymouth County Historical Museum.)

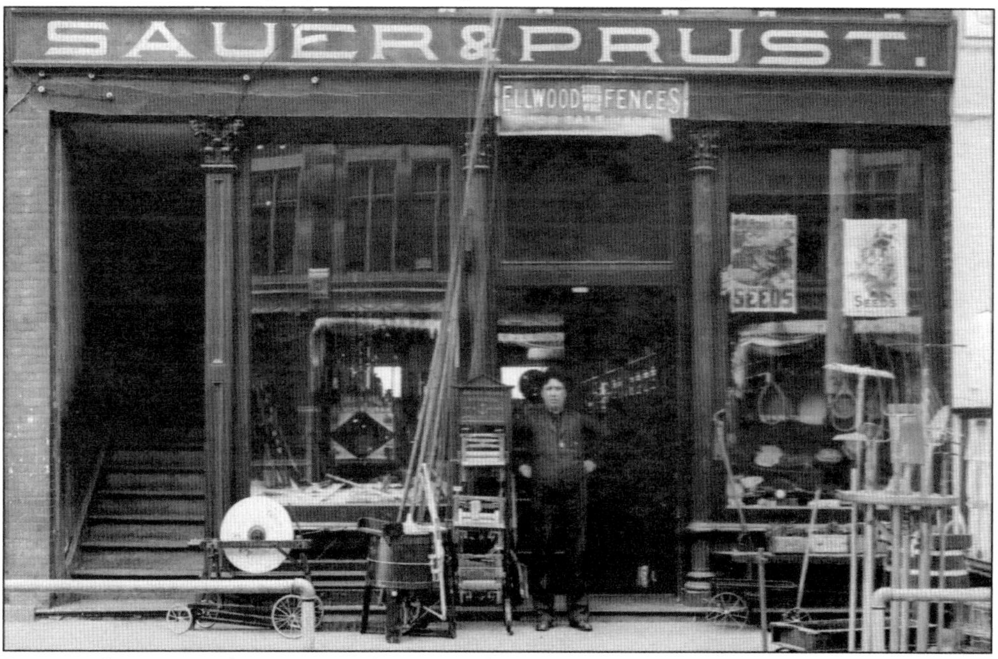

Sauer and Prust Hardware Store of Le Mars has an array of featured hardware items for sale outside the front door of the store. As with most hardware stores of the late 19th and early 20th centuries, a shopper could purchase all kinds of interesting gadgets and newfangled inventions. (Courtesy Plymouth County Historical Museum.)

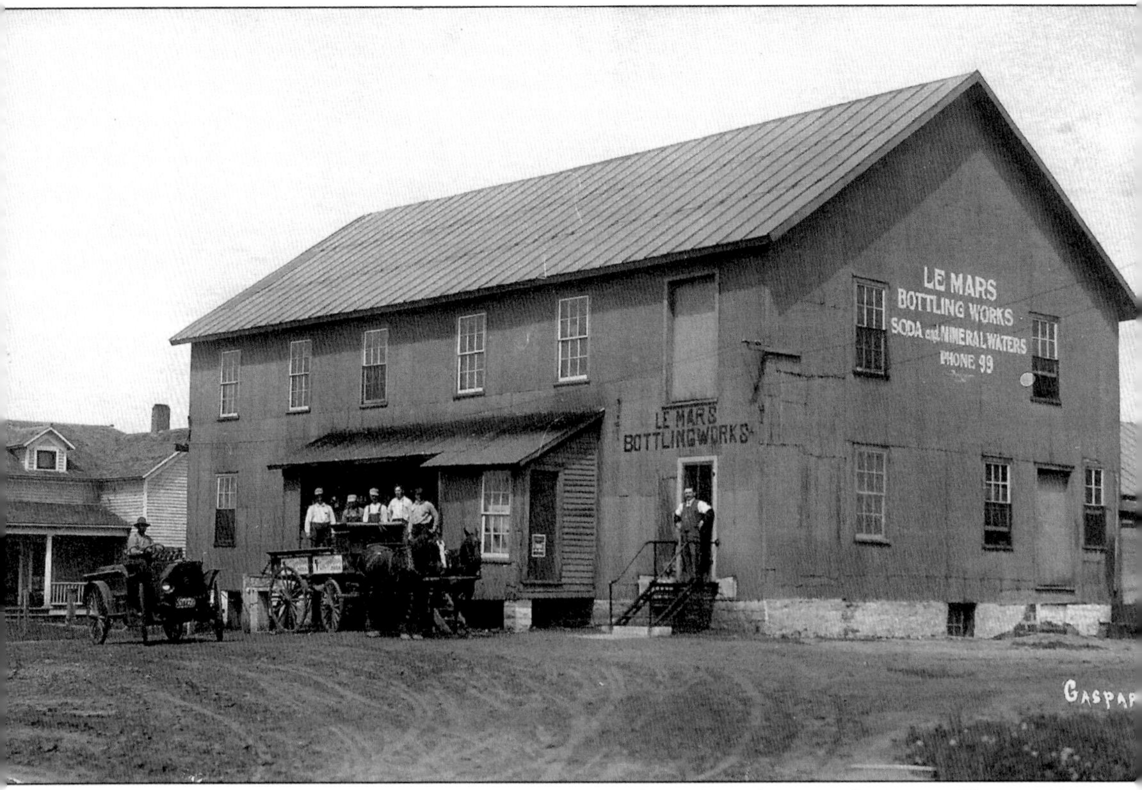

The Le Mars Bottling Works Company advertised "Soda and Mineral Waters, Phone 99" in large letters on its building, located at 629 Main Street. The June 1, 1893, edition of the *Le Mars Sentinel* explained much of how the company operated in a news story about a tragic accident with one of the employees. The article told the story of an explosion, resulting in one of the operators, Isadore Neudermann, losing an arm. A generator for the production of carbonic acid gas used a pressure of 1,500 pounds per square inch. From it are filled the ordinary copper soda fountains, used in drugstores and restaurants. The proprietor of the works had his hand on the stop-cock to shut the gas off. However, a copper soda fountain exploded, one part going up with great violence against the ceiling, striking the young man's right arm in its upward flight. The lower section of the fountain was forced nearly through the door. His arm was badly cut, bruised, and broken. Physicians determined that the arm had to be amputated in order to save his life. (Courtesy Plymouth County Historical Museum.)

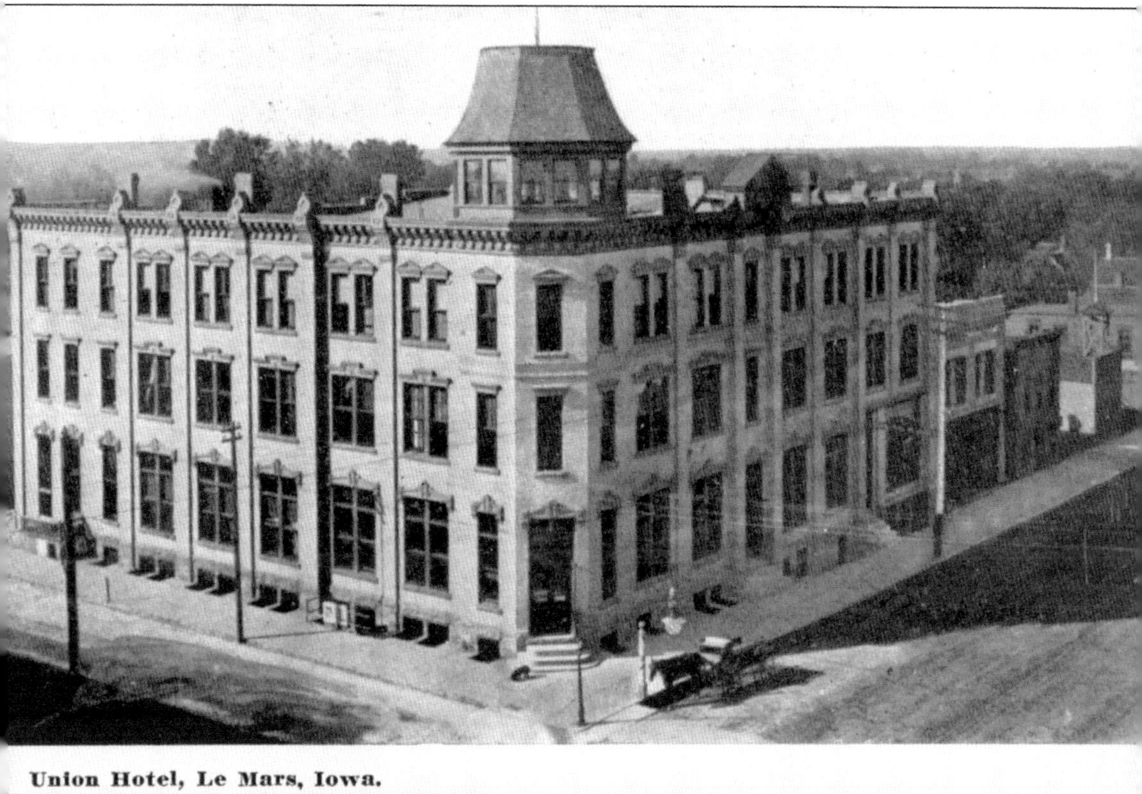

The Union Hotel was a fixture in Le Mars from 1888 when it opened in the spring until the summer of 1968 when it was razed. For over 80 years, this Le Mars landmark stood in servitude to its patrons, located at the corner of Sixth Street and Eagle Street, now the intersection of Plymouth Street and First Avenue SW. The Union Hotel was built on the location of the former Revere House, which was destroyed by fire in 1884. The *Le Mars Sentinel* April 24, 1888, edition proudly reported that it was springtime, Monday, April 23, 1888, before the Union Hotel opened its doors. Those instrumental in opening the hotel were M. A. Moore, P. F. Dalton, Manahan and Wilson, C. H. Kluckhohn, G. W. McLain, A. H. Treat, M. W. Richey, J. W. Myers, G. E. Richardson, W. H. Perry, A. A. Alline, A. S. Garetson (Sioux City), B. Beecher, Spring Brothers, P. H. Diehl, G. Post, A. C. Cotrell, Hermann and Uhlman, and Molampey and Damon. The officers were George E. Richardson, president; M. A. Moore, vice president; W. H. Perry, secretary; and P. F. Dalton, treasurer. Directors were P. F. Dalton, C. H. Kluckhohn, M. W. Richey, George W. Wilson, M. A. Moore, and W. H. Perry. (Courtesy Plymouth County Historical Museum.)

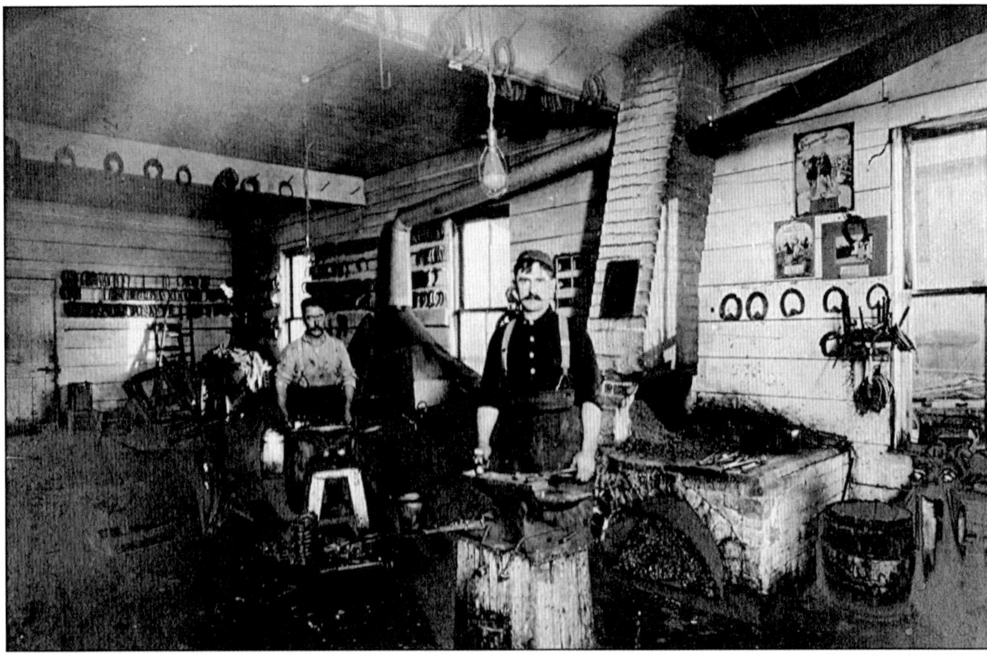

This photograph was simply labeled, "Warren Lillie Blacksmith." The 1900 federal census states that Warren N. Lillie, blacksmith, was head of household with his wife, Bessie L., and Lillian, a three-year-old daughter. They lived in Ward 3 in Le Mars. (Courtesy Plymouth County Historical Museum.)

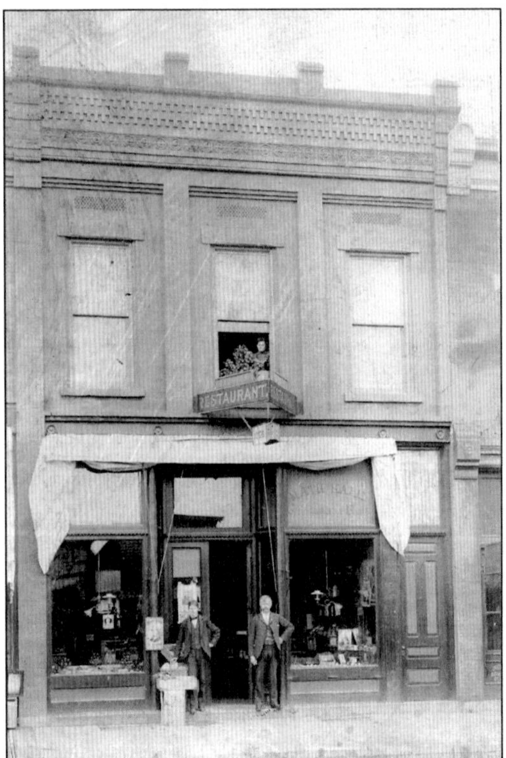

The 1897 Plymouth County directory states that Math Kale was the proprietor of Math Kale Confectionery and Fruit restaurant. His wife was Maggie Kale, who is very likely the woman in the upper window near the restaurant sign. The Kales had four sons. Their oldest son, Joseph, age 18 in 1900, is presumably the young man on the left in the picture, with his father, Math Kale, standing to the right. (Courtesy Plymouth County Historical Museum.)

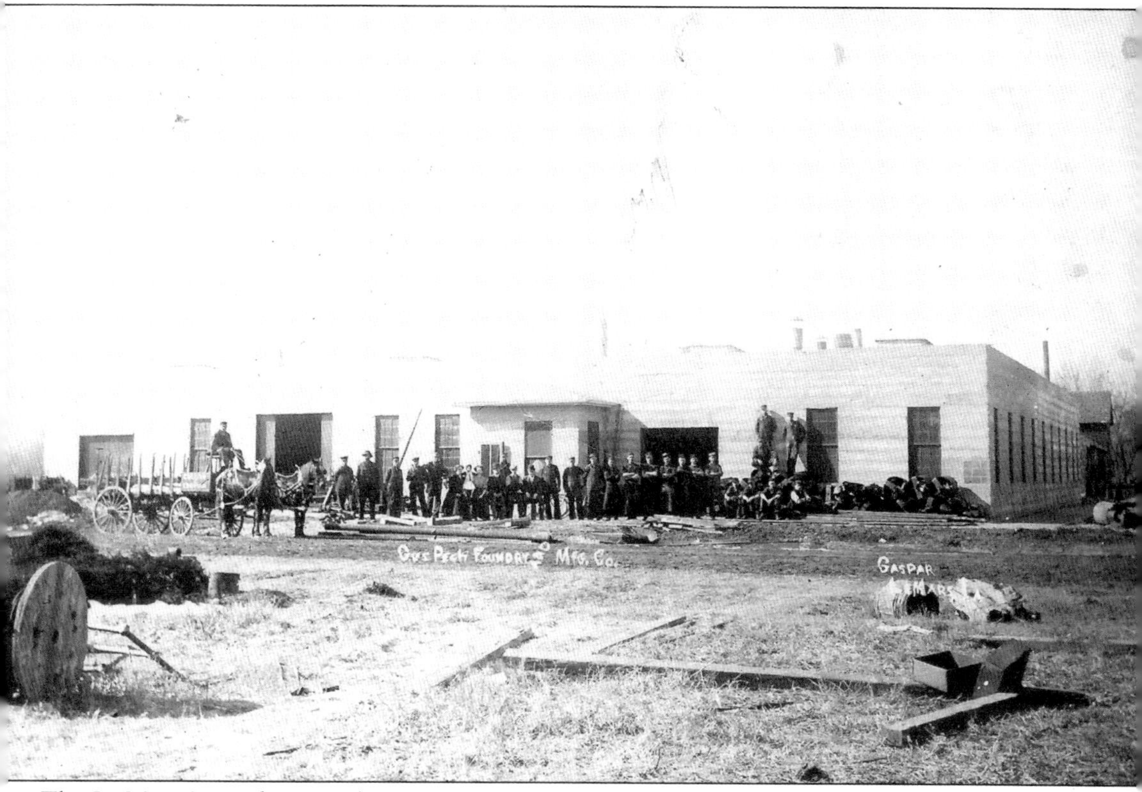

The *Le Mars Sentinel*, September 7, 1909, reported that the Pech Foundry and Manufacturing Company had laid the foundation for its new building on the site formerly occupied by the skating rink and would begin the erection of the frames during that week. The building would be 42 by 108 feet, and the walls were to be built of concrete with an air chamber. The new building would furnish a home for the entire plant, which was located in several frame buildings just across the street. The company's growing business demanded better facilities, and the new home would furnish it commodious and convenient quarters. (Courtesy Plymouth County Historical Museum.)

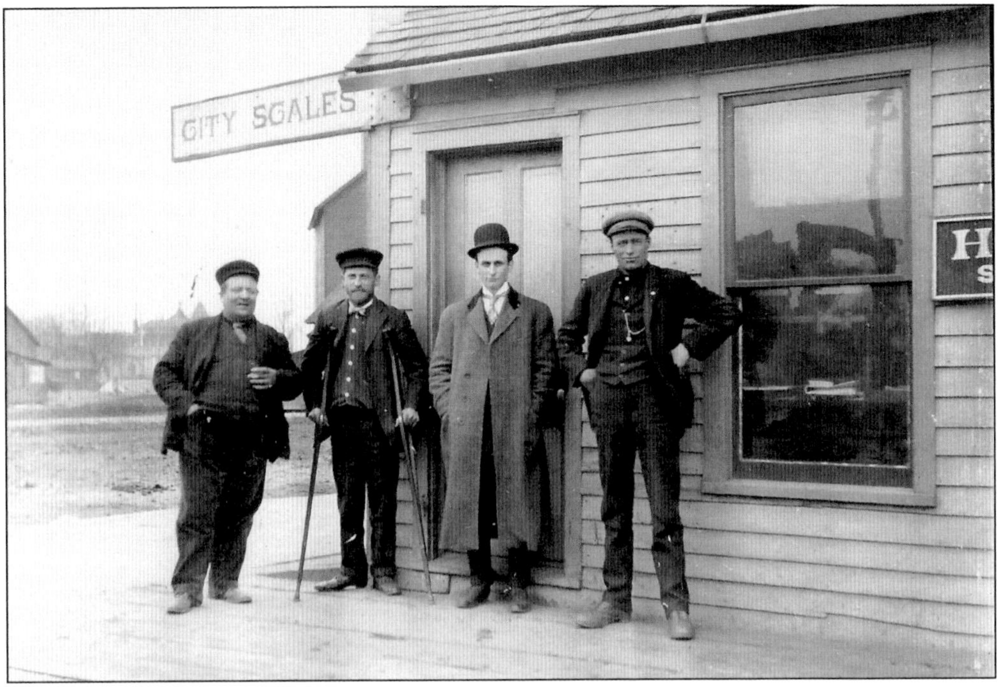

The *Le Mars Sentinel* reported on August 17, 1893, that the city scales were kept quite busy every day at weighing hay and livestock. The man using crutches in the photograph is identified as John Hentges. (Courtesy Plymouth County Historical Museum.)

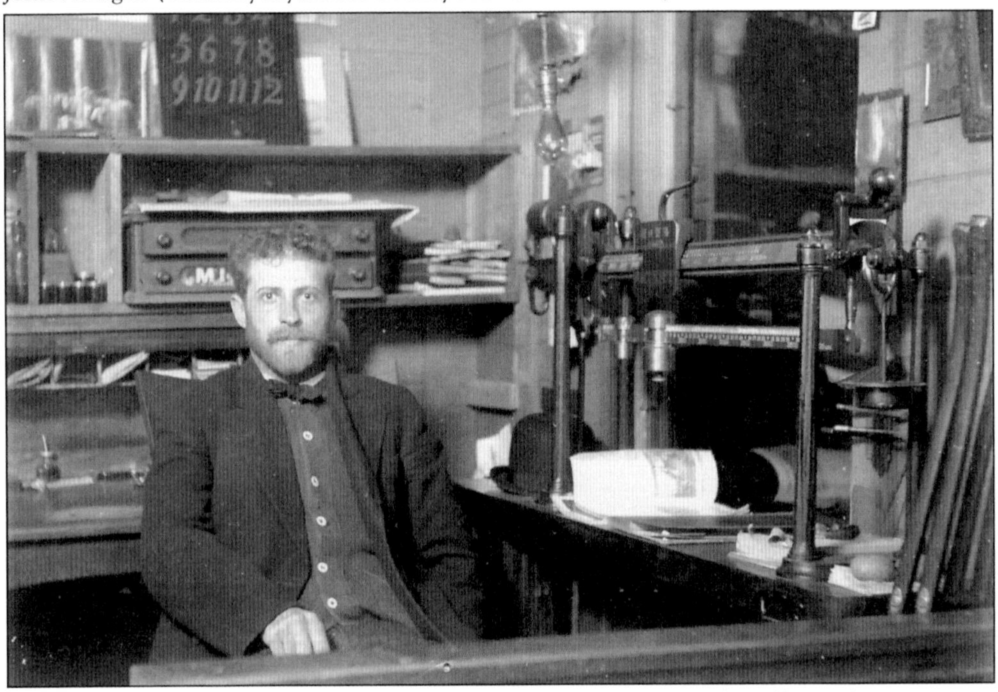

This photograph is an excellent view of the interior of the city scales office. John Hentges is identified as the man in this photograph. Notice his crutches propped against the inside wall on the right side of the photograph. (Courtesy Plymouth County Historical Museum.)

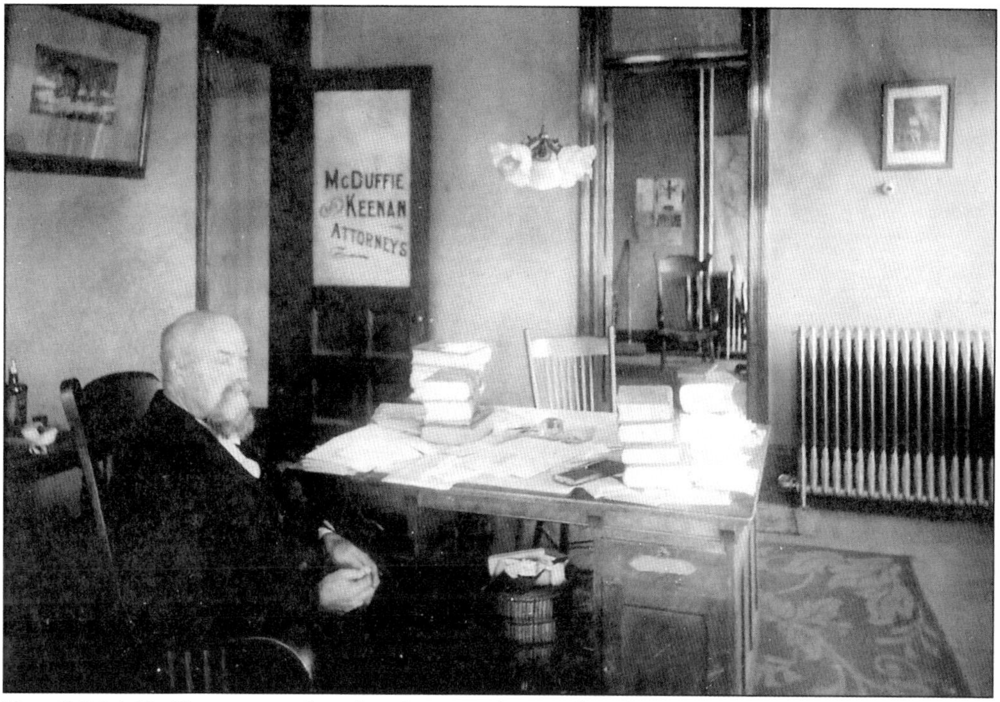

Hon. I. J. McDuffie is pictured in this photograph seated in the attorney's office of McDuffie and Keenan. McDuffie and his family moved to Le Mars in November 1891. (Courtesy Plymouth County Historical Museum.)

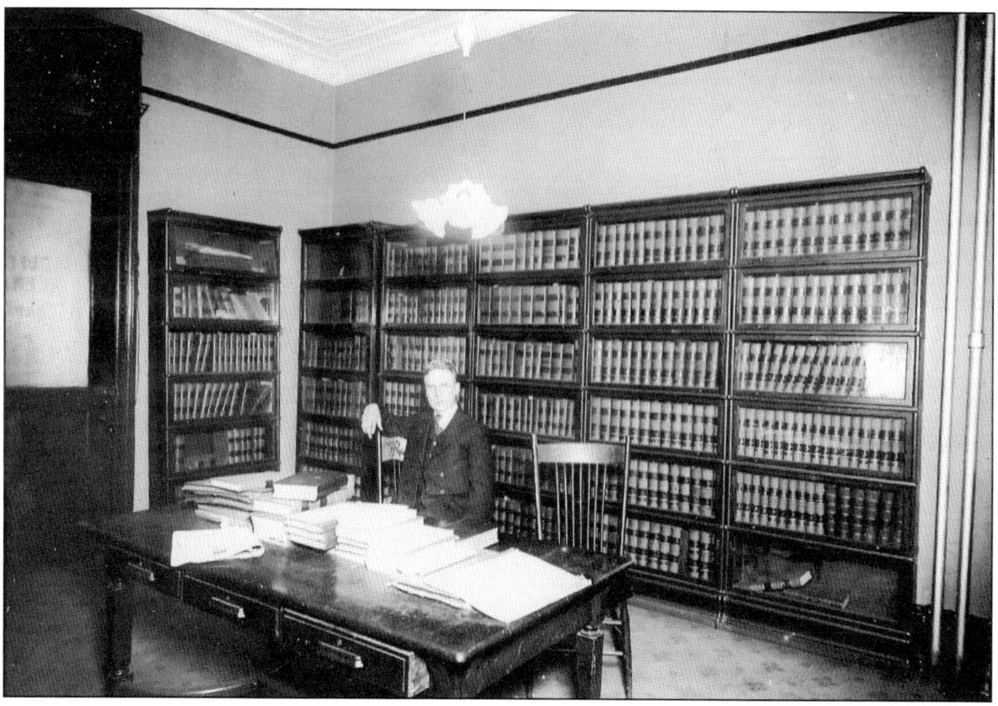
J. T. Keenan is photographed in the attorney's office of McDuffie and Keenan. (Courtesy Plymouth County Historical Museum.)

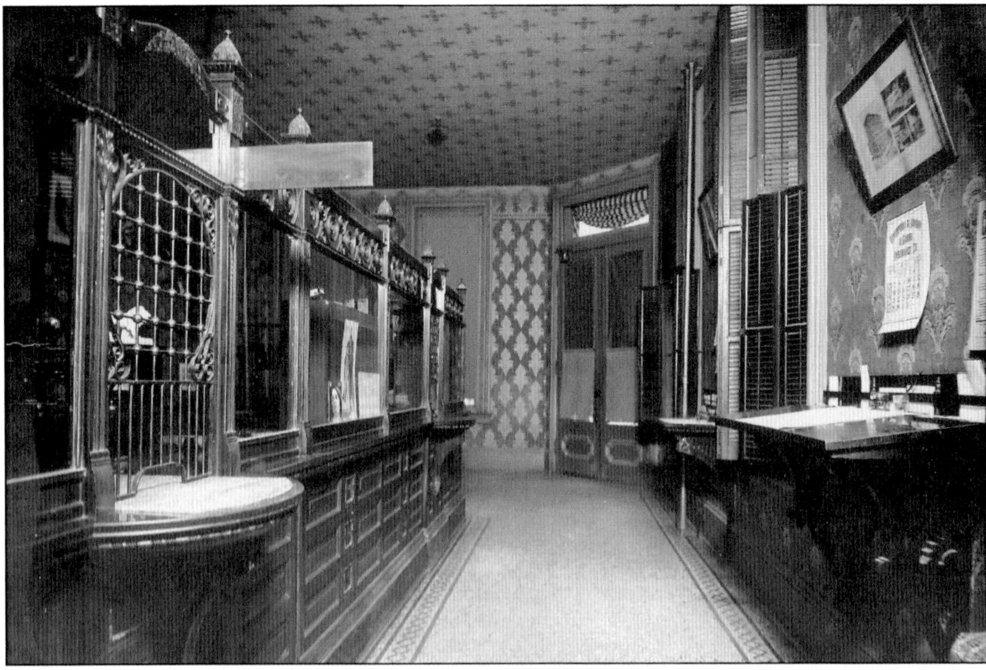

Elaborate wood decor was used inside the German American Bank in Le Mars. These photographs give full view of the inside corridor with beautiful flooring and the solid wood teller cages. The German American Bank was prosperous until World War I. Unfortunately, at that time, the anti-German attitudes of many people led to its demise. (Courtesy Plymouth County Historical Museum.)

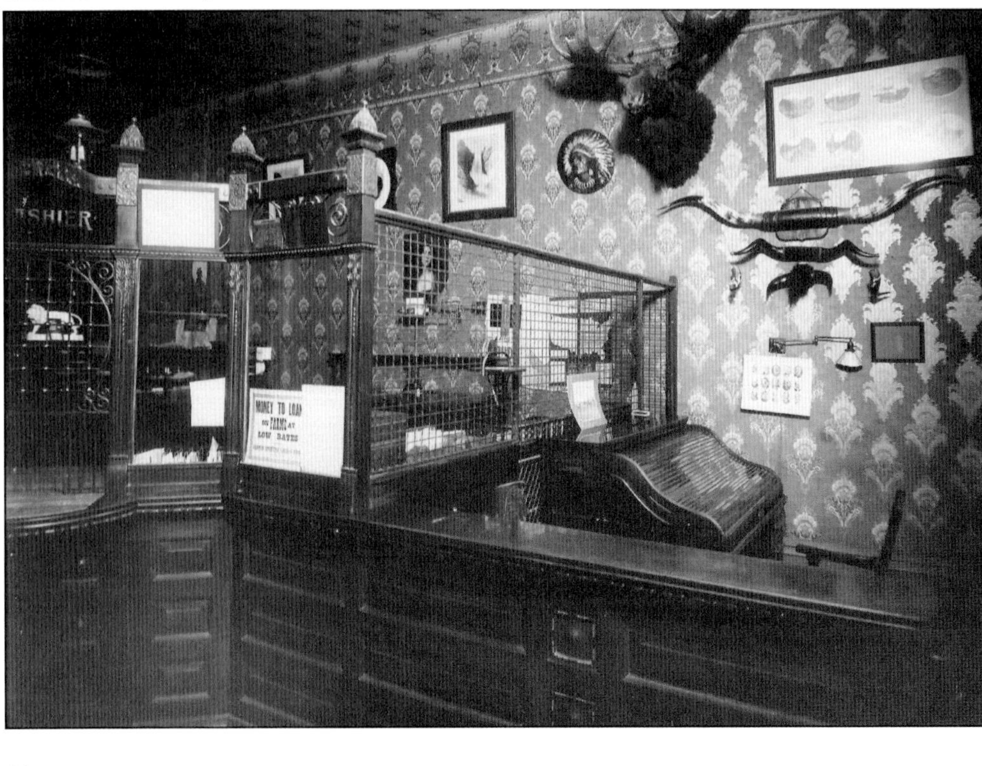

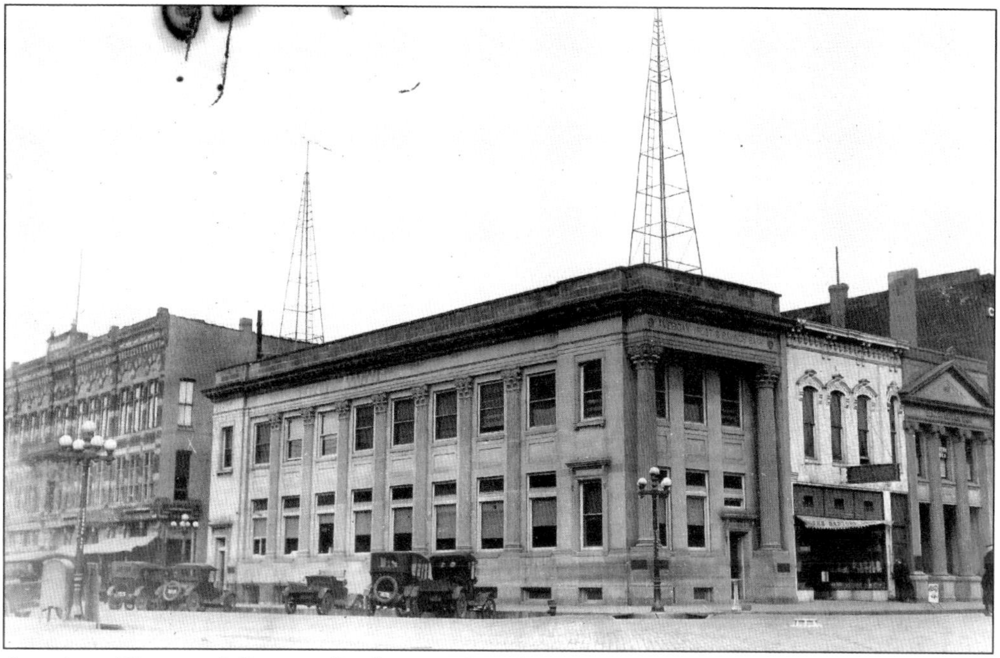

American Trust and Savings Bank existed in Le Mars in 1920 at Central and Plymouth Streets with J. A. Brauch as the owner. The first radio station in Le Mars, operated by Clark Bolser, was located on the second floor of the bank building. (Courtesy Plymouth County Historical Museum.)

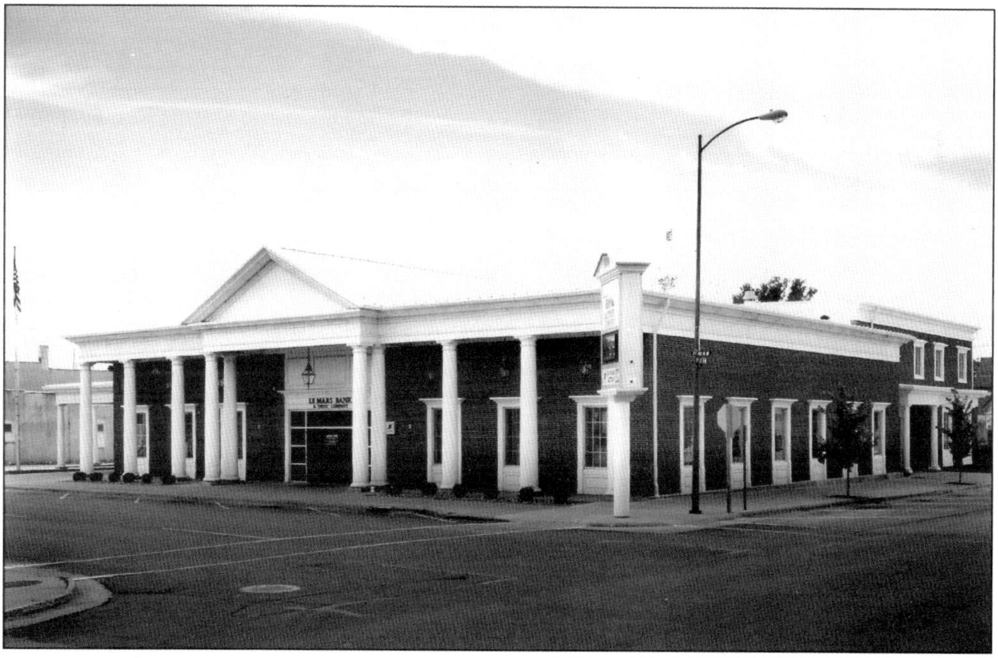

Le Mars Bank and Trust was located in later years at 37 First Avenue NW. Today this same bank is known as Primebank. The bank buildings through the years changed in style, but the banking institution always remained a key component to the local community. (Courtesy Plymouth County Historical Museum.)

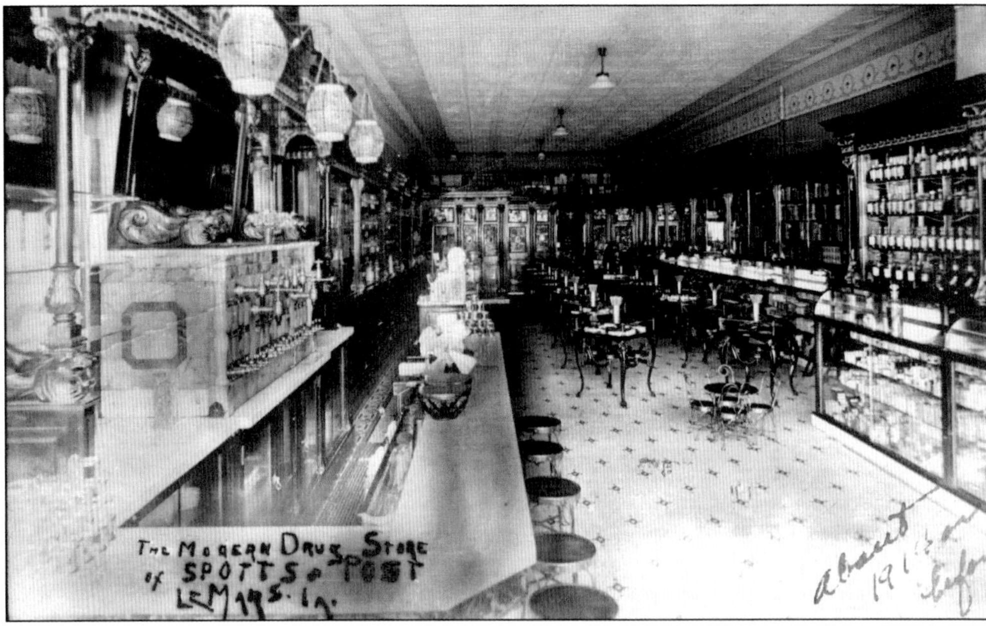

Spotts and Post Drug Store is listed in the 1897 Plymouth County directory at 724 Main Street, Le Mars. "The Modern Drug Store" was its claim. The soda fountain was always the favorite place for patrons and guests. This photograph is dated sometime between 1910 and 1914. (Courtesy Plymouth County Historical Museum.)

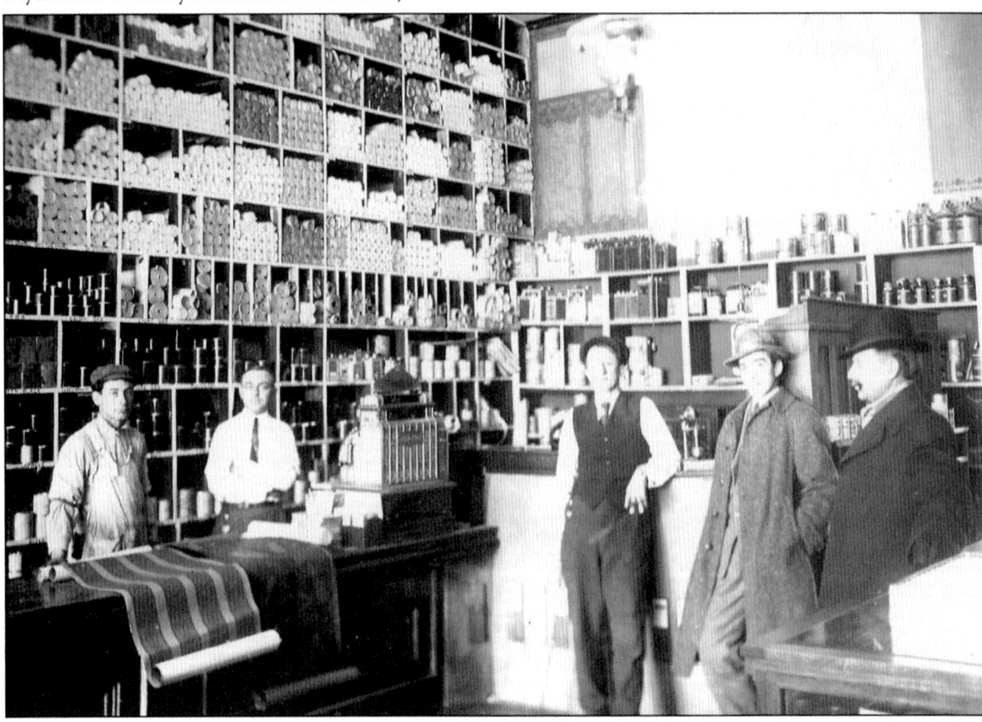

This store in Le Mars had a wide variety of wallpaper for sale, which can be seen on the shelves and counter. Unfortunately, the people in this photograph are not identified. (Courtesy Plymouth County Historical Museum.)

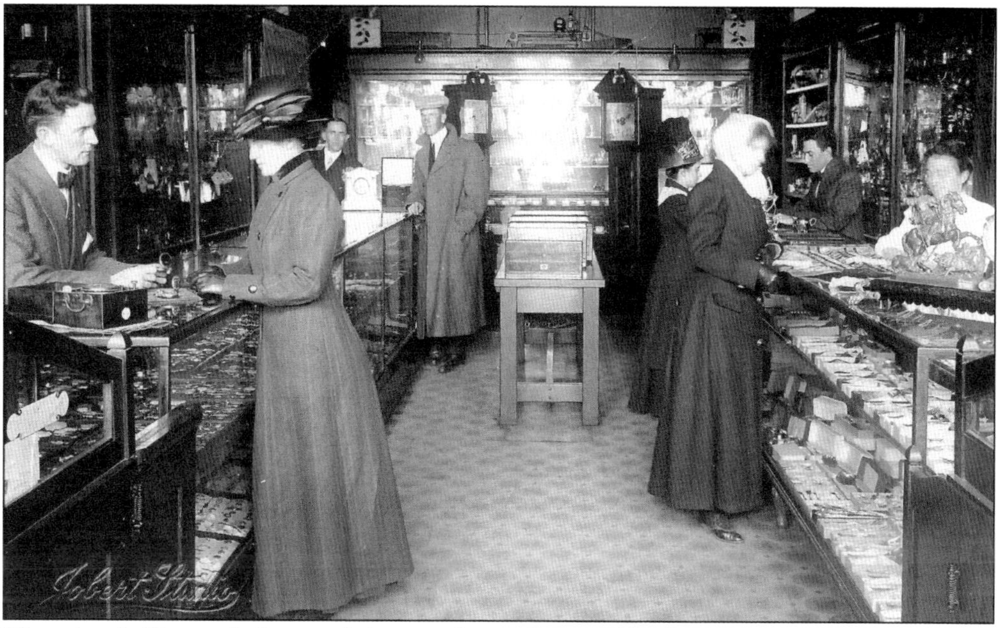

These lovely Plymouth County ladies are doing their weekly shopping in Le Mars. (Courtesy Plymouth County Historical Museum.)

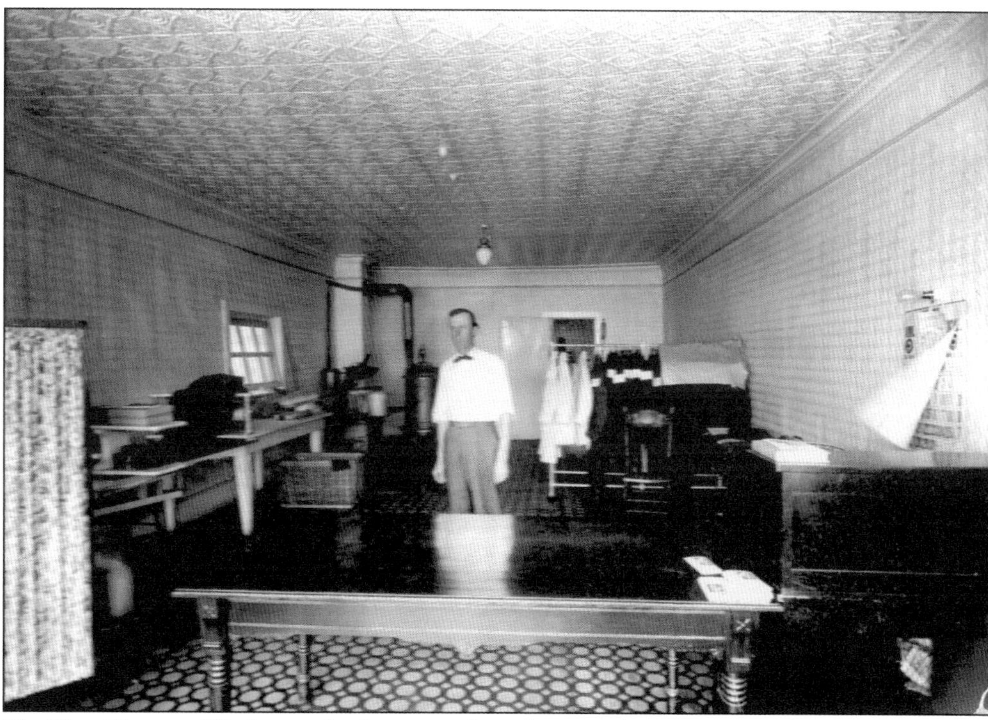

The Troy Cleaning Works was the first up-to-date cleaning plant in Le Mars. (Courtesy Plymouth County Historical Museum.)

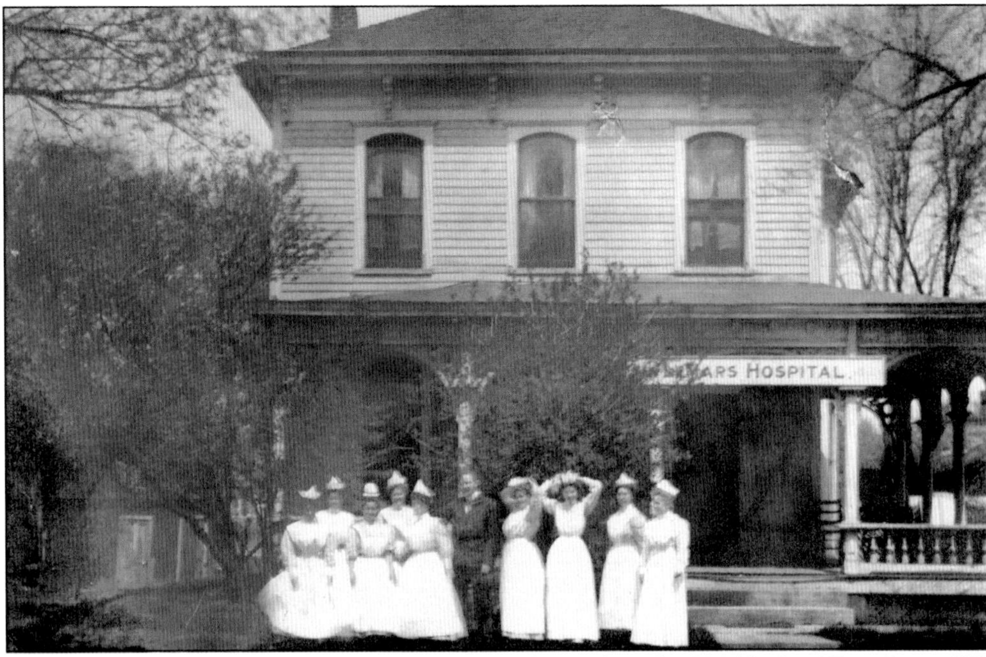

The first Le Mars hospital opened in 1905. It was located in the 200 block of First Street SW. Photographed standing in front of the hospital building are the nursing staff and one gentleman. (Courtesy Plymouth County Historical Museum.)

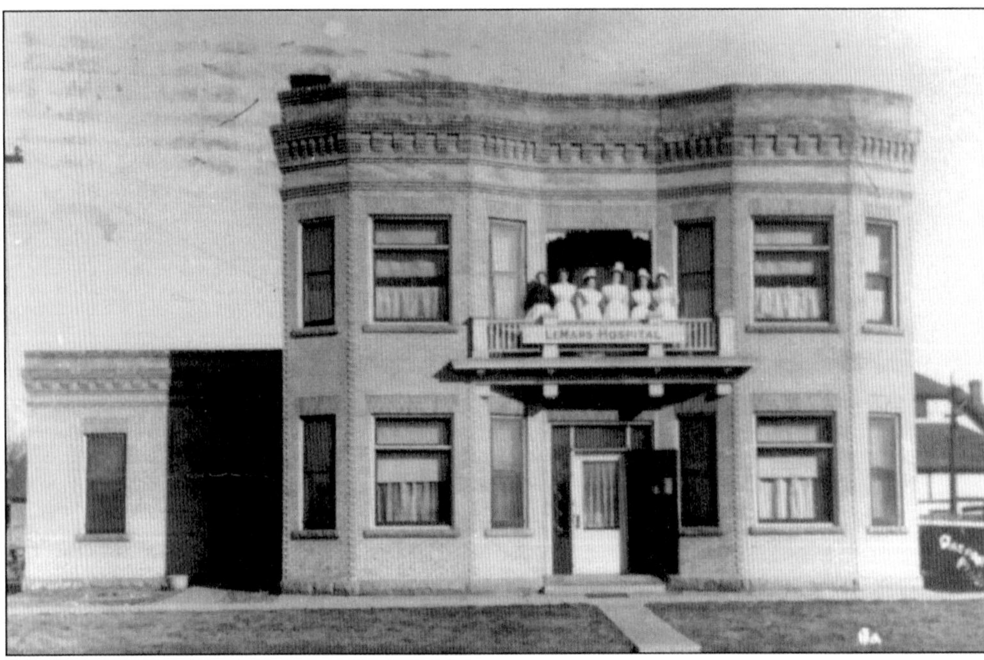

From the time this building was built in 1906 until it closed in 1909, it was known as the White House Bathing Palace. In 1916, it became home to the Le Mars Hospital. This photograph pictures hospital staff standing on the upper balcony. In later years, this same building was used for apartment housing. (Courtesy Plymouth County Historical Museum.)

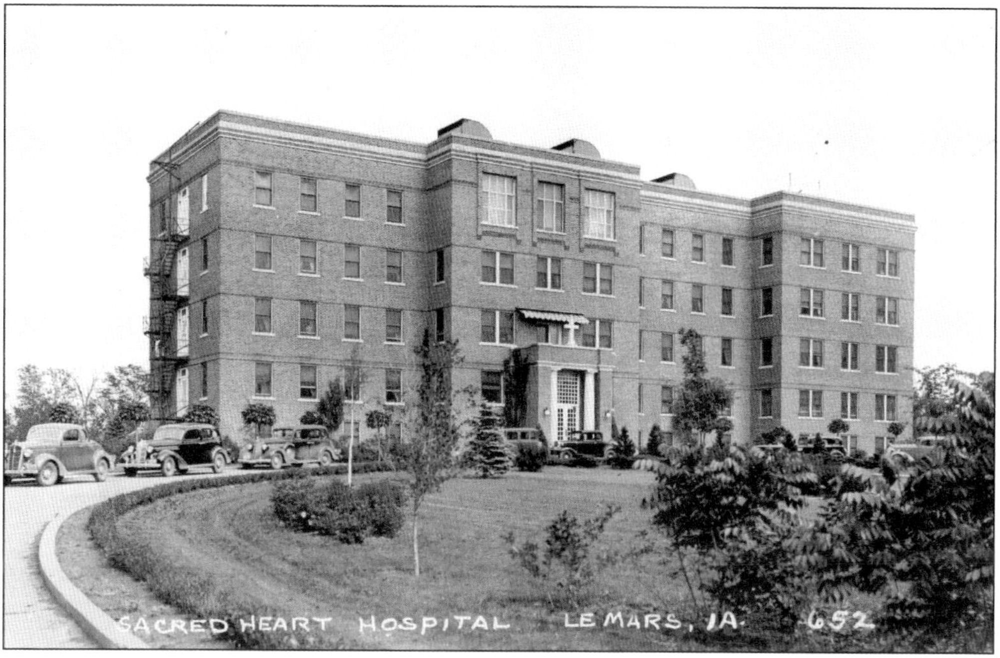

Sacred Heart Hospital in Le Mars was opened in 1923. In 1966, this building was sold to the City of Le Mars and continued as Floyd Valley Hospital until 1976. In that year, Floyd Valley Hospital moved to its new facility a short distance away. (Courtesy Plymouth County Historical Museum.)

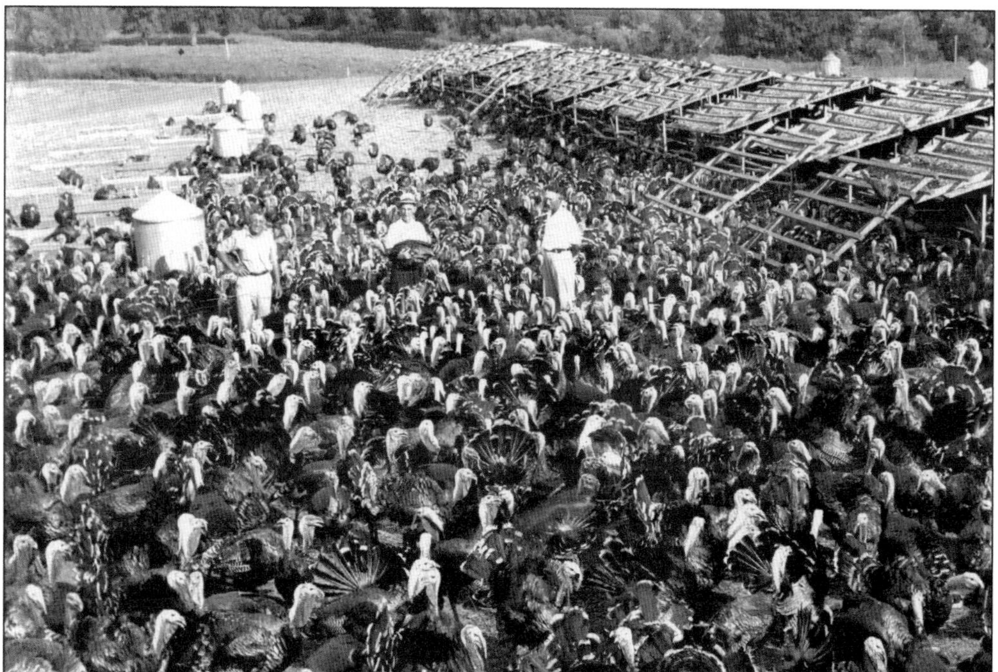

The Ray Dorr turkey farm at Le Mars in the 1930s is photographed with three employees standing in the flock of turkeys. The man on the right is employee Charlie Ewin of Le Mars. The middle unidentified man is holding a turkey. (Courtesy Linda Ewin Ziemann.)

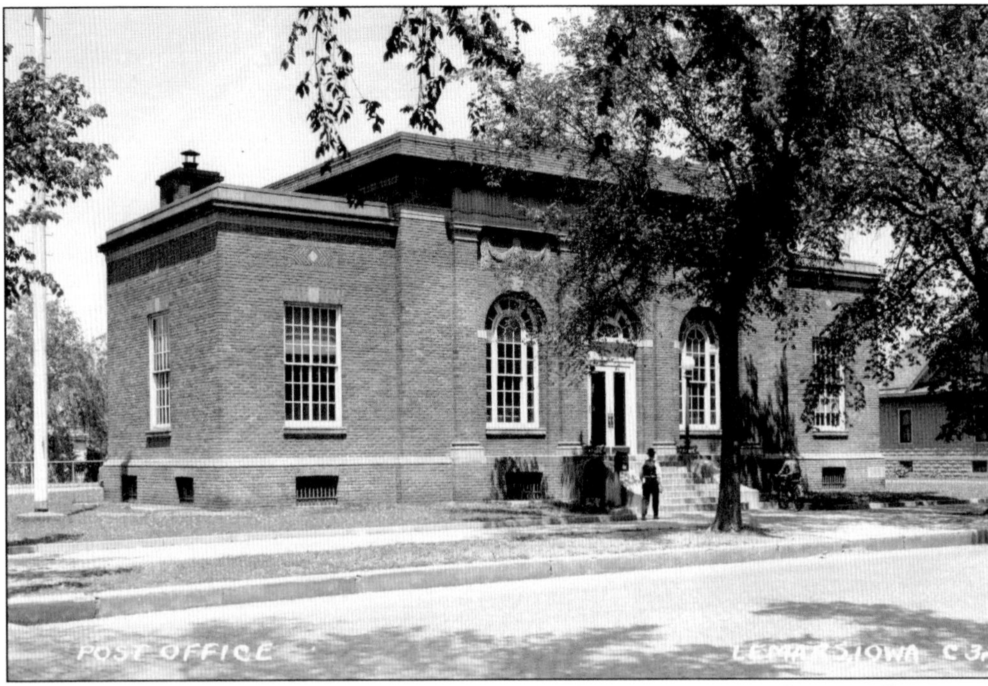

The federal building served as the Le Mars Post Office from 1916 to 1971. The post office moved to its new facility in 1971, and the old post office building was leased to the Le Mars Community Theatre. (Courtesy Linda Ewin Ziemann.)

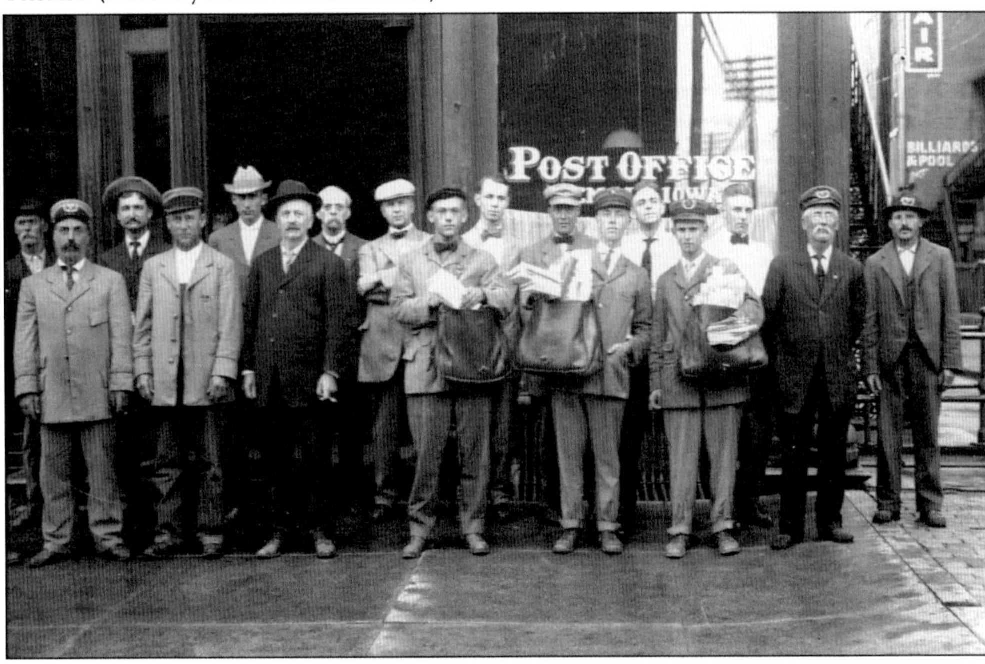

Le Mars postal mail carriers pictured in 1917 are, from left to right, ? Briggs, Marshall Mann, George Hammet, Ted Rees, ? Flickinger, Web Freeman, Tom Treet, Egbert Whittman, Oze Bartels, Anton Sartori, unidentified, Harvey Boyd, Ray Edmonds, Leonard Andrews, Lee Harker, ? Billings, and Joe Forsyth. (Courtesy Plymouth County Historical Museum.)

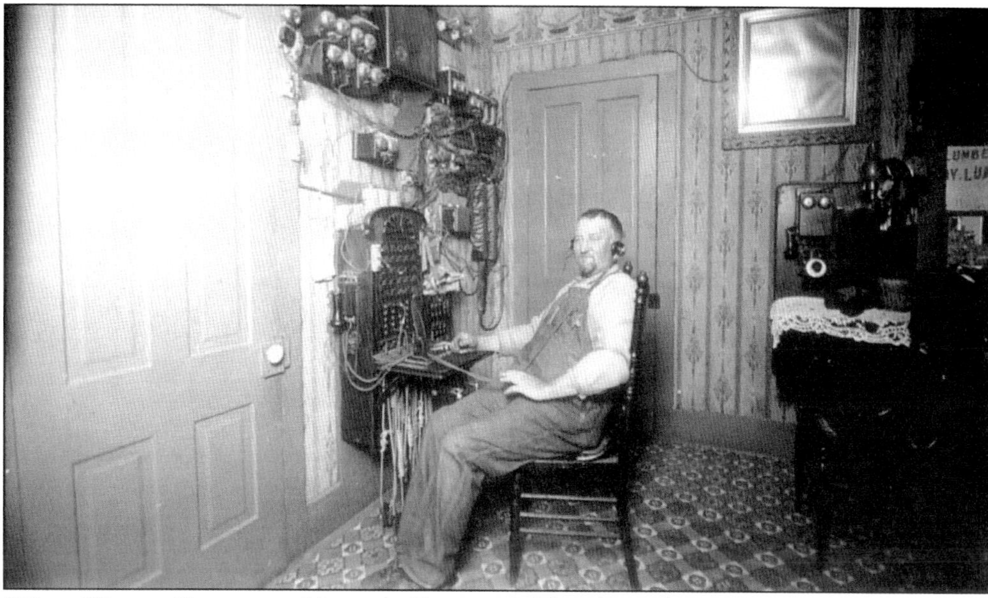

Cilbert Wyman Harrison and his wife, Florence Adeline (Peron) Harrison, owned and operated the Hinton Telephone Exchange, operating first out of the back of their general store in 1905 and then in their home in 1915. Cilbert wired all the rural lines and placed the telephone poles east and west of Hinton into Moville, Lawton, and James. The Harrisons' daughter, Violet Jones, took over the family business. Her son Lamar Jones Sr. made the switch to a rotary system in 1960. (Courtesy Justin Herbst)

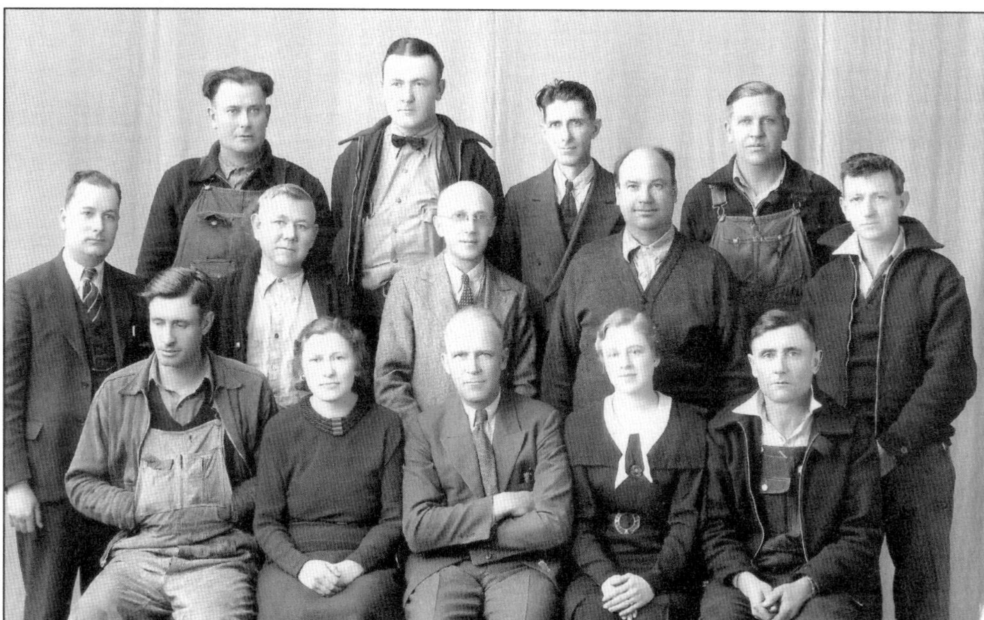

Iowa Public Service workforce employees in the early 1930s are, from left to right, (first row) Jim Hamilton, Ann Kemp, George Hannosch, Ethel Williams, and Jack Shearon Sr.; (second row) Shrimp Battern, Hans Hanson, Rudy Bartels, Jim Woomer, and Bill Rohde; (third row) Tom Long, George Gondon, Max Foster, and Ed Wulf. (Courtesy Plymouth County Historical Museum.)

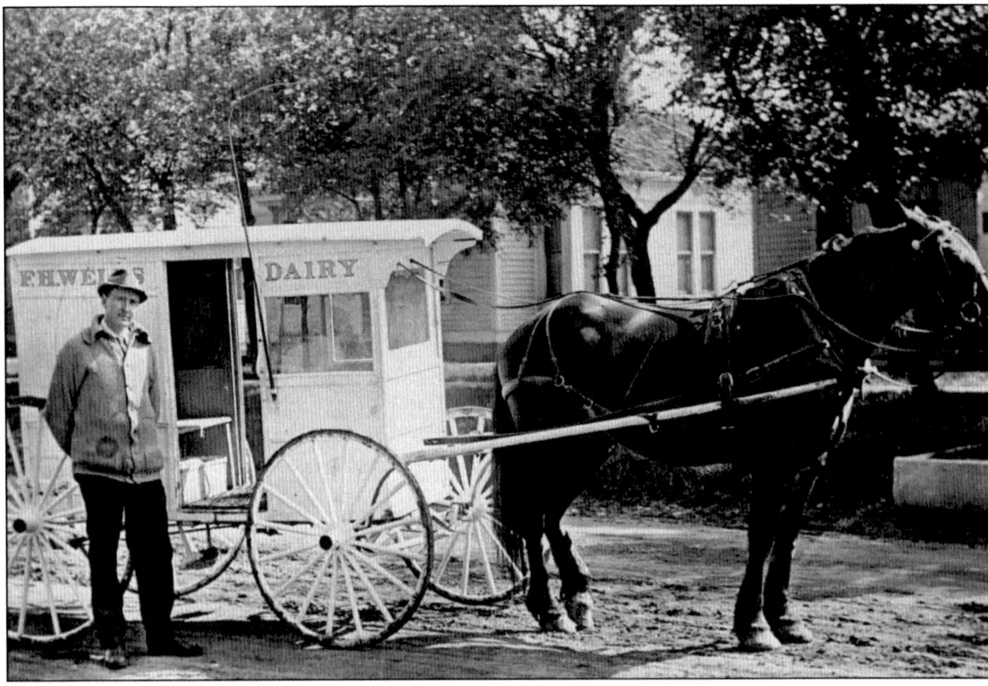

Wells Dairy was founded in 1914 by Fred H. Wells, when he purchased a horse, a delivery wagon, a few cans and jars, and the goodwill of the business from Ray Bowers. (Courtesy Plymouth County Historical Museum.)

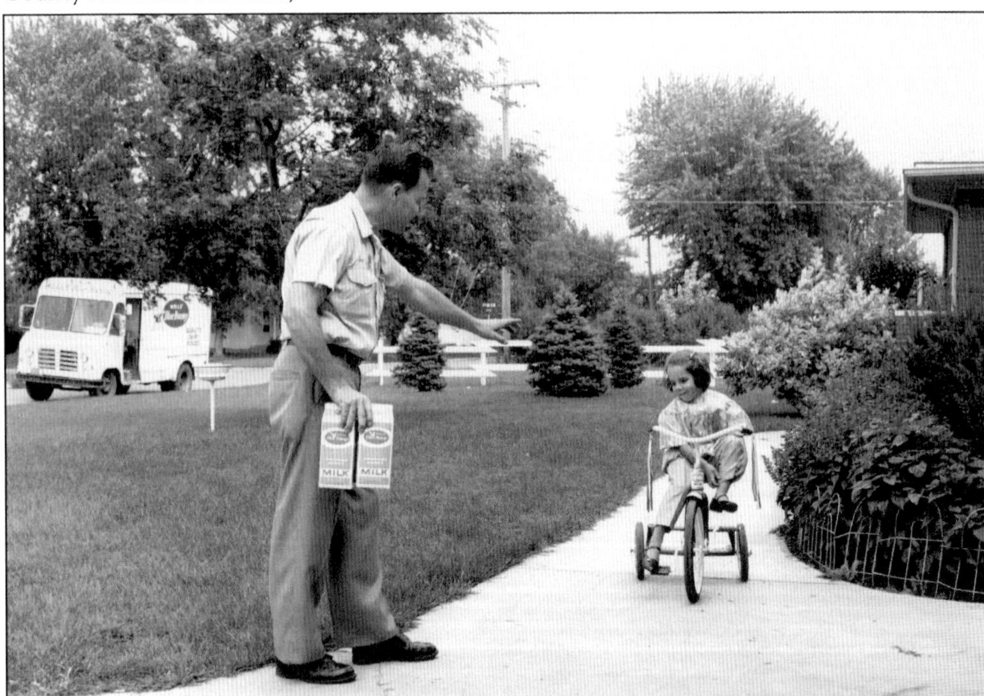

The Wells deliveryman in this later photograph is identified as Stan Weiler. (Courtesy Plymouth County Historical Museum.)

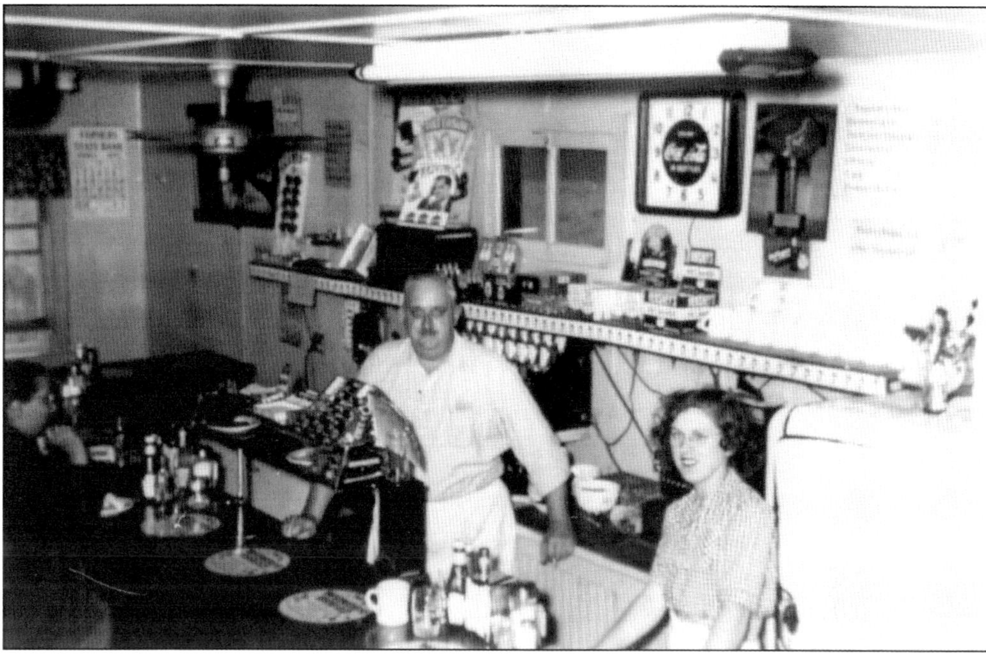

Charles Miller and his wife, Ida, moved to Le Mars in 1940. They operated Miller's Lunch on north Highway 75 from 1943 to 1990. Miller's Lunch was a favorite stop for truckers and everyone who liked good hamburgers. Charles and an unidentified waitress are anticipating the arrival of customers. The customer seated to the far left in the photograph above is Vida Brouillette. The photographs were taken by Freeman "Frenchy" Brouillette about 1950. (Courtesy Plymouth County Historical Museum.)

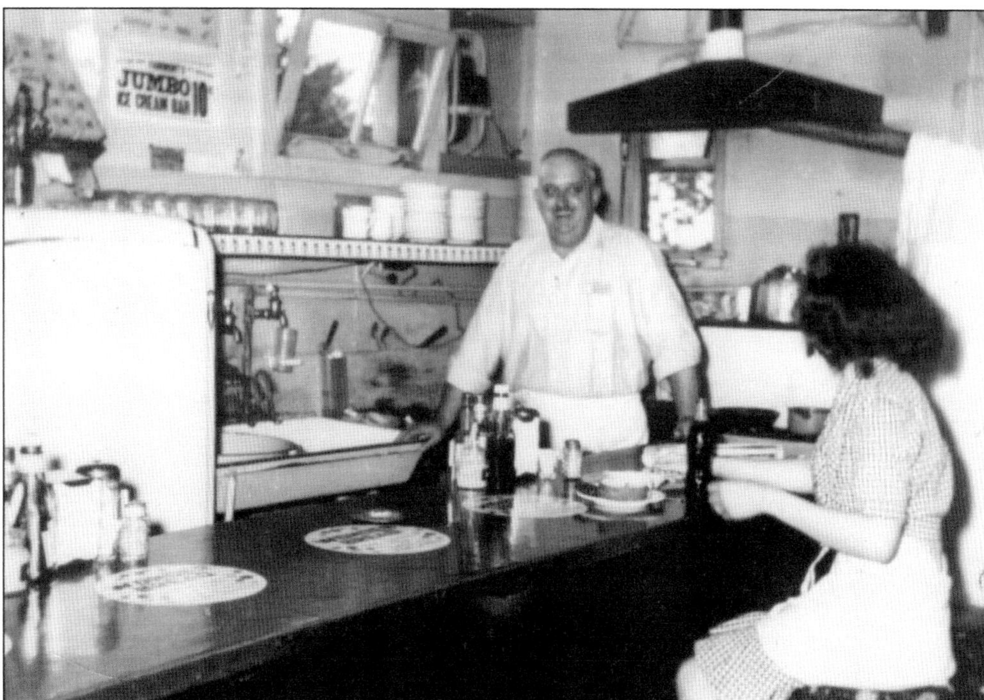

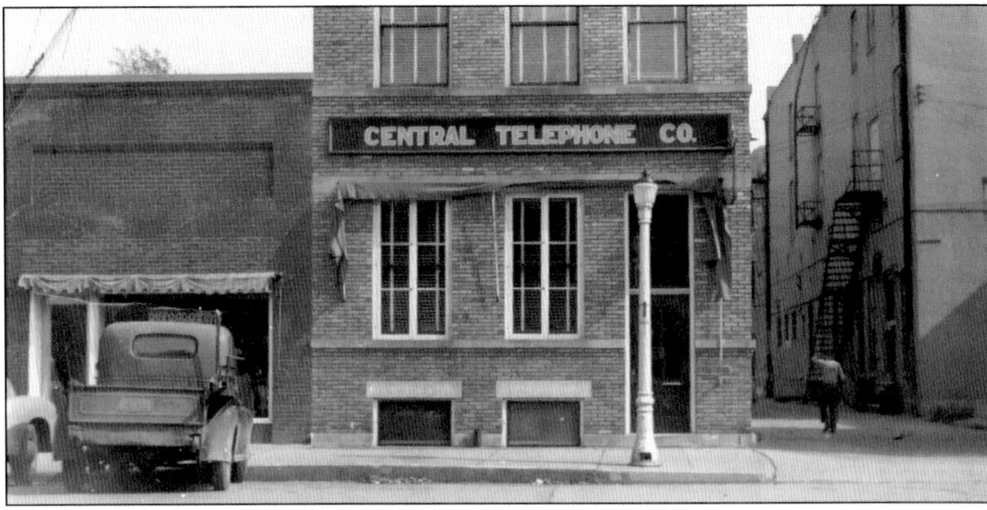

The Central Telephone Company was a member of the Iowa Independent Telephone Association. The building was located at 22 First Avenue NW according to the November 1955 telephone directory for Le Mars. (Courtesy Plymouth County Historical Museum.)

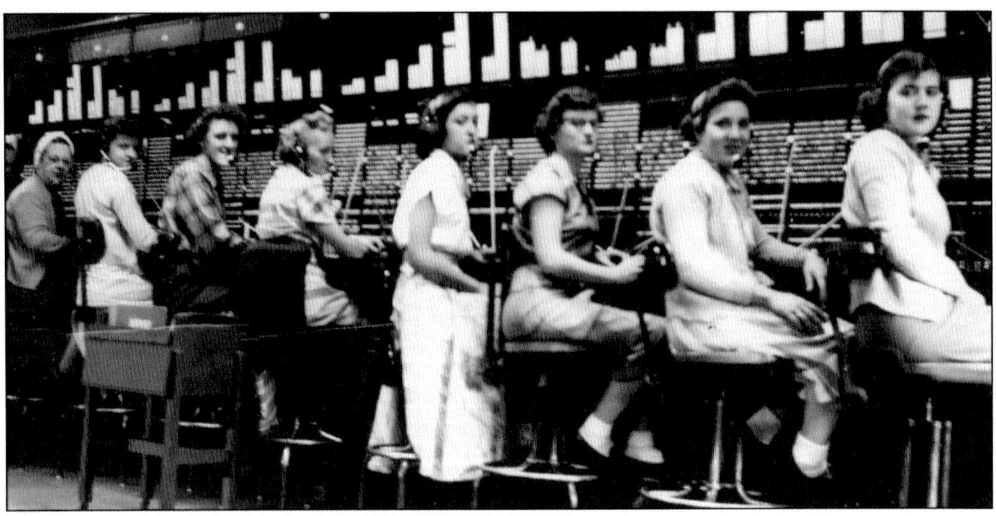

Le Mars Central Telephone Company operators are, from left to right, Mae Carey, Marthetta Reddix, Phyliss Wilde, Emma Trafford, Beverly Domonick, Joan Clifford, Marion Wilhelmi, and Donna Nielsen. (Courtesy Plymouth County Historical Museum.)

Three

ENTERTAINMENT AND EVENTS

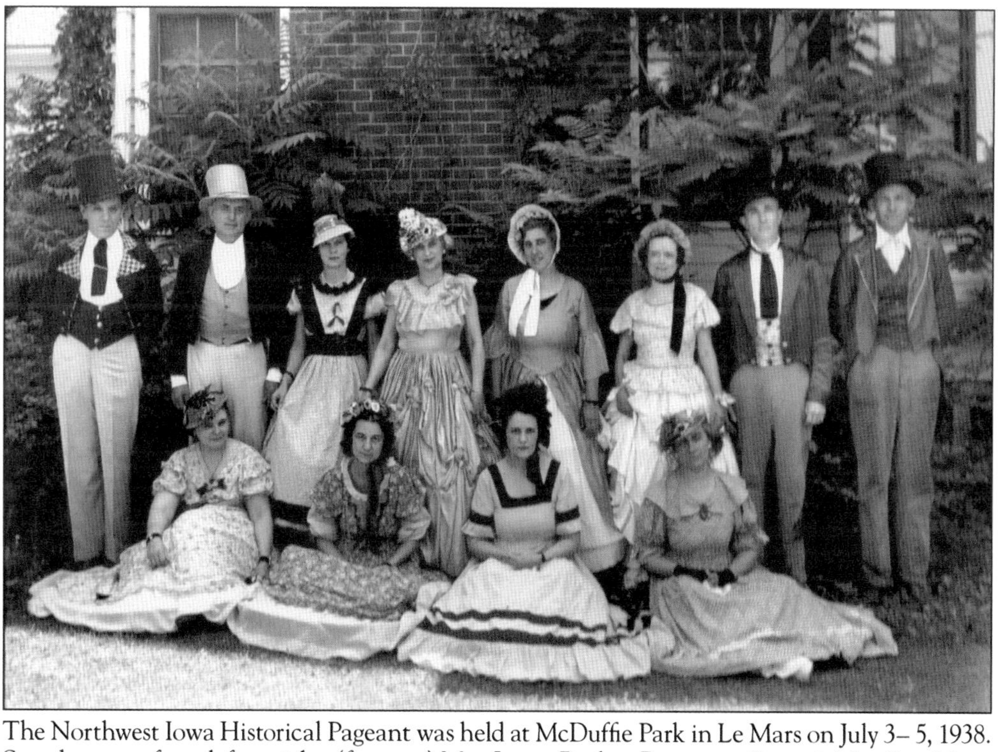

The Northwest Iowa Historical Pageant was held at McDuffie Park in Le Mars on July 3– 5, 1938. Seen here are, from left to right, (first row) Mrs. James Becker, Rosemary Sartori, Mrs. Pete Haas, and Mrs. R. J. M. Long; (second row) Homer Steeg, Jake Hoorneman, Ann Kanago, Mrs. Billy Arendt, Mrs. George Koenig, Mrs. George Sturges, George W. Sturges, and Russell Green. (Courtesy Plymouth County Historical Museum.)

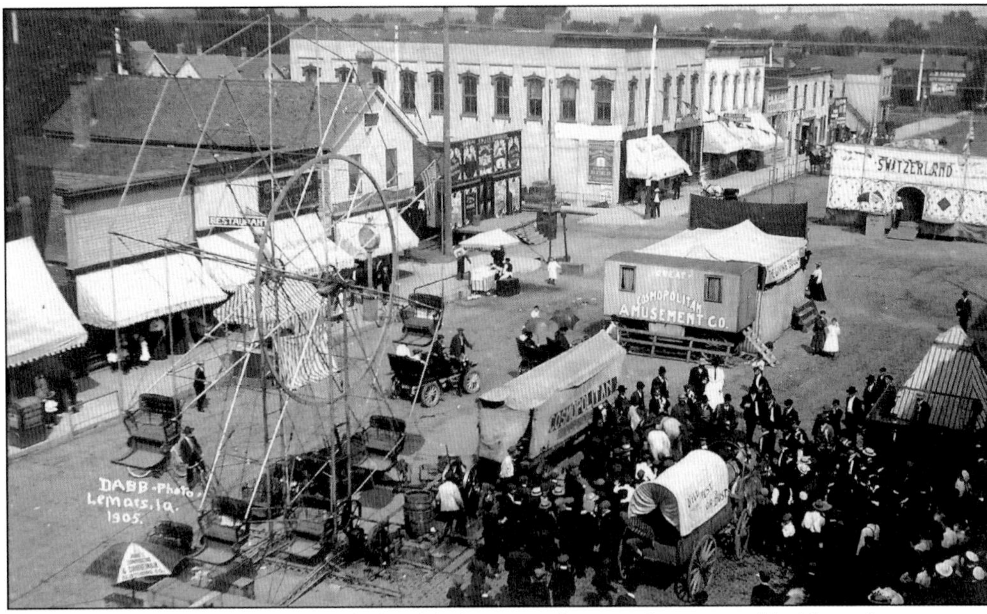

Dabbs Photo of Le Mars captured this fabulous aerial view of a carnival held on the streets of Le Mars in 1905. The *Akron Register-Tribune*, August 17, 1905, stated that Joseph Sampson, J. F. Keenan, Lou Walker, and John Hentges Jr. comprised a party of well-known county seat citizens distributing advertising matter about the Le Mars carnival to be held September 4–9. (Courtesy Plymouth County Historical Museum.)

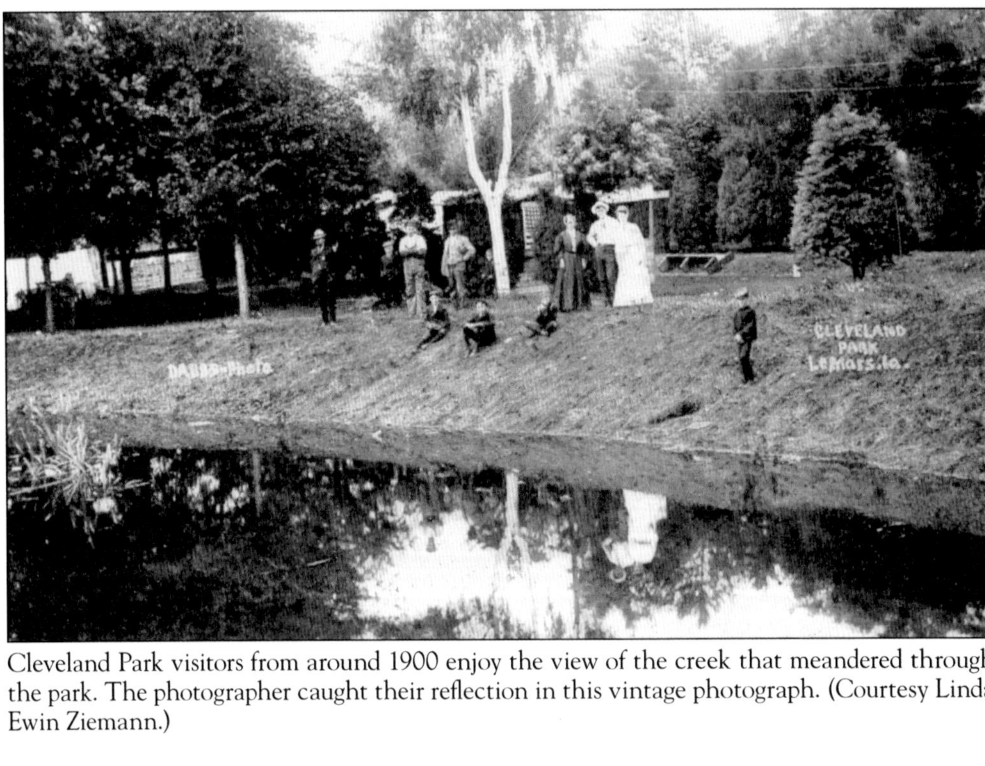

Cleveland Park visitors from around 1900 enjoy the view of the creek that meandered through the park. The photographer caught their reflection in this vintage photograph. (Courtesy Linda Ewin Ziemann.)

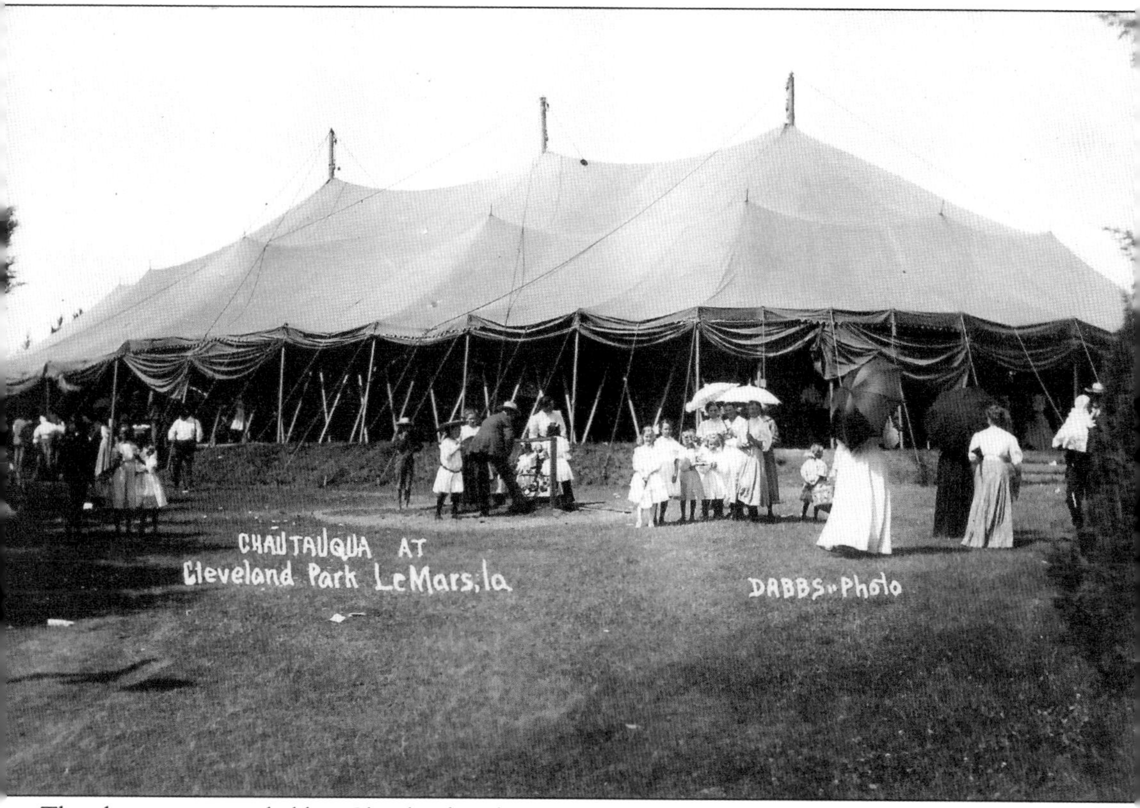

The chautauqua was held at Cleveland Park in Le Mars. At its peak in the mid-1920s, circuit chautauqua performers and lecturers appeared in more than 10,000 communities in 45 states to audiences totaling 45 million people. The circuit chautauqua meant a chance for the community to gather for three to seven days to enjoy a course of lectures on various subjects. Audiences also saw classic plays and Broadway hits and heard a variety of music, from metropolitan opera stars to glee clubs to bell ringers. Many saw their first movies in the circuit tents. The goal of the circuit chautauqua was to offer challenging, informational, and inspirational stimulation to rural and small-town America. The last of the chautauqua meetings in Le Mars were held in 1930, declining because the automobile and radio were filling the cultural communications gap more efficiently. (Courtesy Plymouth County Historical Museum.)

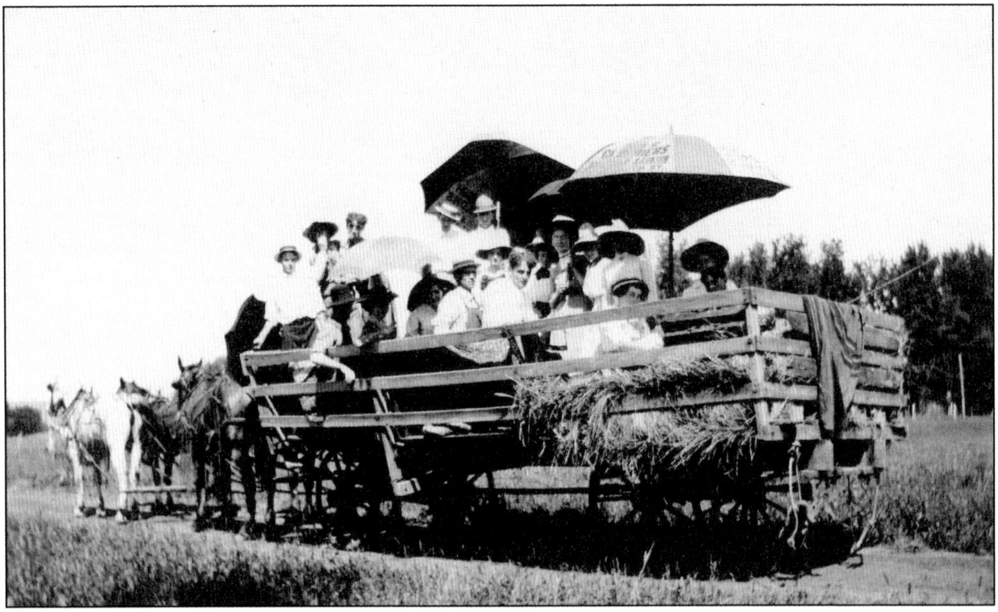

In the early 1900s, Adaville young people enjoyed a special hayride outing. They are Mr. and Mrs. Ray Oaks, Veta Stinton, Clarence Bristow, Myrtle Herman, Phoebe Chamberland, Laura Bristow, Ruth Brown, Ronald Brown, Viola Parker, Grant Brown, Alice Brown, Wesley Brown, Mary Brown, Charlie Brodie, Bertha Ott, George Taylor, Neva Stinton, Emery Lias, and French. (Courtesy Nancy Tindall Yoder.)

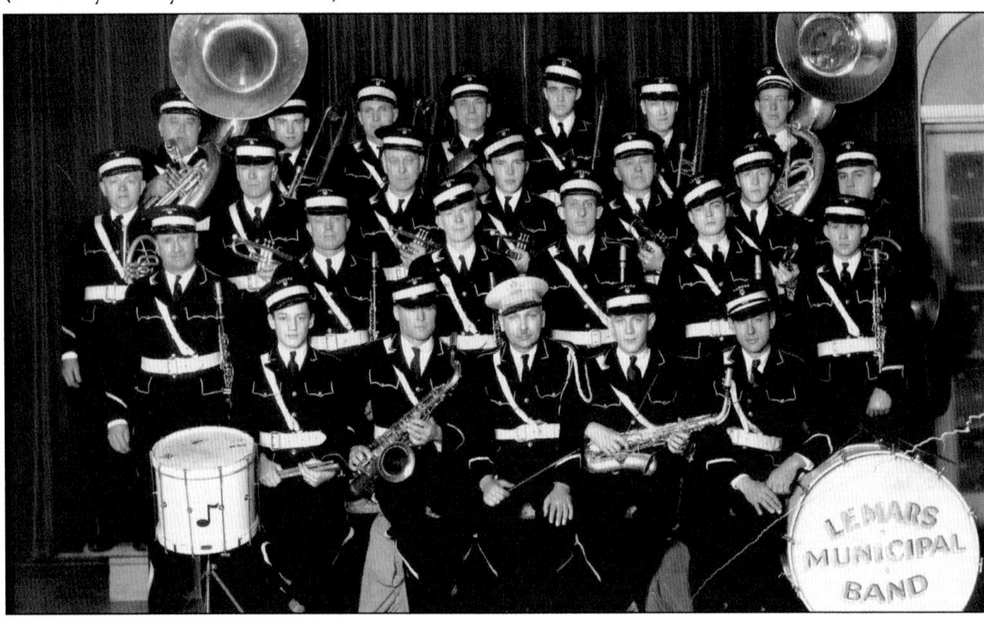

The 1938 Le Mars Municipal Band members are, from left to right, (first row) Bob Merritt, M. Lake, Ira Vail (conductor), J. Becker, and J. Runcie; (second row) Gordon Stokes, ? Schmidt, Vets Kale, Jim Muller, H. Petersen, and L. Weidauer; (third row) Joe Overman, Hans Sonnichsen, Art Hansen, H. Eilers, ? Hansen, Harvey Smith, and Sy Lucken; (fourth row) Bill Hartter, unidentified, unidentified, ? Nelle, ? Boudy, A. Honneld, and unidentified. (Courtesy Plymouth County Historical Museum.)

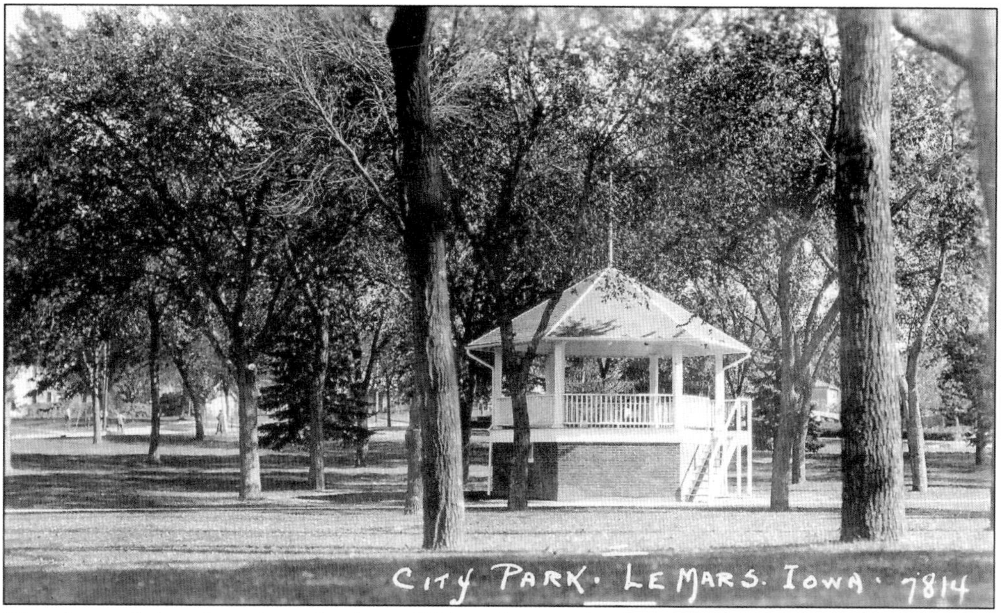

The city park bandstand was built in 1924, with steps leading to the stage floor on the south side, and it contained a step-down basement. The park also had a fishpond and a combination drinking fountain. The Beuther Memorial was a brick and ceramic public fountain, providing two drinking fountains for people (one on each end). In the center was a lower fountain for animals to use to quench their thirst. The memorial became known as the "dog's drinking fountain." By the 1960s, the original bandstand and the memorial were gone. In May 1981, a dedication was held for the newly constructed bandstand replacement in Foster Park, formerly known as City Park. (Courtesy Plymouth County Historical Museum.)

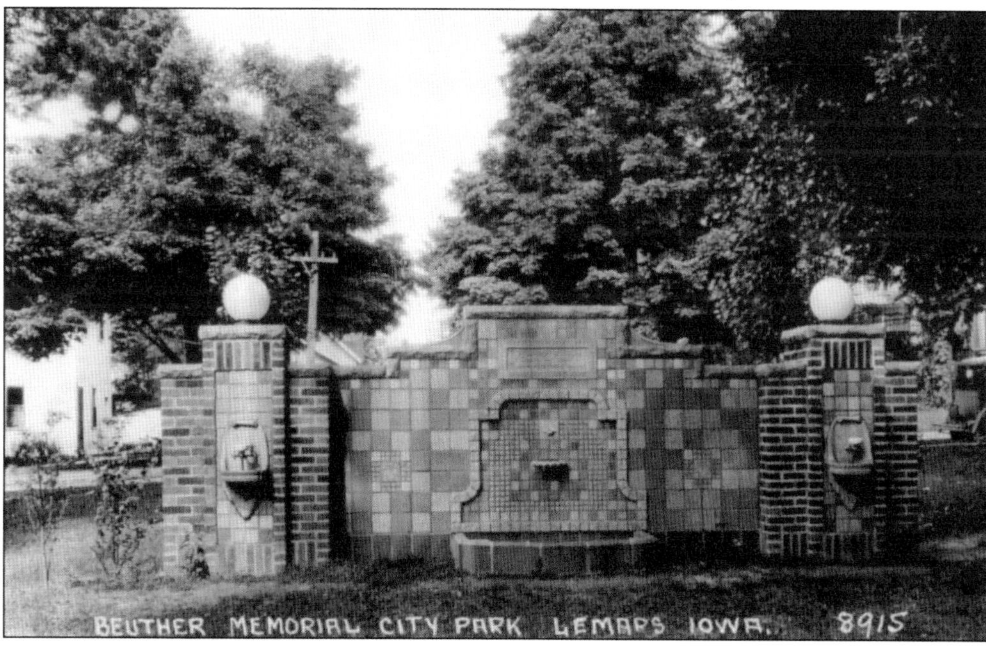

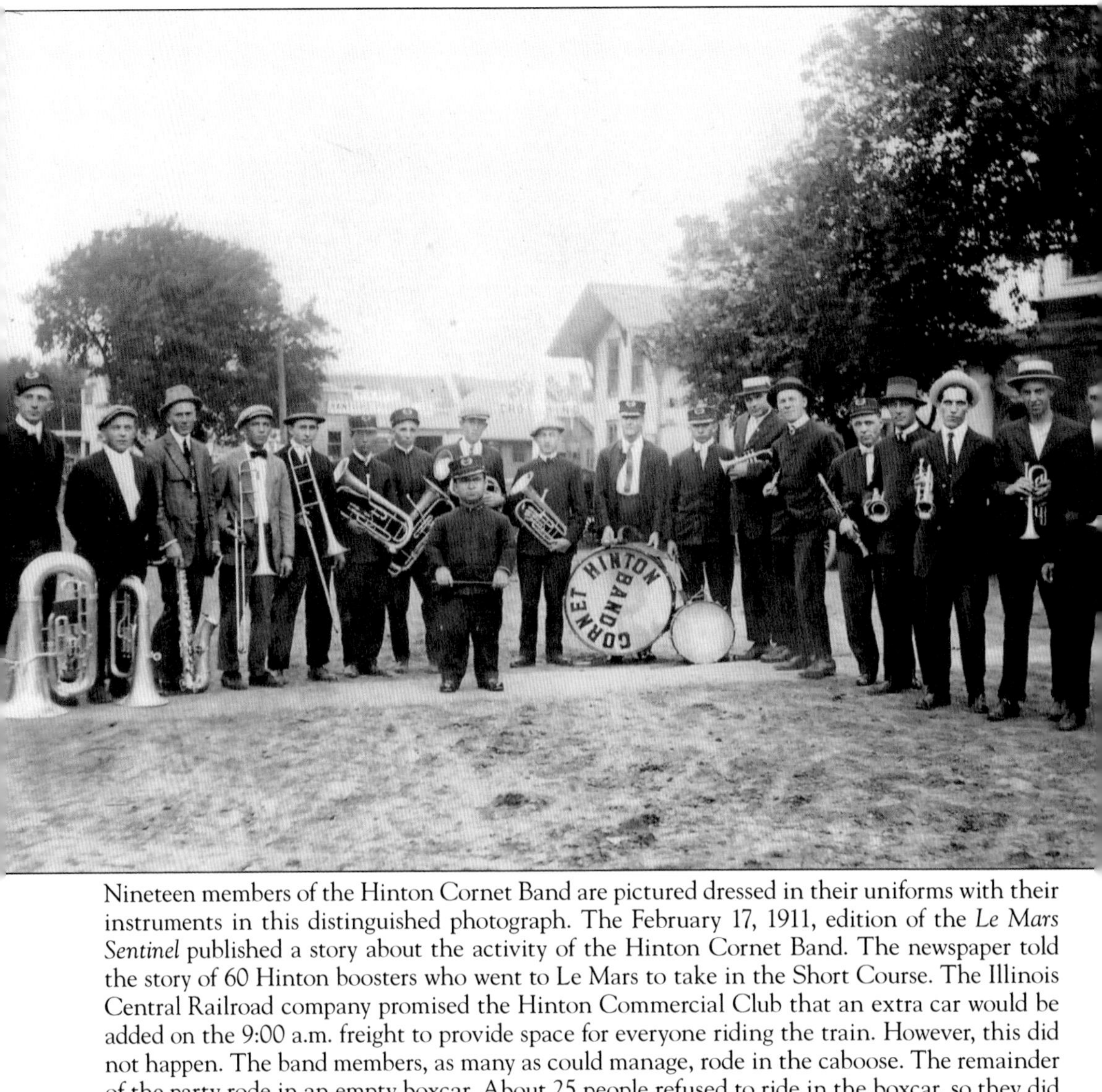

Nineteen members of the Hinton Cornet Band are pictured dressed in their uniforms with their instruments in this distinguished photograph. The February 17, 1911, edition of the *Le Mars Sentinel* published a story about the activity of the Hinton Cornet Band. The newspaper told the story of 60 Hinton boosters who went to Le Mars to take in the Short Course. The Illinois Central Railroad company promised the Hinton Commercial Club that an extra car would be added on the 9:00 a.m. freight to provide space for everyone riding the train. However, this did not happen. The band members, as many as could manage, rode in the caboose. The remainder of the party rode in an empty boxcar. About 25 people refused to ride in the boxcar, so they did not go to Le Mars. The Hinton Cornet Band furnished music during the day. They performed very well, in spite of the fact that they had to play in the cold air on the street. The entire crowd boarded the 3:45 p.m. train for home, all thinking Le Mars was a very entertaining town. (Courtesy Plymouth County Historical Museum.)

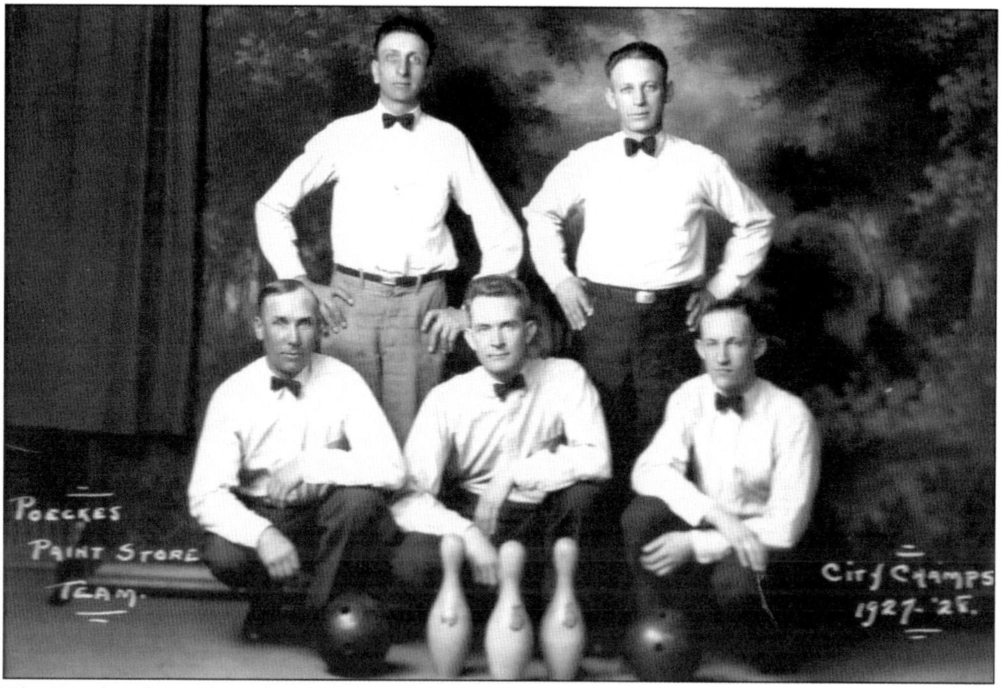

The Poeckes Paint Store bowling team was city champs in 1927–1928. Those pictured are, from left to right, (first row) Dan Ariosa, Vets Kale, and Hank Poeckes; (second row) Bill Zeig and Fred Frink. (Courtesy Plymouth County Historical Museum.)

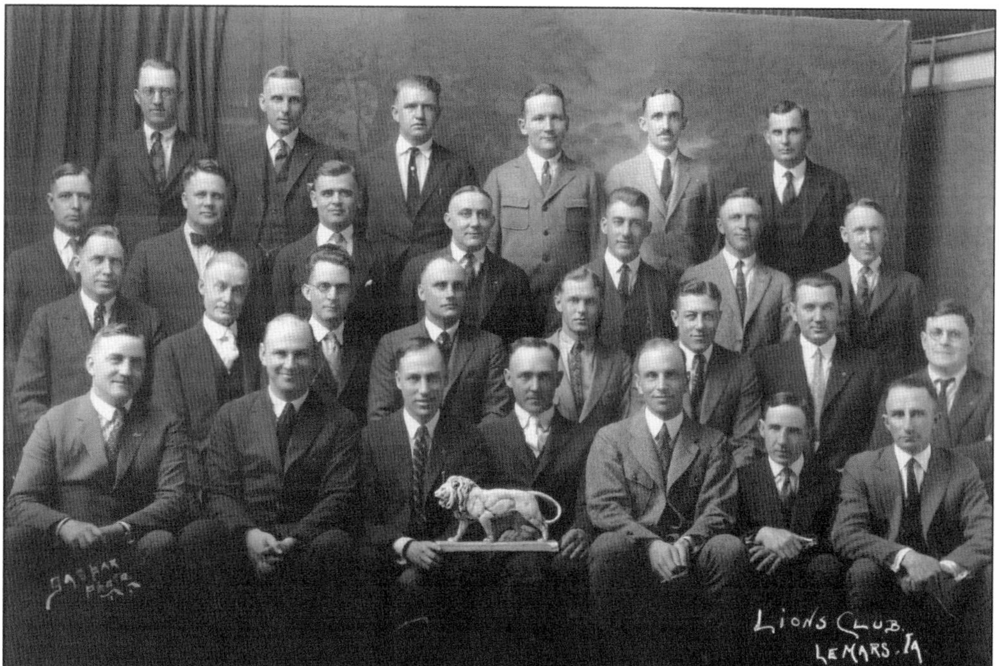

The Le Mars Lions Club was founded in 1921 and became an important center of leadership and sociability in the community. This photograph did not provide any identification of names or date. (Courtesy Plymouth County Historical Museum.)

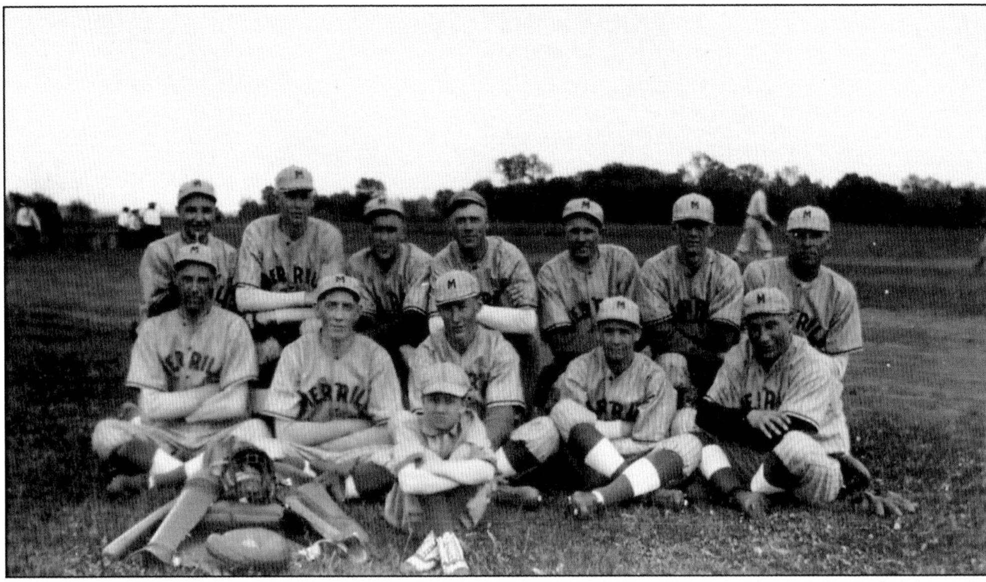

The Merrill baseball team members were photographed together, with the ball field in the background. Clarence Roland Hemphill is the person on the top row, first from left. (Courtesy Pat Hemphill.)

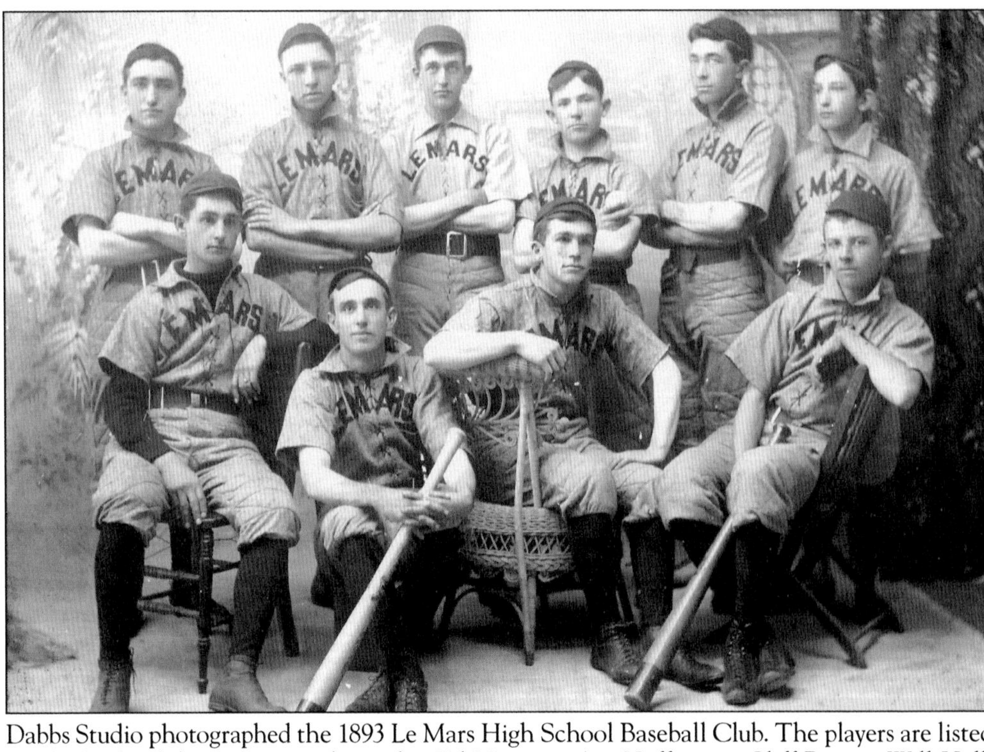

Dabbs Studio photographed the 1893 Le Mars High School Baseball Club. The players are listed on the back of the picture in this order: Ed Hentges, Art Hoffmann, Cliff Brown, Will Hall, Claude Brown, Louie Gilbert, Art Wilson, Carl Adamson, Guy Struble, and Art Hillebrand. Hillebrand later coached at Princeton. (Courtesy Plymouth County Historical Museum.)

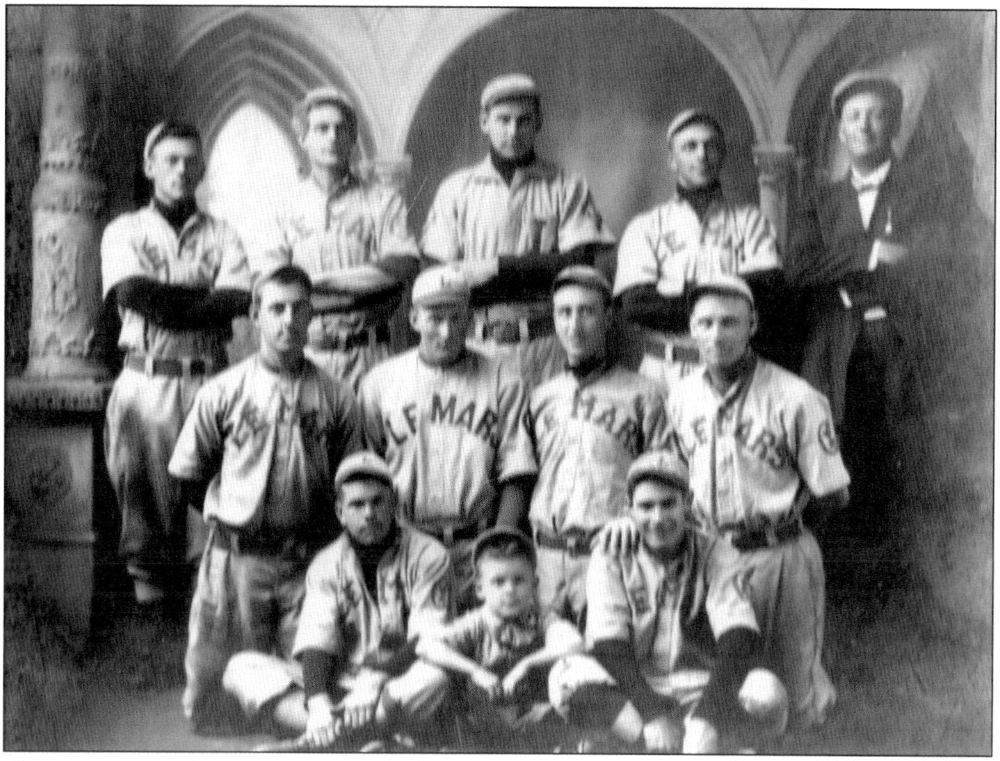

These are two early photographs of the Le Mars baseball team. There are no names or dates on either of the photographs. (Courtesy Plymouth County Historical Museum.)

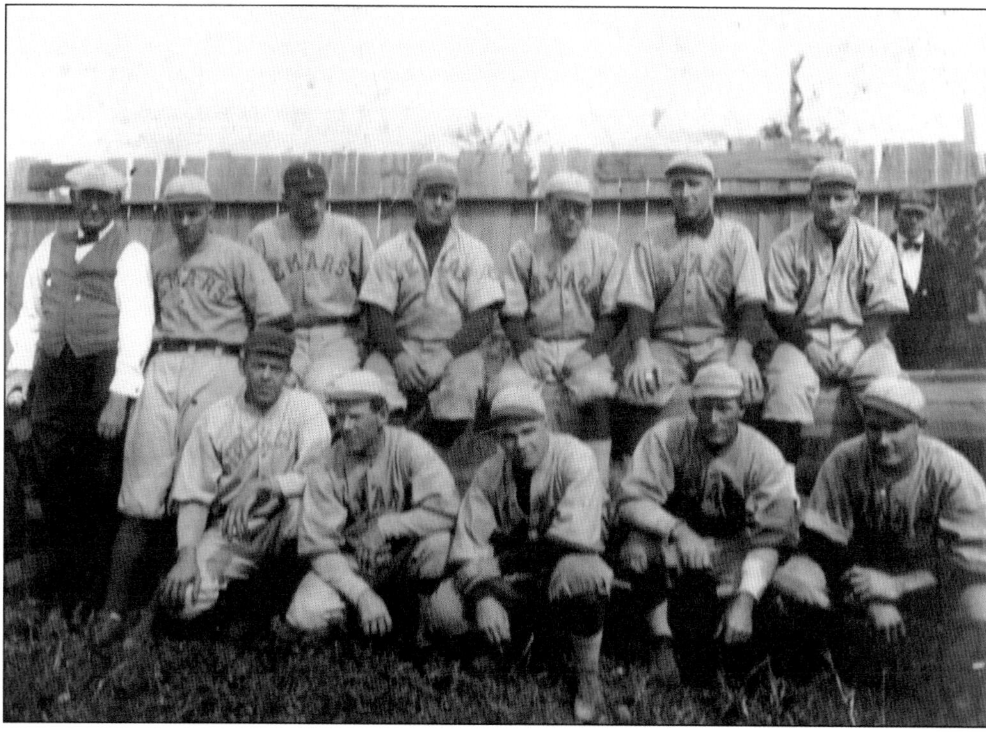

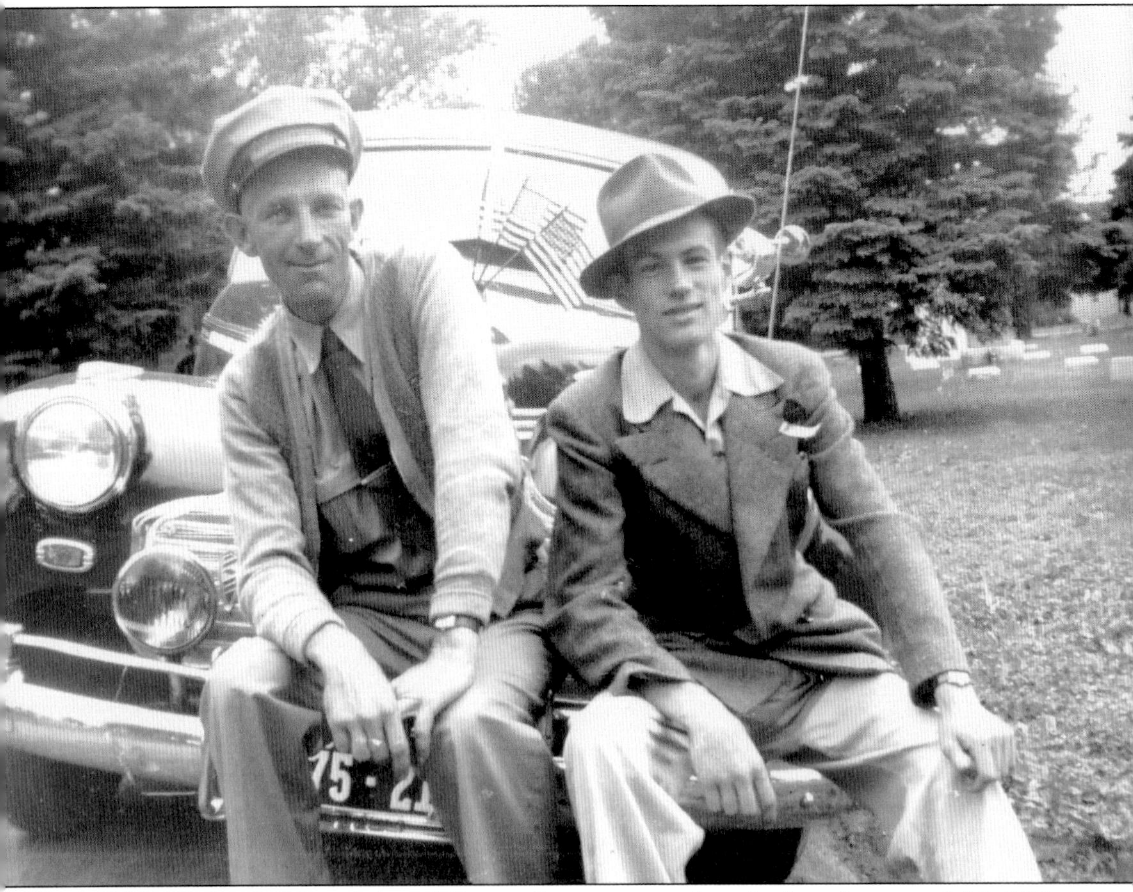

Clarence Stevenson, at left, and Vernon Ewin are seated on the front bumper of this 1941 car. Notice the parade flags in the center of the windshield of the car. The picture was taken on Memorial Day 1941, with the Le Mars City Cemetery in the background. The annual Memorial Day parade had just taken place. The parade route started in the downtown area, proceeded to the Catholic cemetery, and ended at the Le Mars City Cemetery. (Courtesy Linda Ewin Ziemann.)

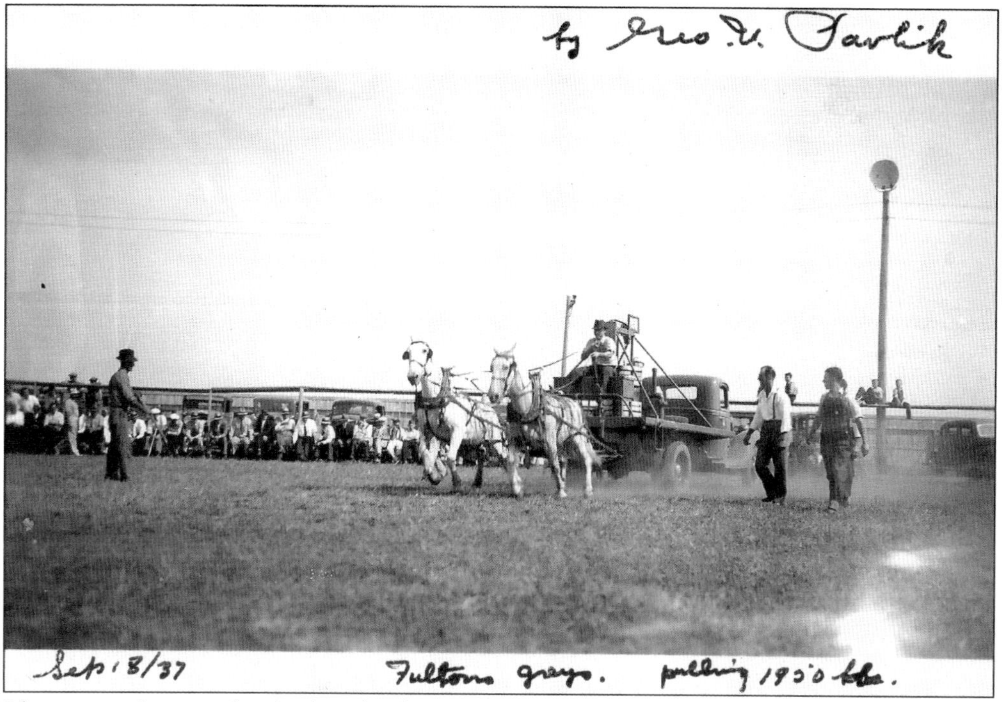

These two photographs display the fun and adventure at a local horse show. The pictures are dated the same day, September 18, 1937. George Pavlik was the photographer. (Courtesy Plymouth County Historical Museum.)

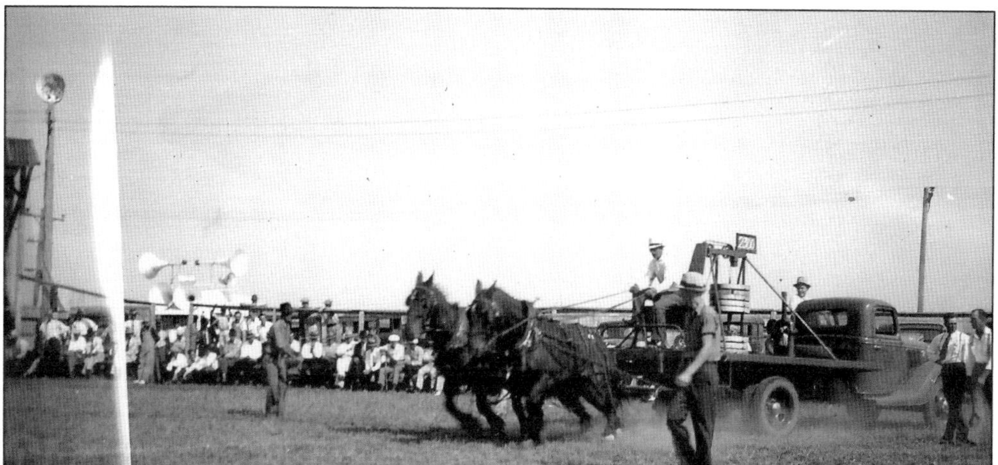

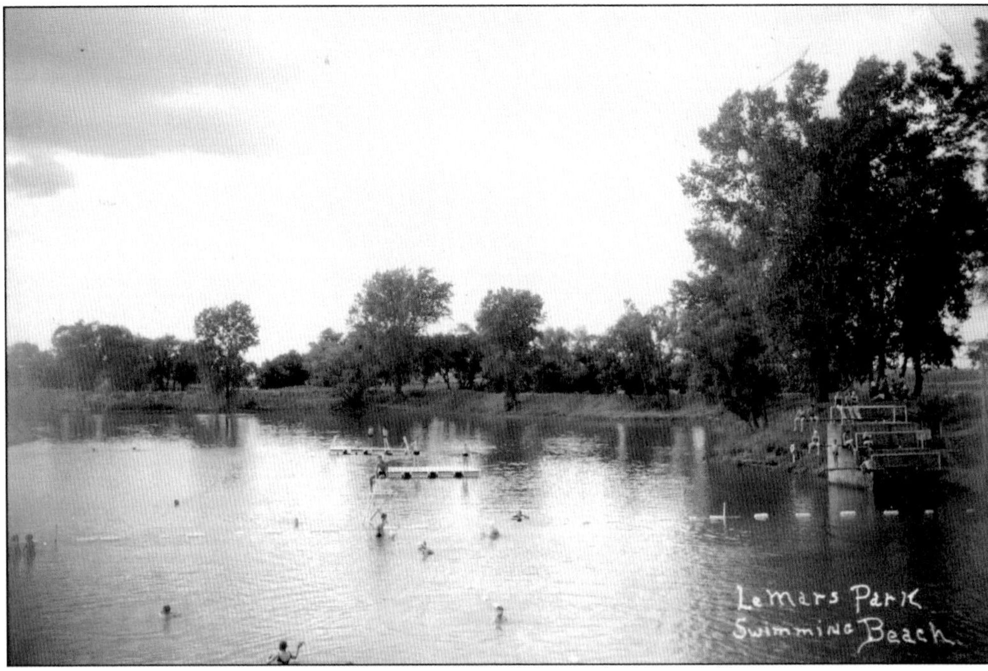

The Le Mars Park swimming beach, also known as "the pit," was home to much enjoyment and fun in the water during the summer warm weather for several decades. The structures were built by the WPA during the Depression years. (Courtesy Plymouth County Historical Museum.)

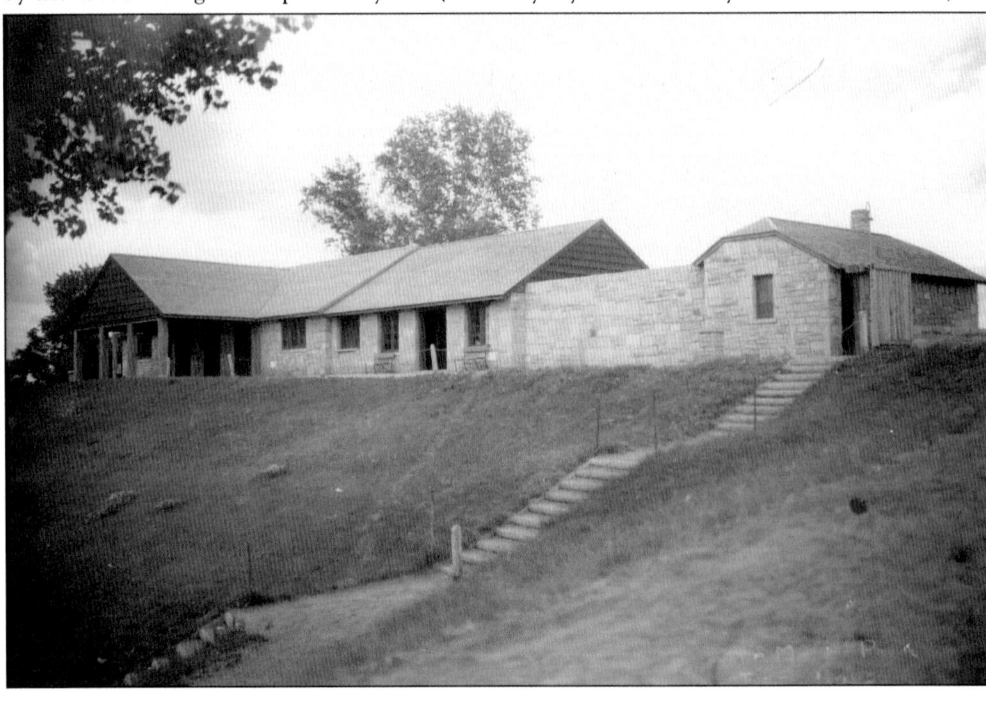

Four

Farm to Market

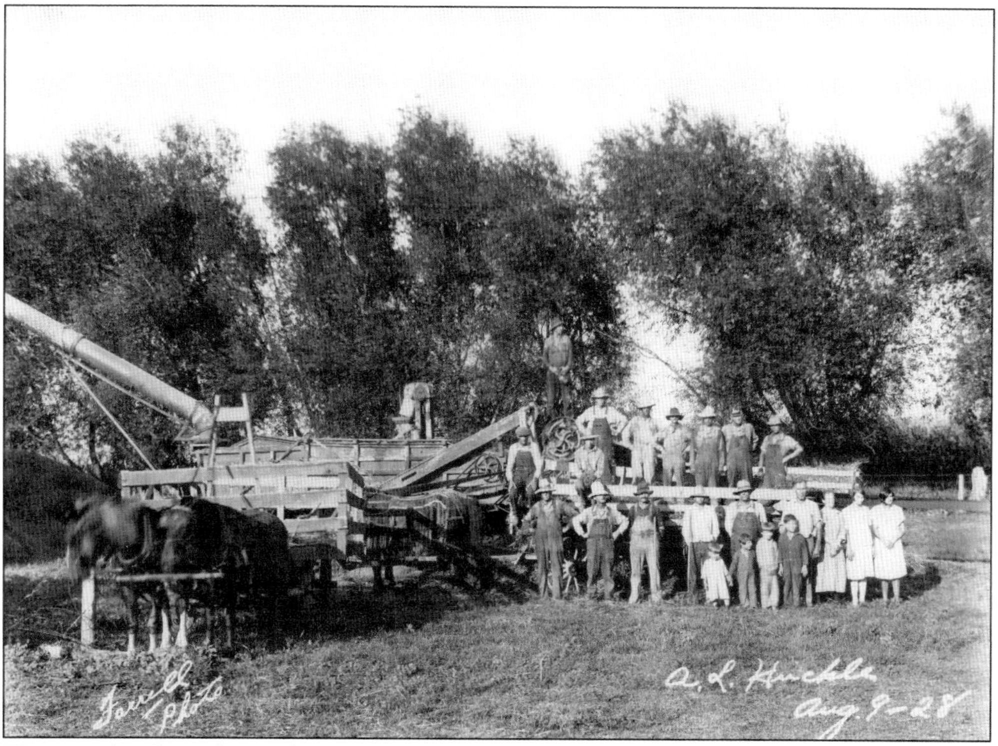

This was threshing day in the summer of 1928 at the A. L. Huckle farm west of Le Mars. Seen here are, from left to right, (first row) Martin Huckle, Eva Huckle, Rita Huckle and William (Bill) Huckle; (second row) Emil Grosenheider, Andrew McClintock, J. D. Tindall, unidentified, unidentified, A. L. Huckle, Anna Huckle, Minnie Grosenheider, and Eva Stevens; (third row, seated on edge of the rack) Hans Martfield and Richard Tindall; (fourth row, standing on the rack) unidentified, unidentified, Pete Petersen, Carl Harms, Henry Adden, and Hilbert McClintock. (Courtesy Nancy Tindall Yoder.)

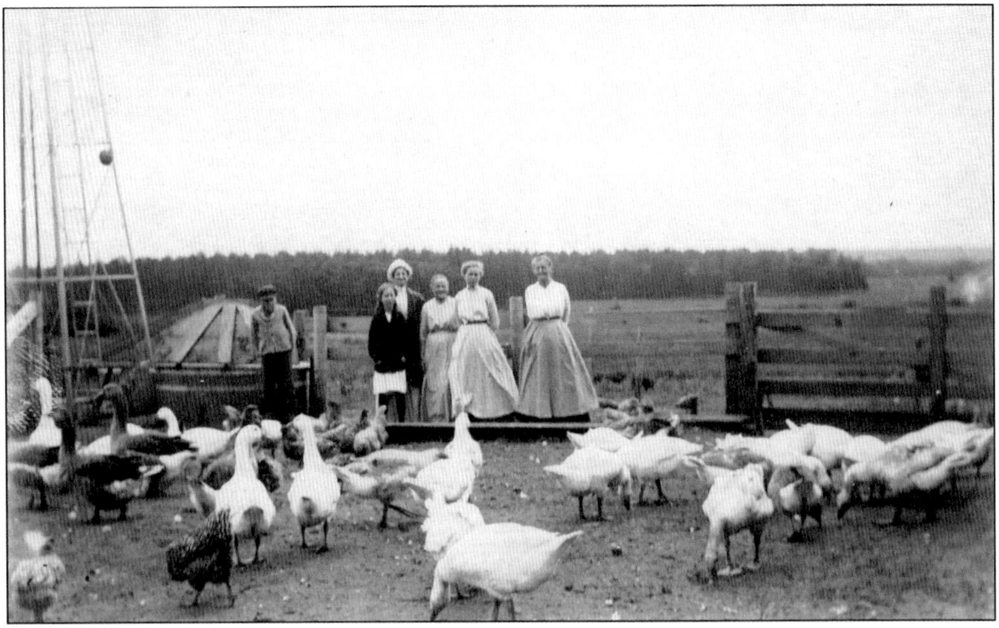

This farmyard geese photograph was taken at the home of Eddie and Mary Alice Lancaster, near Seney in 1917. Those in the picture are, from left to right, Vincent Lancaster, Gladys Kennedy, Sadie Alderson, Alice Lancaster, unidentified, and Nannie Alderson. (Courtesy Linda Ewin Ziemann.)

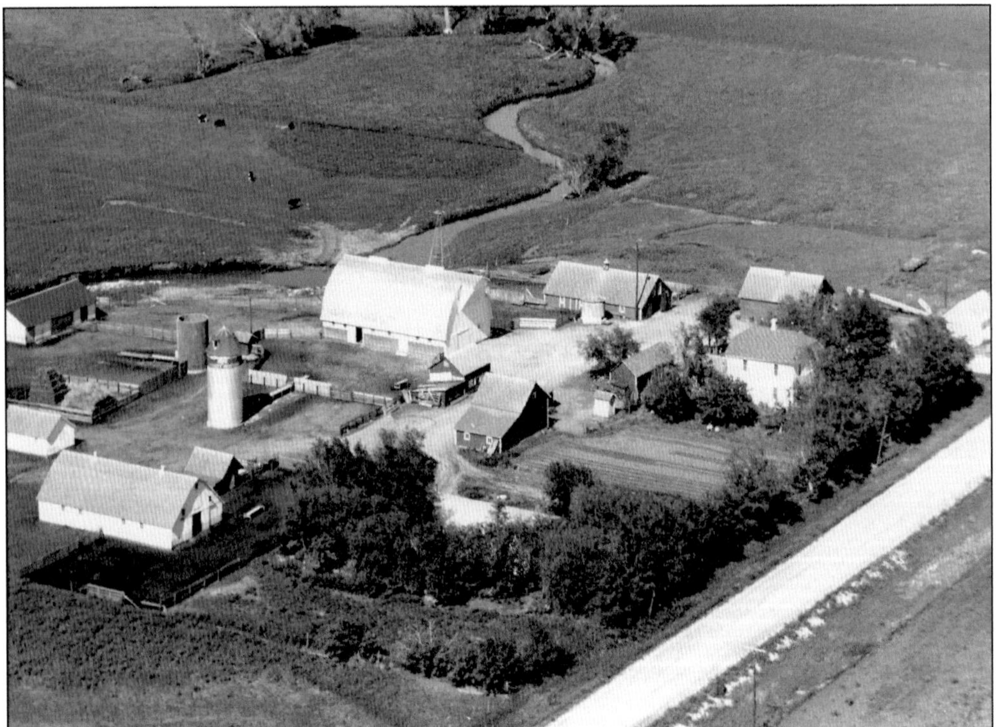

This is an aerial view of an unidentified Plymouth County farm building site. (Courtesy Plymouth County Historical Museum.)

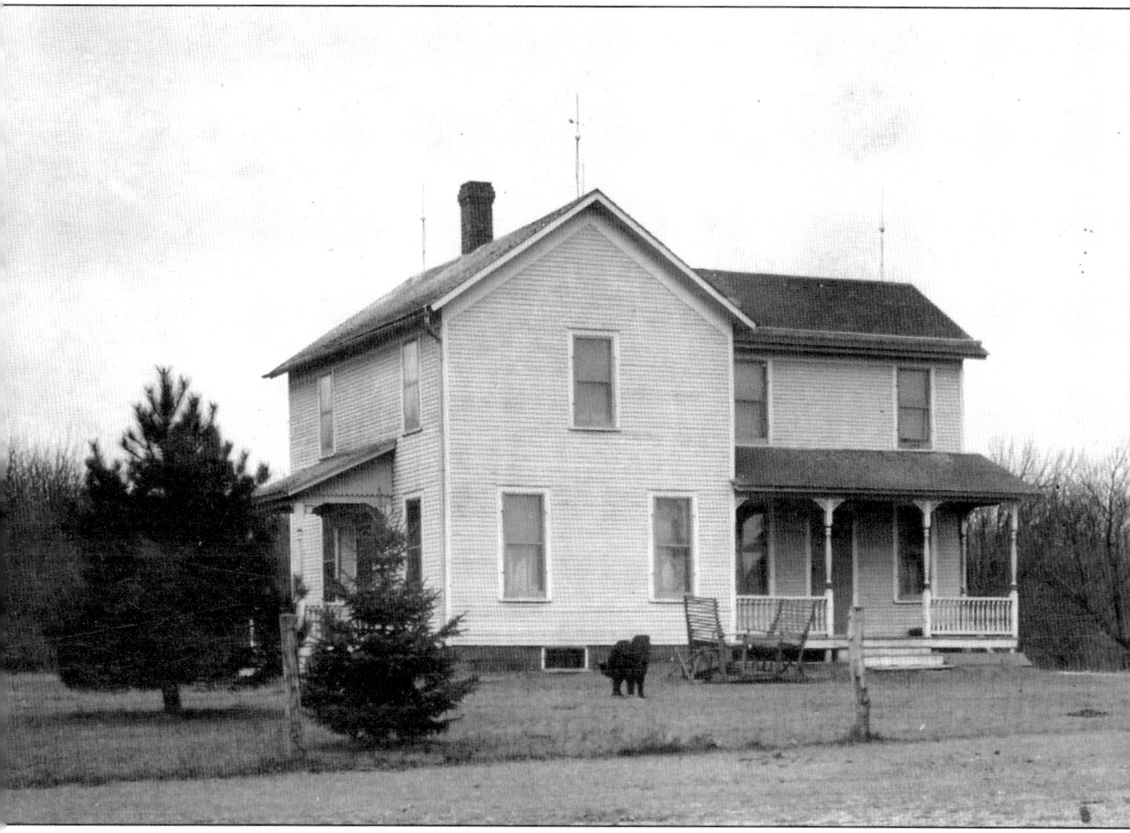

This farm owned by George H. Burrill was located east of Union Township Presbyterian Church. George's fourth daughter, Faye, married Henry Dempster. Henry, Faye, and their son Lowell lived on this farm when their daughter, Thelma, was born at home in 1920. George originally bought this farm in 1909 from Noah Carpenter, who sold the corner acre on which the Union Township Presbyterian Church was built. (Courtesy Duane and Vivien Reeves.)

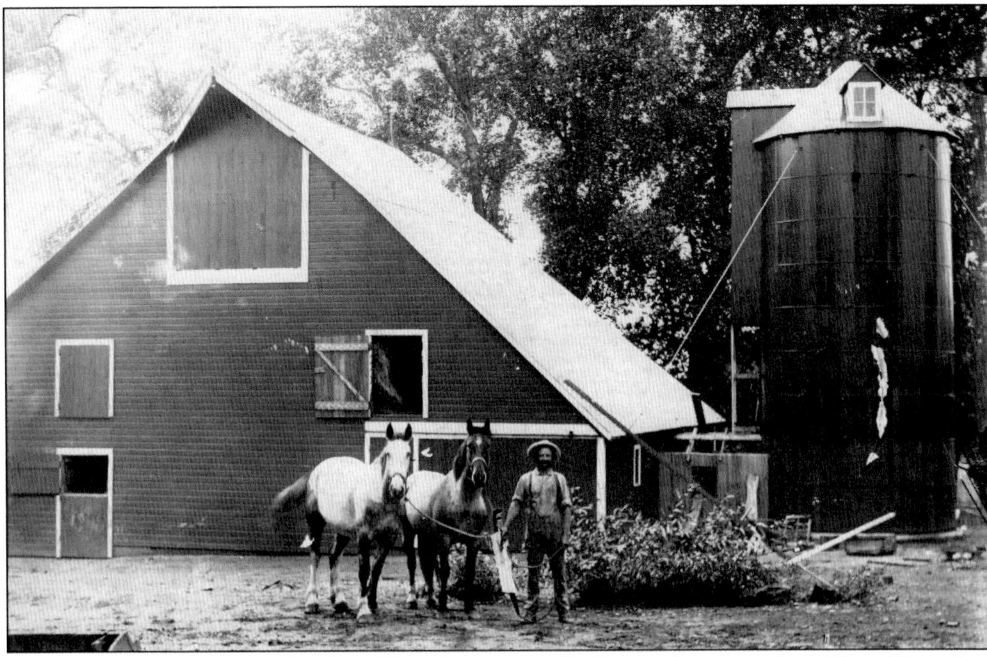

This photograph is believed to be of Bert Reeves on the Reeves homestead, in Elgin Township, one and a half miles northeast of Seney prior to 1900. Bert's grandfather John Reeves first received the patent on this homestead on January 10, 1874. It is a Century Farm and has been farmed by five generations of the Reeves family. (Courtesy Duane and Vivien Reeves.)

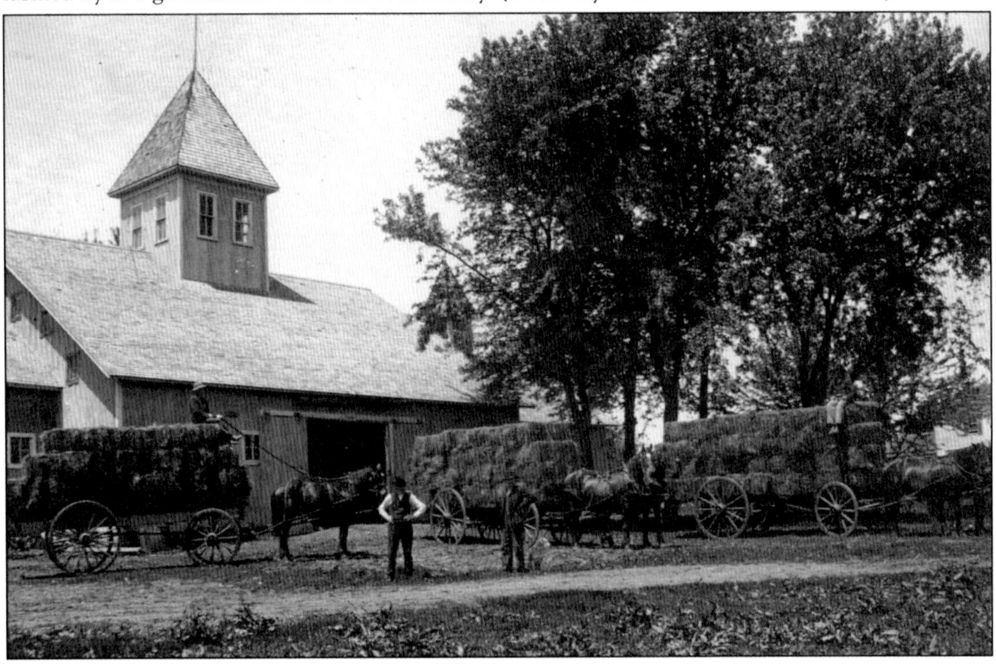

Cap Morton-Sullivan ranch was located one mile west and one mile north of Le Mars. The results of the harvest are stacked in the hay wagons in front of the barn. The second sons of affluent Englishmen were sent to this ranch to learn farming. (Courtesy Plymouth County Historical Museum.)

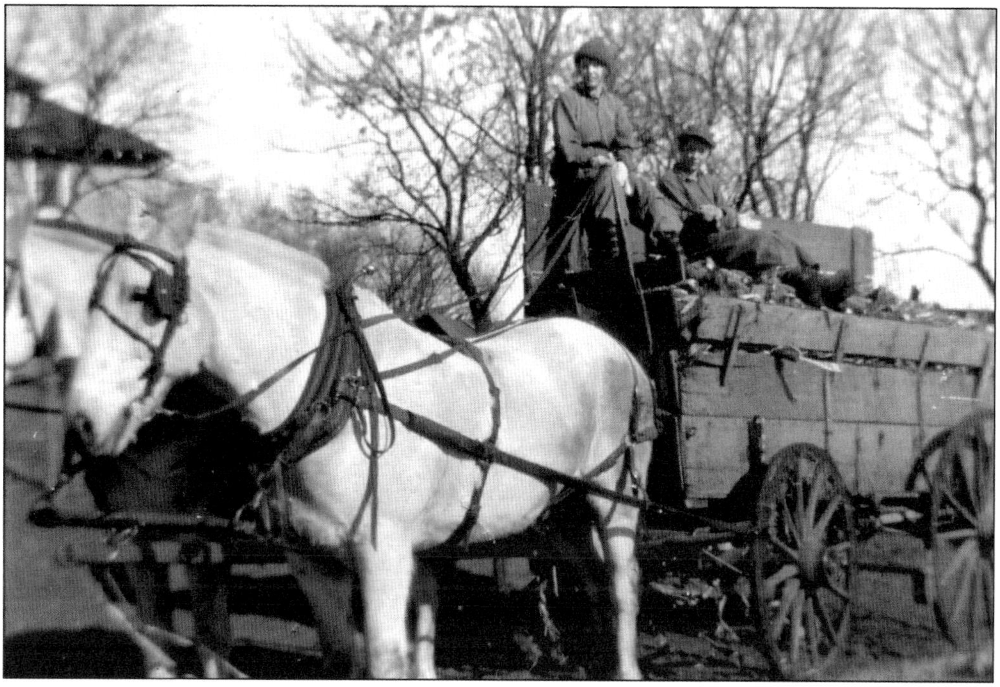

Freda (at left) and Ferne King, daughters of Warren J. and Birdie King, of Adaville are pictured riding on top of a wagonload of picked corn. Both of these girls were teenagers in 1921. (Courtesy Linda Ewin Ziemann.)

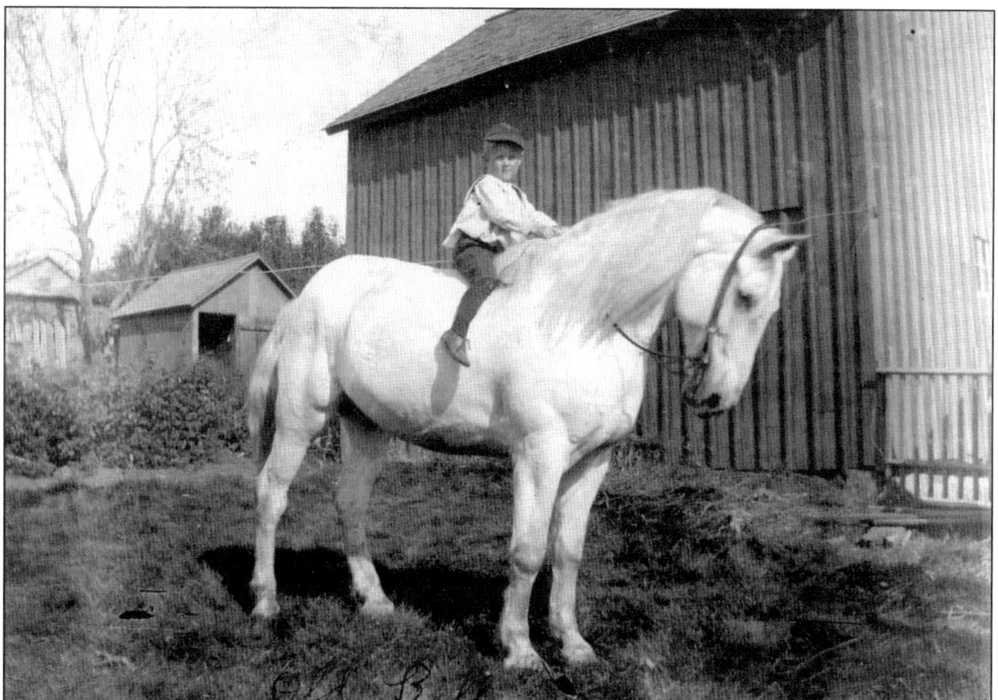

Stanley King, youngest child of Warren J. and Birdie King, is sitting on Old Bill, the family horse. This photograph can be dated to about 1920. (Courtesy Linda Ewin Ziemann.)

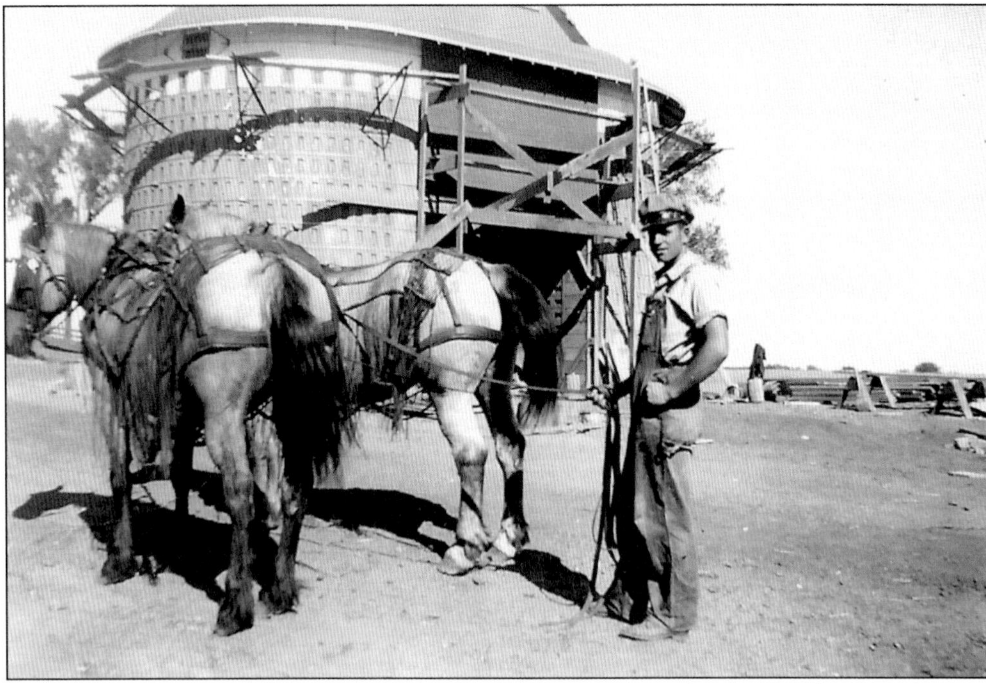

Alfred Tone is photographed with his team in front of a circular corn crib near Akron in 1940. Alfred is the son of Grace (Adams) Tone and Esla Alfred Tone of Hawarden. He hired out to support himself and help his family, as was common practice on the farms. (Courtesy Tim Tone.)

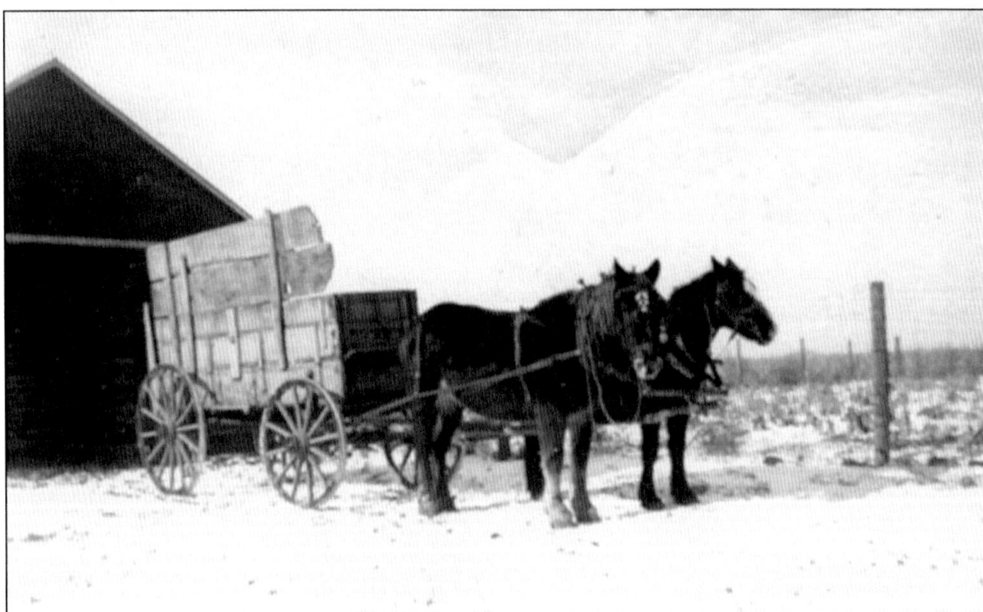

This is a photograph of a horse and wagon with a backboard on the Robertson homestead west of Brunsville. In the 1930s, hand-harvested ears of corn were tossed and bounced off the backboard into the bed of the wagon. The workers harvested the corn from the stalks with glovelike corn hooks as they walked alongside the wagon. (Courtesy Tim Tone.)

This is a photograph in the mid-1930s of Sid Locer's last team of draft horses on his farm west of Brunsville, before machines took over. Their names are lost to time, but they are remembered as a good team. (Courtesy Tim Tone.)

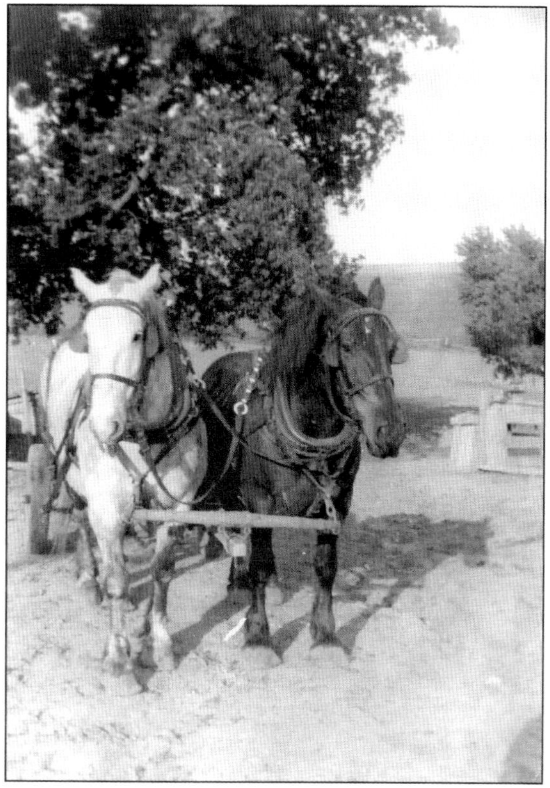

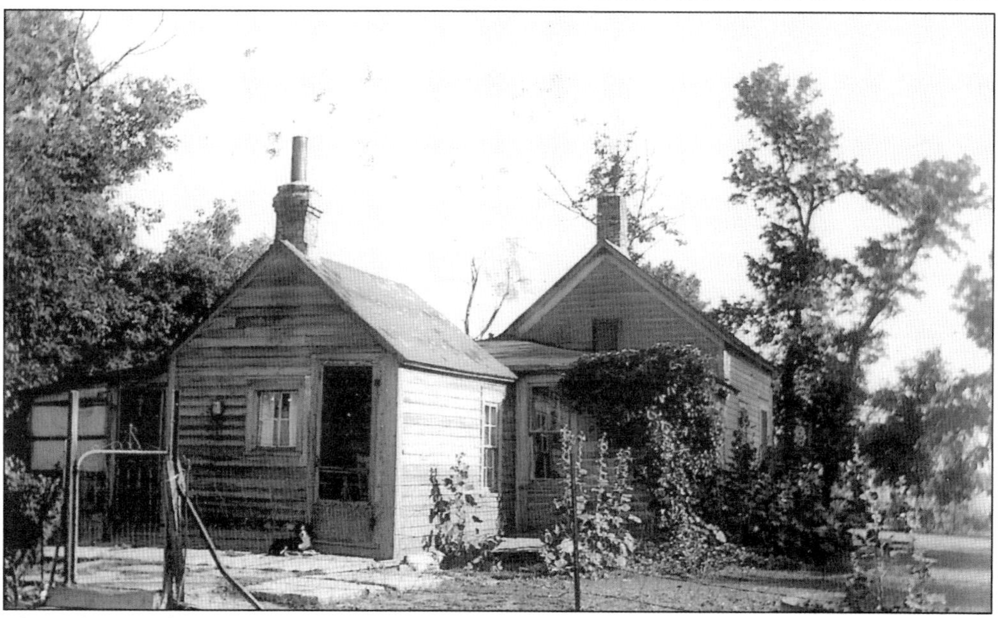

The Robertson homestead place was located a mile north and two miles west of Brunsville. The back original part of the house was expanded as the family grew. Duncan Robertson and Belle (Ross) Robertson owned farms scattered throughout Plymouth County, but this was the home place. Sid Locer and Bessie (Robertson) Locer were the last of the Robertson family to live in this house before a new one was built in the 1960s. (Courtesy Tim Tone.)

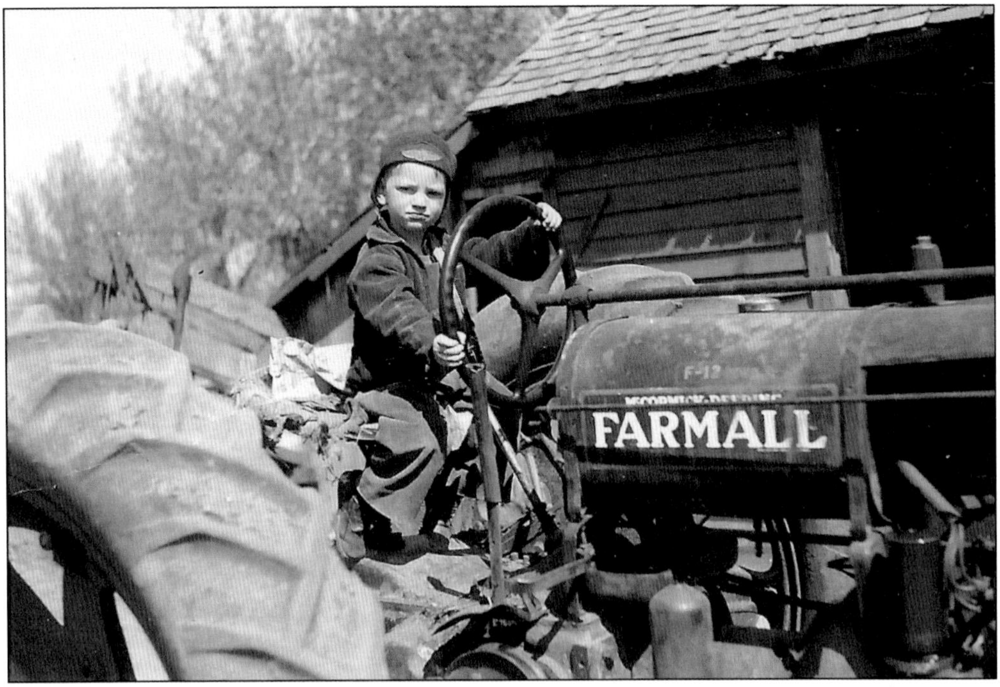

Dan Tone is seated on an International McCormick-Deering Farmall F12, wearing his aviator hat, in 1947. He is a son of Alfred Tone and Dorothy (Locer) Tone. He grew up on the farm and later became a college professor at the University of Nevada–Reno. (Courtesy Tim Tone.)

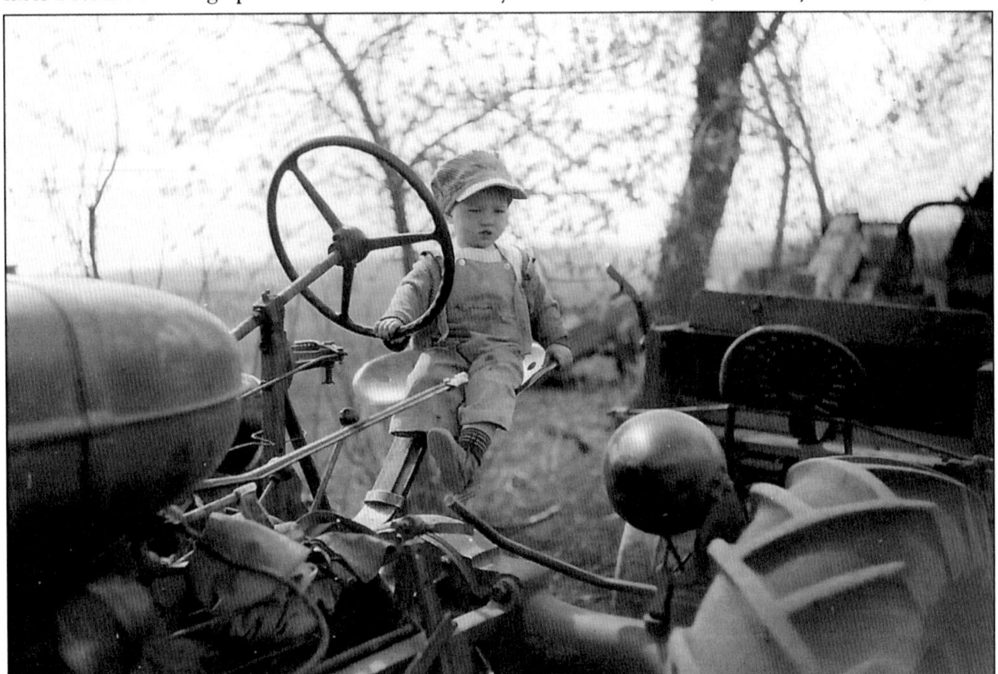

Paul Tone is riding on a Massy pulling a manure spreader in 1947. He is a son of Alfred Tone and Dorothy (Locer) Tone. He grew up on the farm and later lobbied congress for student financial aid. (Courtesy Tim Tone.)

Dan Tone, son of Alfred Tone and Dorothy (Locer) Tone, finds a good use for a fruit crate and looks into the camera giving the "V for Victory" sign for his dad. His father, Alfred, was at that time crossing the Rhine after the Battle of the Bulge in World War II. Alfred returned home, continued farming, and raised a large family near Crathorne. (Courtesy Tim Tone.)

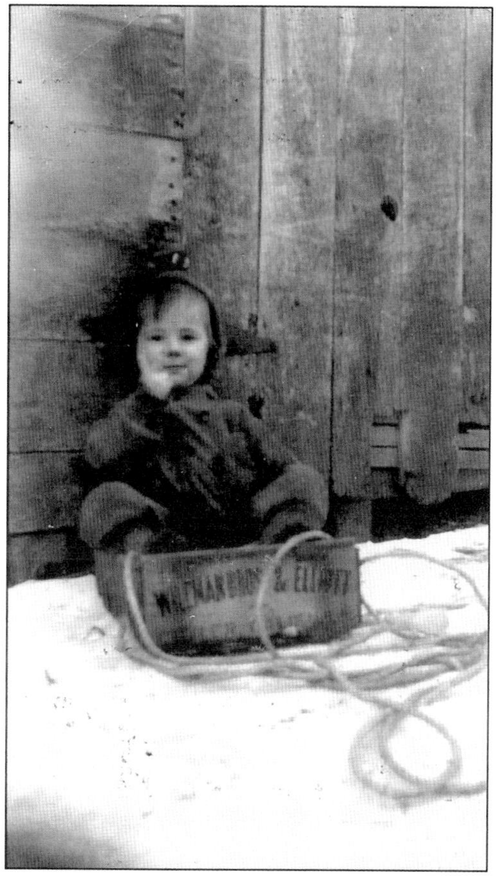

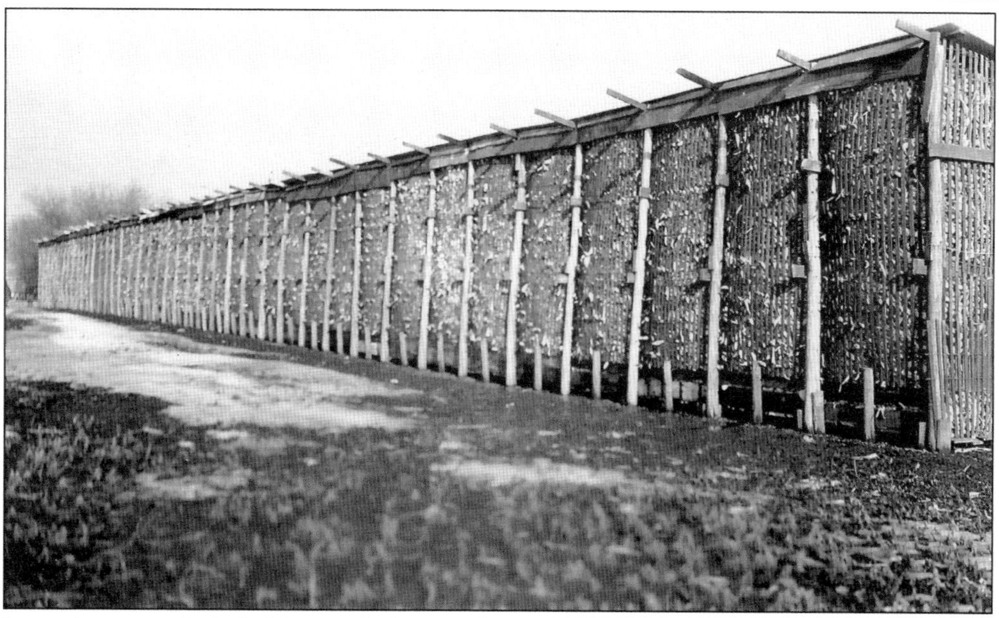

Larson's corn crib is bulging with bounty from the harvest. (Courtesy Plymouth County Historical Museum.)

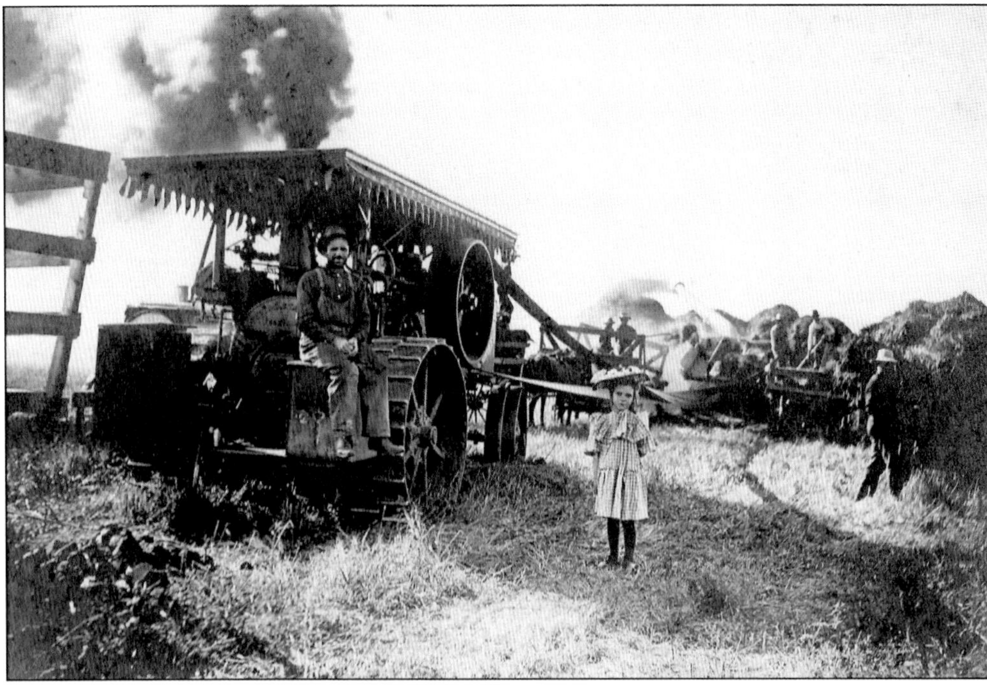

Threshing time was a joint effort by many farmers and helpers in the community. This photograph shows the steam-operated threshing equipment, with a young girl standing in the field near the rig. (Courtesy Plymouth County Historical Museum.)

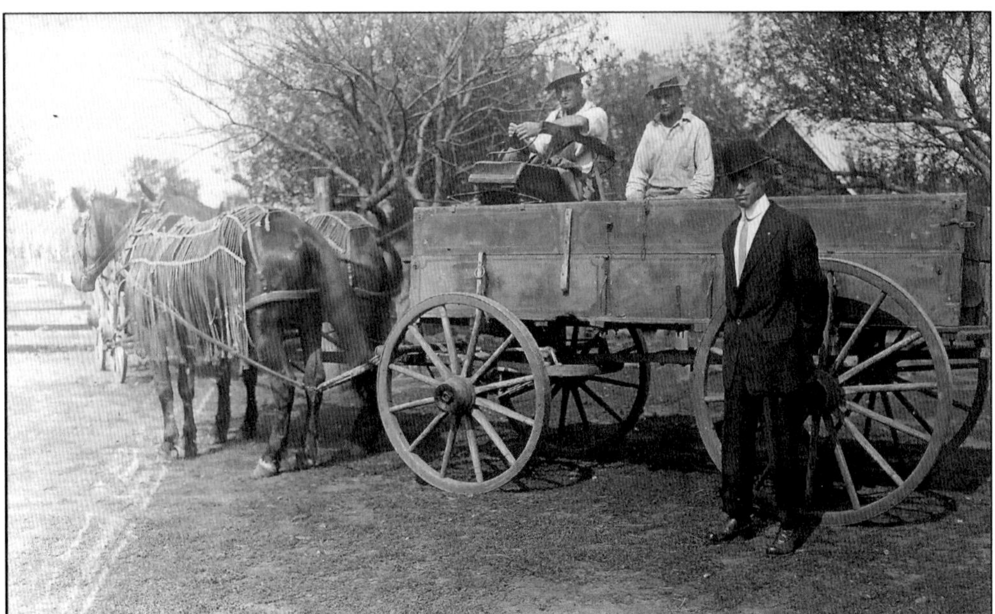

The horse team adorned with fly netting pulling a wagon was a common scene. The men are making ready for the corn harvest. (Courtesy Plymouth County Historical Museum.)

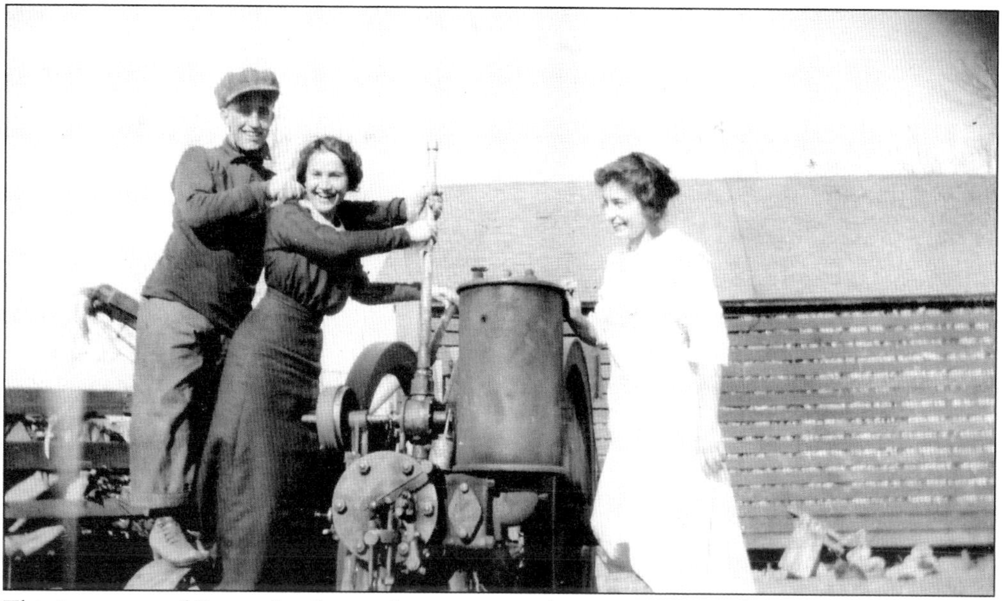

This is a group of Brown family members enjoying the opportunity to have their picture taken with some equipment. Lillian and Wesley Brown are the couple on the left in this photograph. (Courtesy Sue Hunter Miller.)

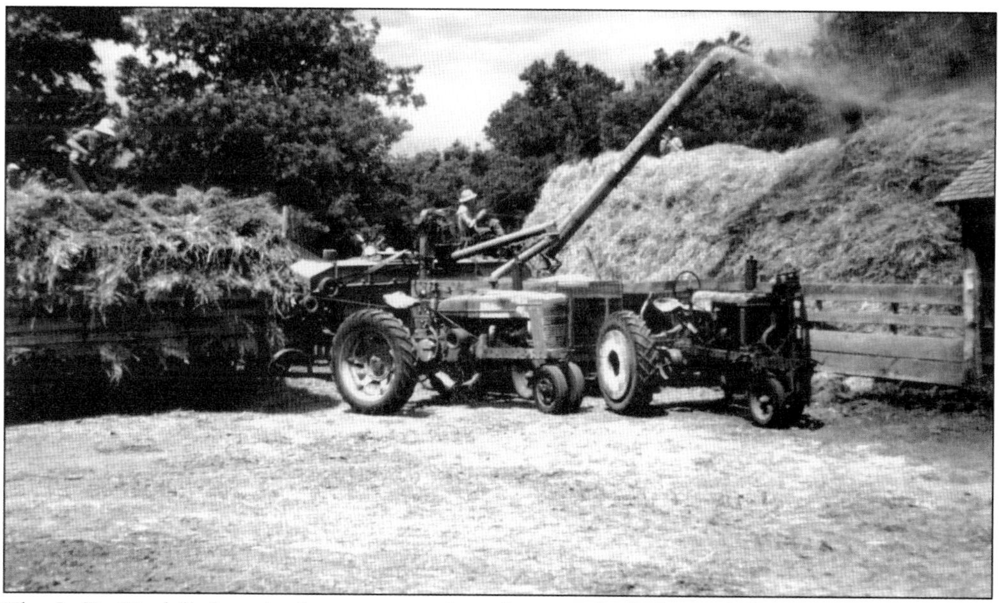

The J. D. Tindall farm is the scene in this photograph. Bob Tindall is on top of the hay wagon. The neighborhood farmers worked together to complete the harvest. (Courtesy Nancy Tindall Yoder.)

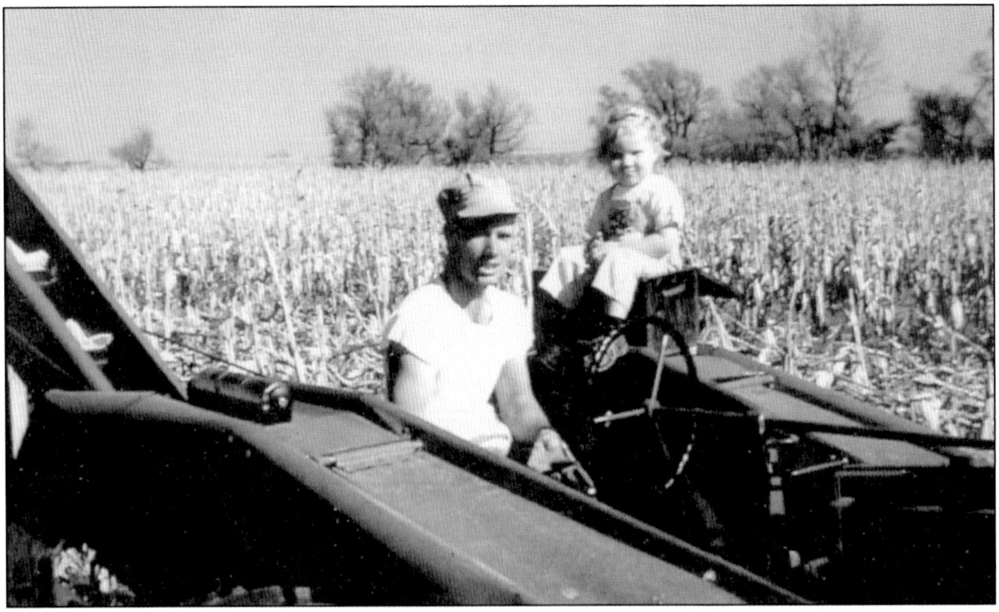

Stanley Tindall took a lunch break during corn-picking time. His young daughter, Nancy, loved to be with him, and the toolbox was the perfect seat for her. (Courtesy Nancy Tindall Yoder.)

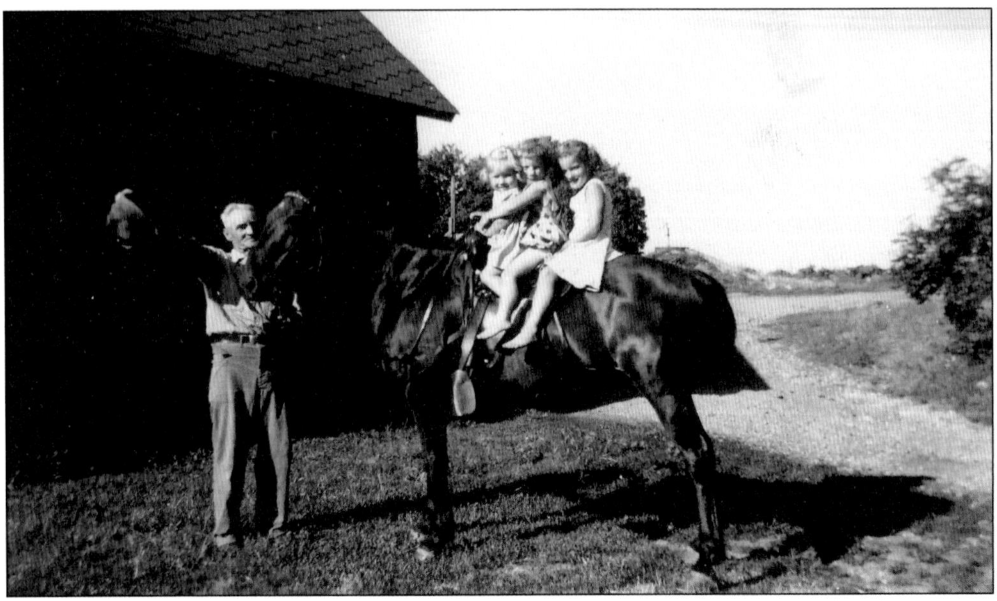

J. D. Tindall holds the lead rope as his three granddaughters, Nancy, Beverly and Barbara, enjoy a ride on the horse. (Courtesy Nancy Tindall Yoder.)

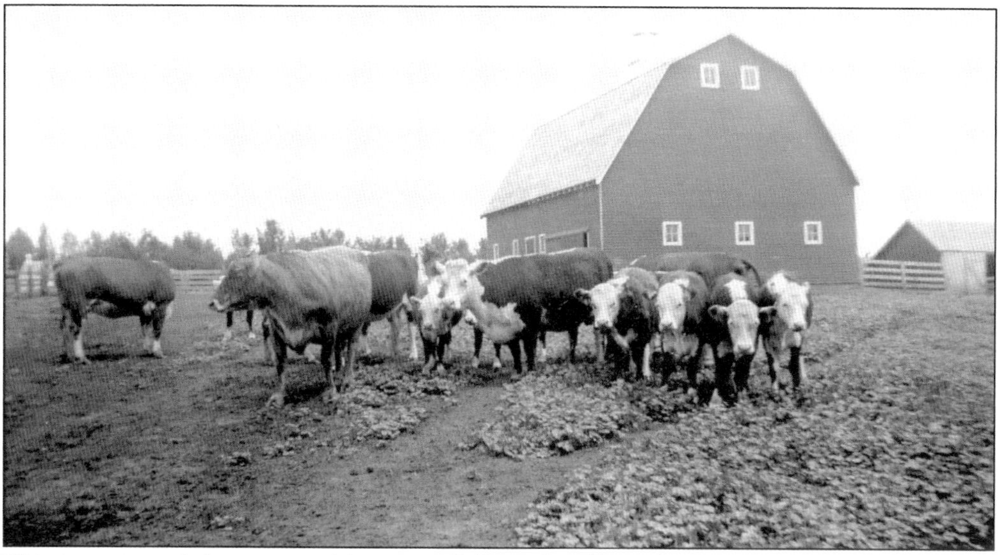

This is a view of the cows and barn, in 1942, at Orville and Fern Cooper's farm. (Courtesy Marvin Cooper.)

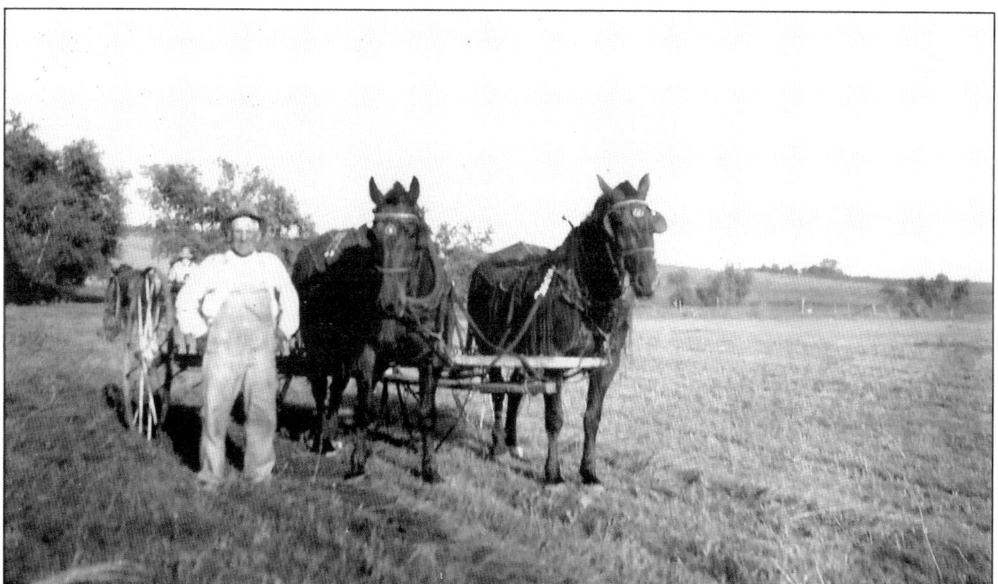

Ed Heimgartner is photographed with his team of horses in 1954. (Courtesy Plymouth County Historical Museum.)

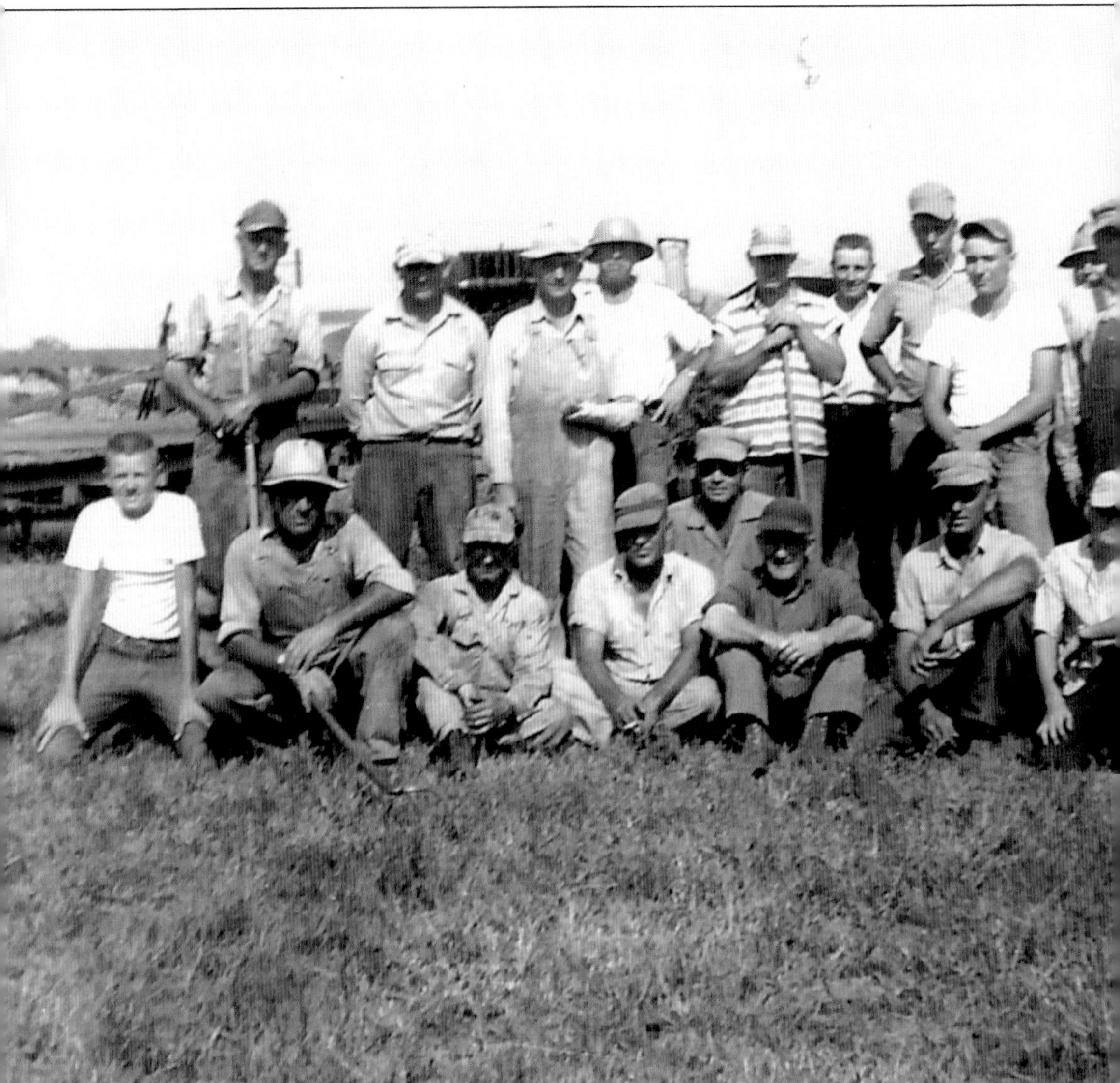

A threshing bee was held at the Hollis Wills farm near Seney in 1960. Friends and neighbors gathered to help bring in the harvest at the time of a death in the Wills family. The men pictured are, from left to right, (first row) Calmer Olson, Bob Lundgren, Hollis Wills, Vernon Penning, Bob Becker, Glen Hinds, Bill Berkenpas, and Darrell Hinds; (second row) Don Berkenpas, Glenn Detloff, Marshall Rees, Orville Cooper, Dave Hawkins, Art Meis, Ken Klave, Orval Rees, unidentified, and unidentified. (Courtesy Plymouth County Historical Museum.)

Five

Towns and Community Scenes

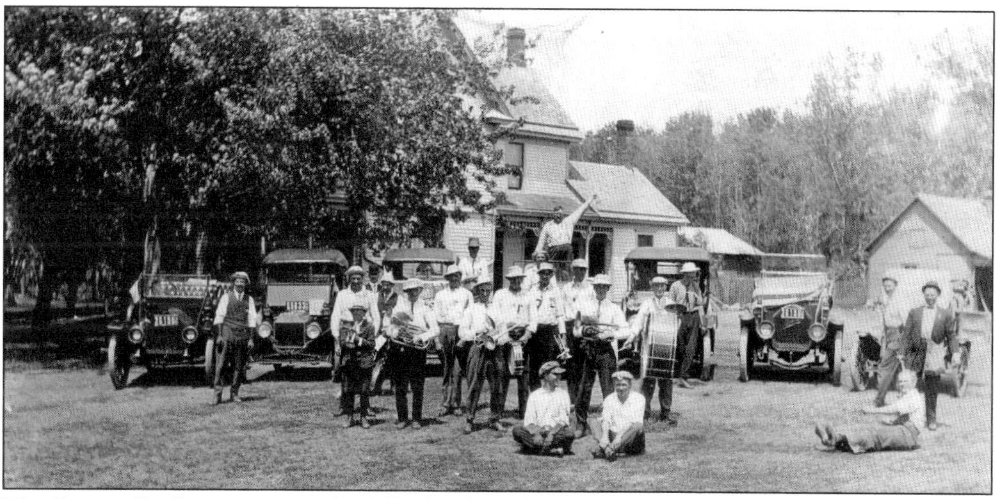

The Brunsville Boosters pose playfully for this fabulous group photograph in 1914, at the Nic Molzen farm, five miles west of Brunsville. A brass and drum band appear to be the core group standing in the center of the photograph. Other members of this booster delegation pose in the picture with grins and antics. Especially interesting is the young man seated on the ground, center right. Careful investigation reveals a watermelon rind sticking out from under his cap. The cars are adorned with American flags. Louie Borchers is identified as the booster member who is standing high on the hood of one of the cars, waving a flag vigorously. Henry O. Jelken is standing in the center of the photograph holding the big bass drum. All evidence from the picture leads to the idea that the Boosters were getting ready to participate in a local Fourth of July celebration parade in their hometown of Brunsville. (Courtesy Vernon and Karen Harrington.)

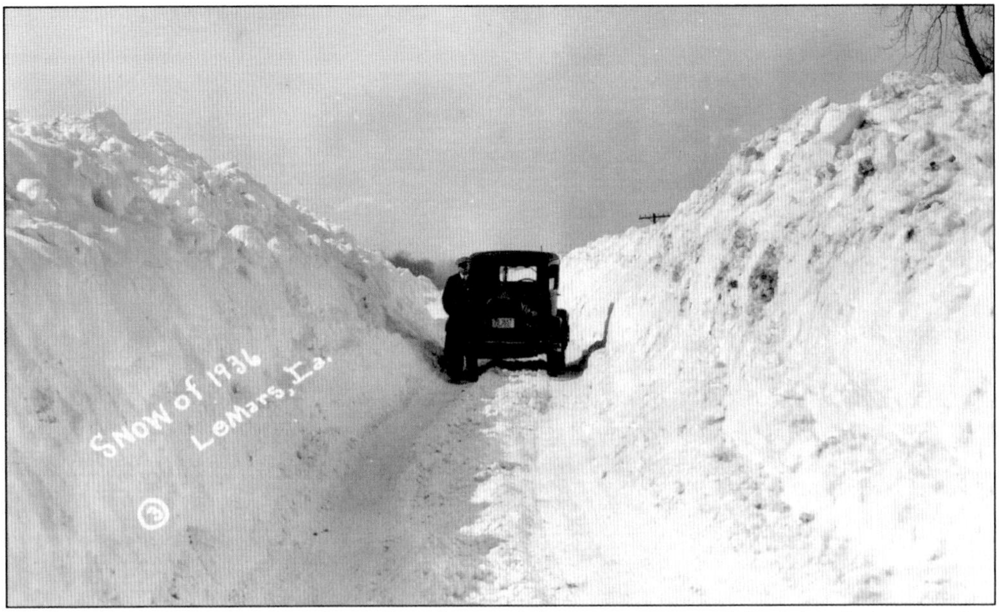

The winter of 1936 proved very hazardous for travel due to severe snowfalls. A local photographer took these pictures February 3–6, showing just how treacherous it was to travel from town to town on snow-covered roads in Plymouth County. (Courtesy Plymouth County Historical Museum.)

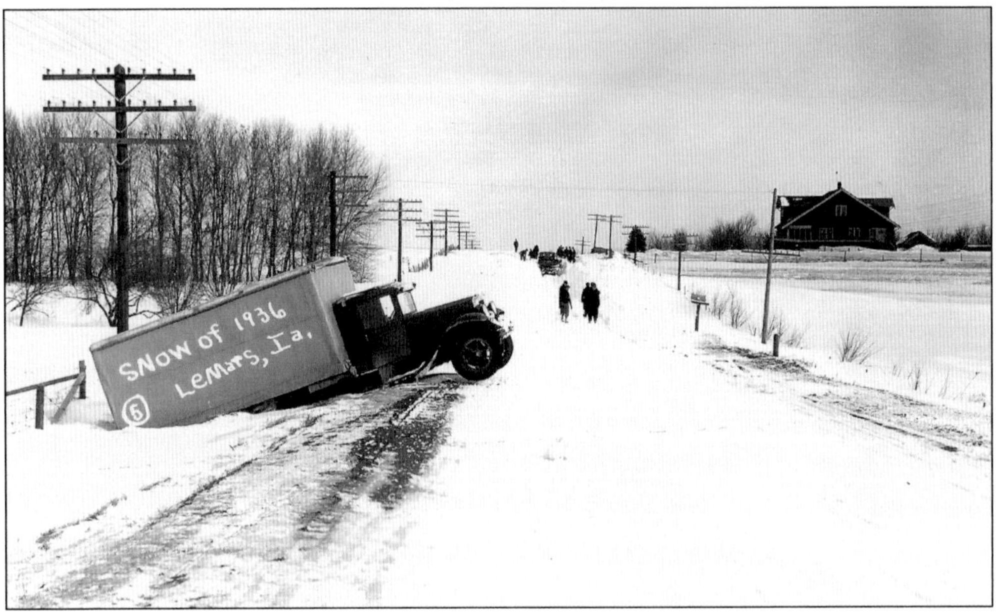

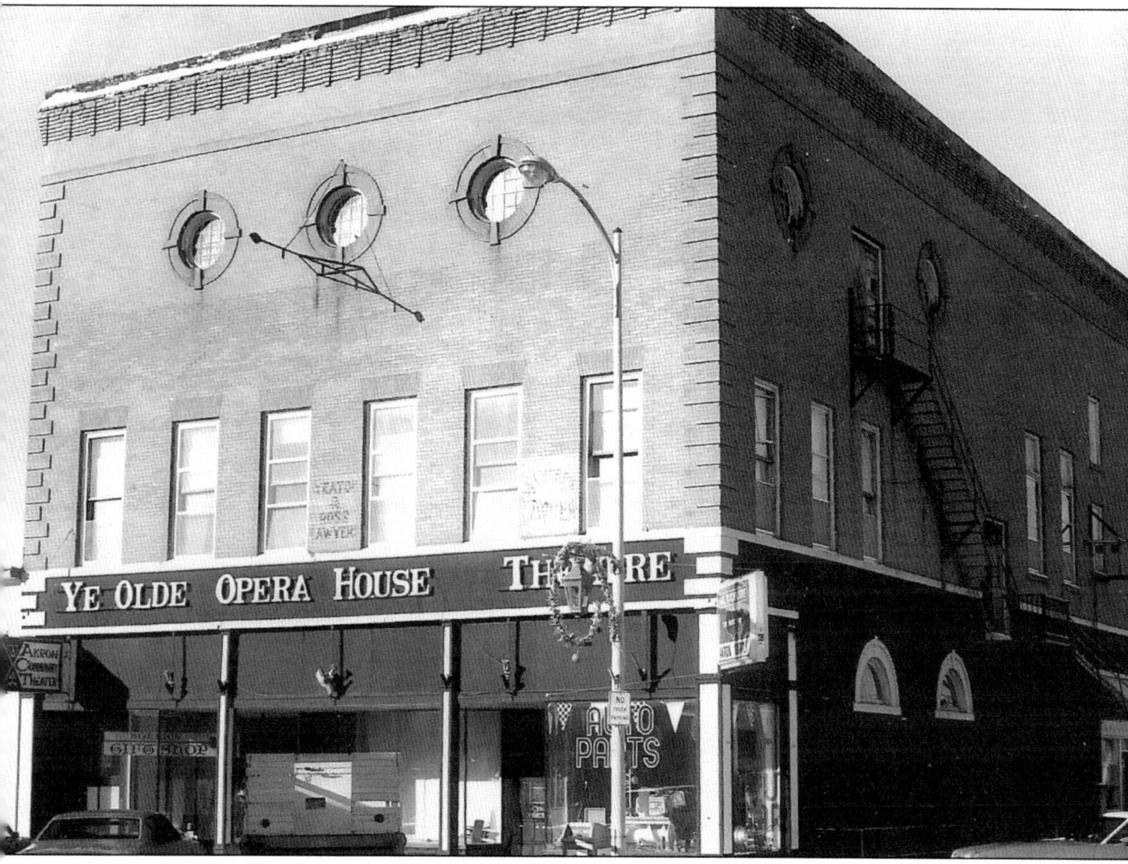

The opera house in Akron was in lot No. 1, block No. 4, in Akron. The property has been owned by several different people through the years. In 1969, the Akron Community Theatre purchased it. Many hours of cleanup and renovation followed, bringing the building back to life. It became known as Ye Olde Opera House Theatre. (Courtesy Plymouth County Historical Museum.)

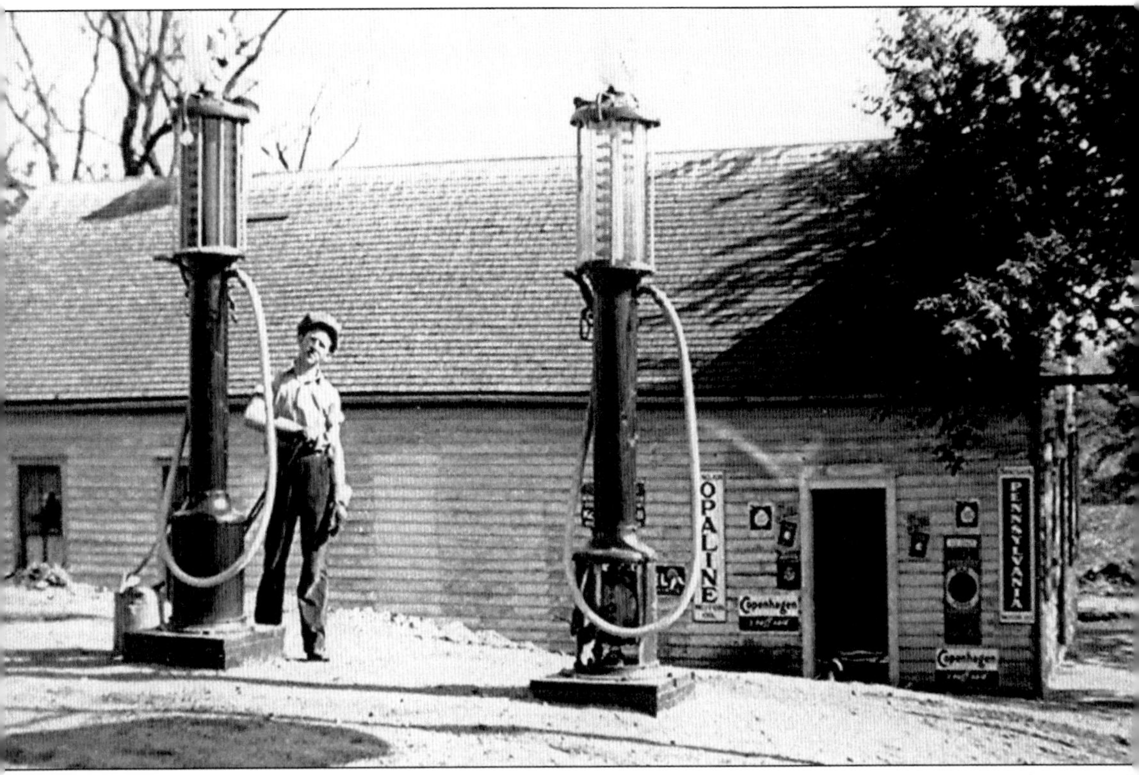

The Adaville store was built by O. R. Gaston and opened for business on May 1, 1892. Gaston taught at the Adaville school while his wife, the former Ella Morehead, ran the store. Gaston sold the store in 1900 to L. L. Morehead and a Mr. Larsen. They later sold the store to Joe Picus. There were three rooms in the east side of the store building that served as living quarters for some of the proprietors or their employees. Marls Goodrich, one of the proprietors of the store, wrote that his dad purchased the store in 1920 from the Grave brothers. His dad had a full line of groceries, plus some clothing, hardware, and Model-T Ford parts. He had a grocery truck and went out in the country and sold groceries and picked up eggs, butter, and cream. The store also sold McCormick-Deering farm machinery and had a truck to haul grain and livestock. During the Great Depression, the store was closed for eight years. The store opened again and had several different owners. Armand Brown bought the store, beginning operation of it in 1946 with the help of his wife. The store closed its doors for the last time in 1956, with the acreage sold in 1958. The store building was torn down sometime in the early 1960s. (Courtesy Kathy Goodrich Crum.)

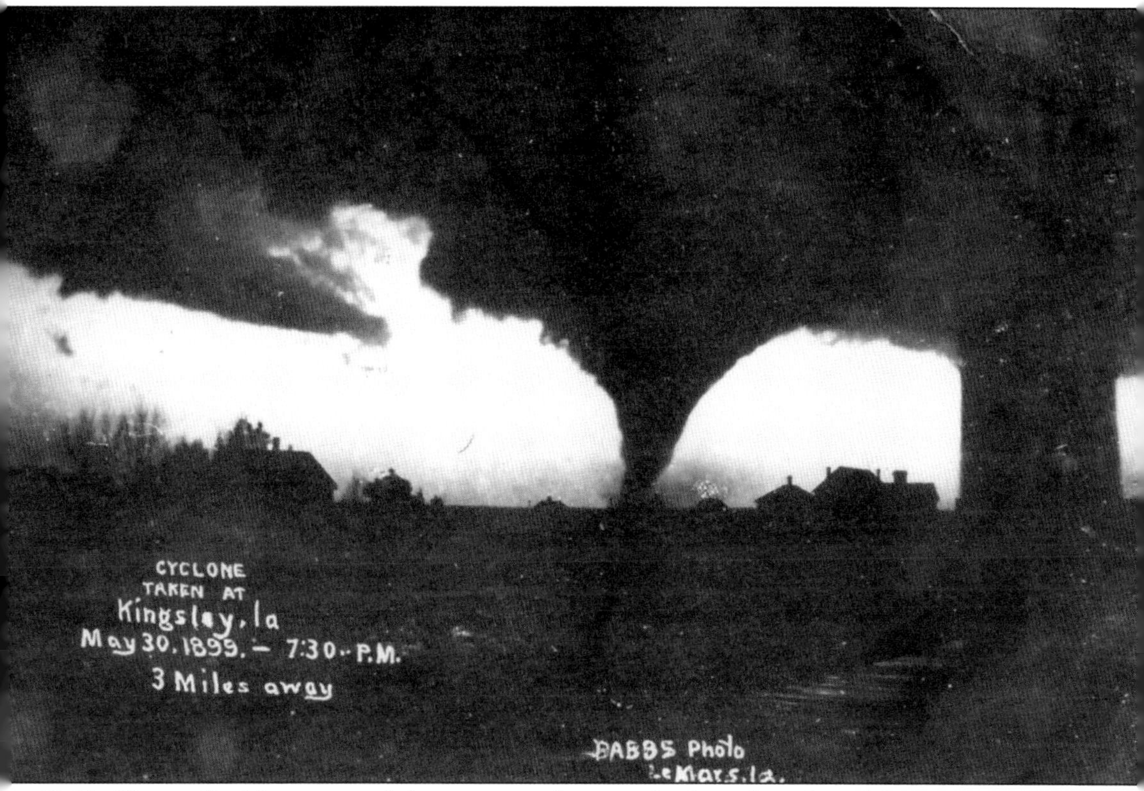

Dabbs Photo of Le Mars captured this stunning photograph of a cyclone funnel dropping out of the sky, located approximately three miles from Kingsley. Standing in Kingsley with his camera, the photographer grasped the silhouettes of houses in town. The picture is dated May 30, 1899, 7:30 p.m. (Courtesy Plymouth County Historical Museum.)

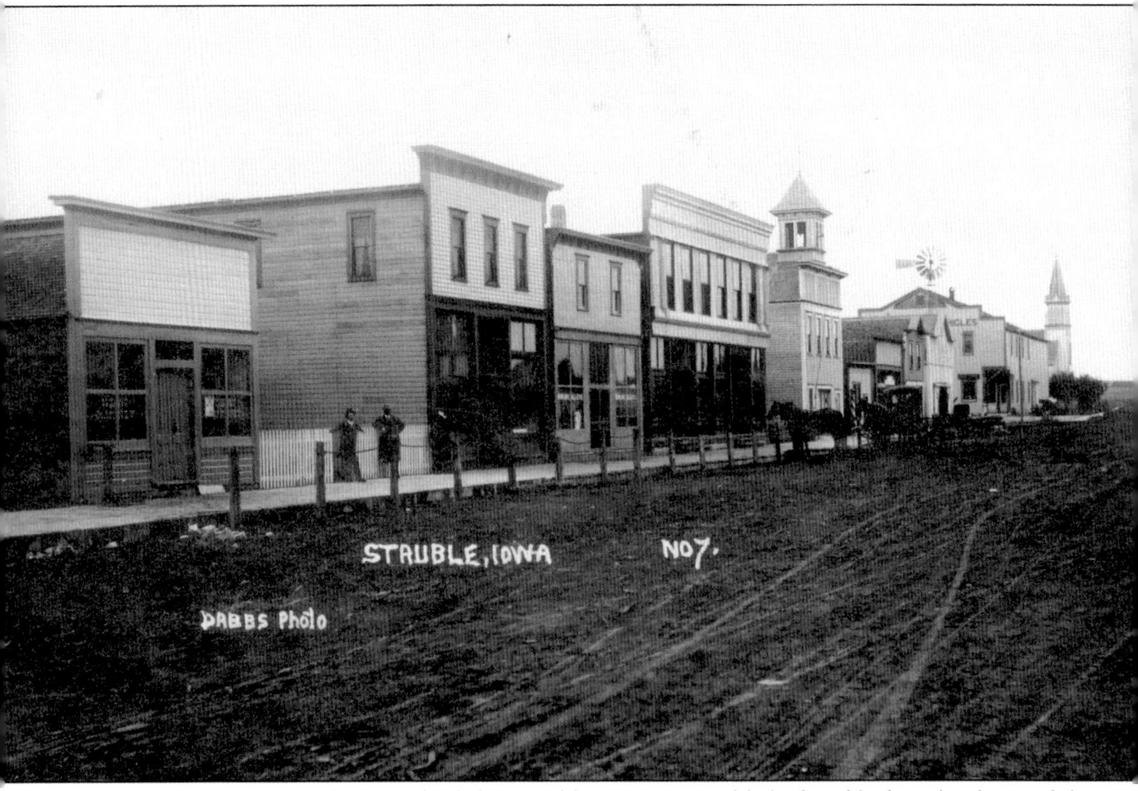

Dabbs Photo Studio photographed this Struble street scene, likely dated before the dawn of the 20th century. Notice at the very end of the street, on the edge of town, is a local church. The steeple of the church rises above all other buildings. The steeple is a reminder to townspeople to come and worship. (Courtesy Plymouth County Historical Museum.)

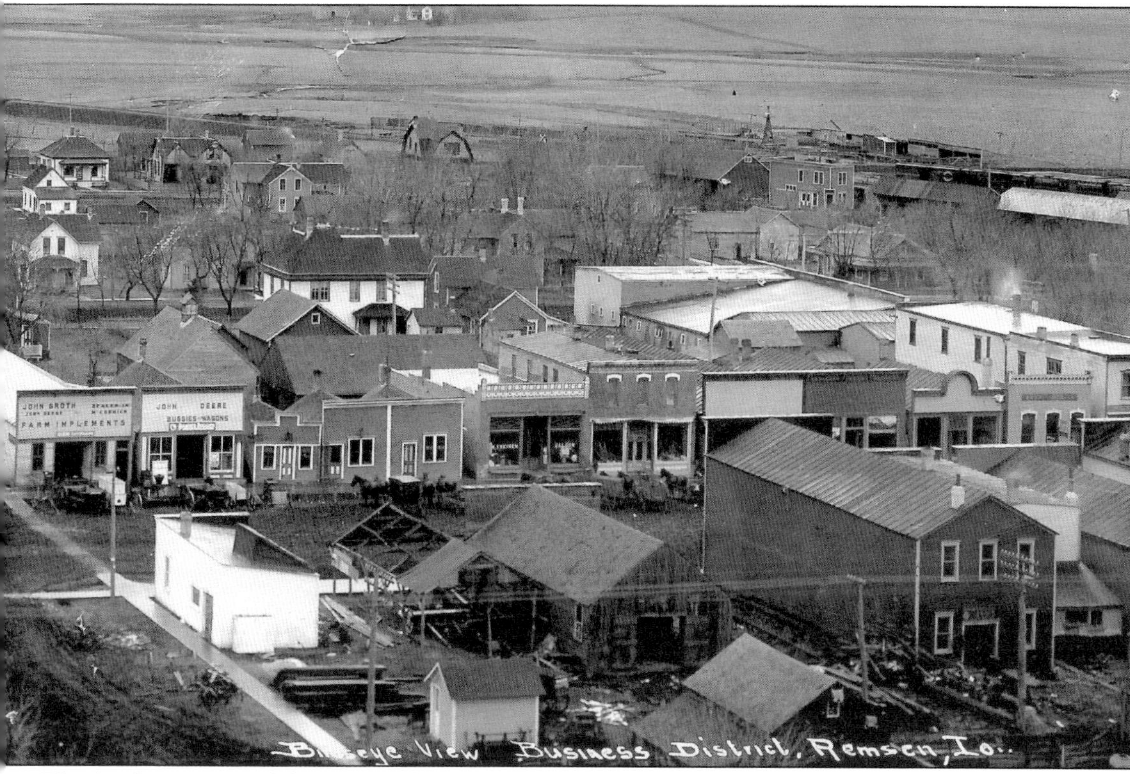

This bird's-eye view of the Remsen business district gives a clear view of the John Deere dealer buildings. On the left side of the picture there are two buildings together with a sign that reads, "John Groth, John Deere dealer in McCormick Farm Implements." Over the door of the second building the sign says "Buggies and Wagons." (Courtesy Plymouth County Historical Museum.)

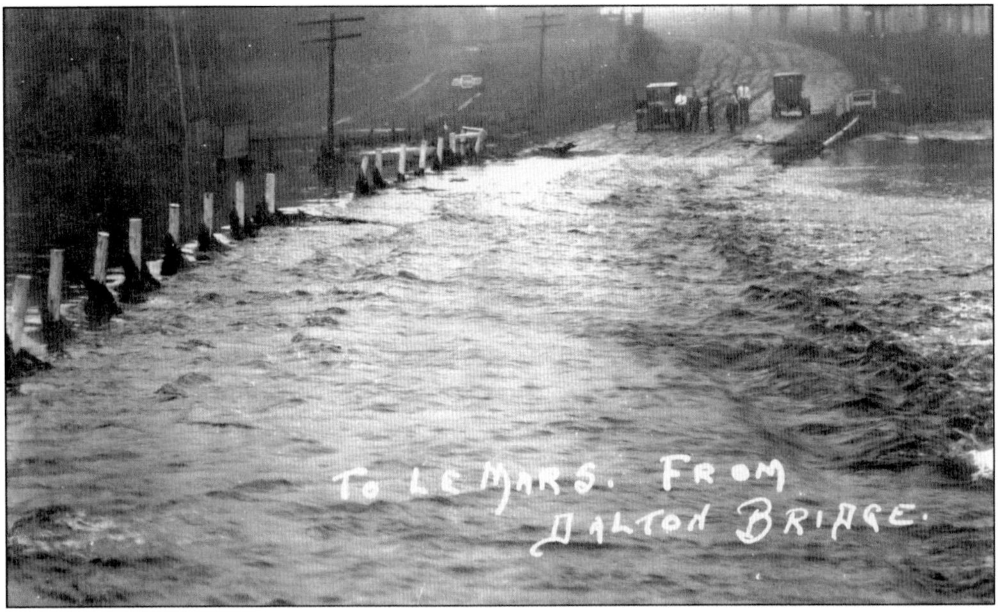

The Floyd River bridge at Dalton was washed out by floodwaters in the year 1905. The aerial view of Dalton was photographed before the road going through town, now known as Highway 3, was paved. The picture also shows the rural schoolhouse and school yard in the upper portion of the photograph. Several generations of children studied in that school building. (Courtesy Plymouth County Historical Museum.)

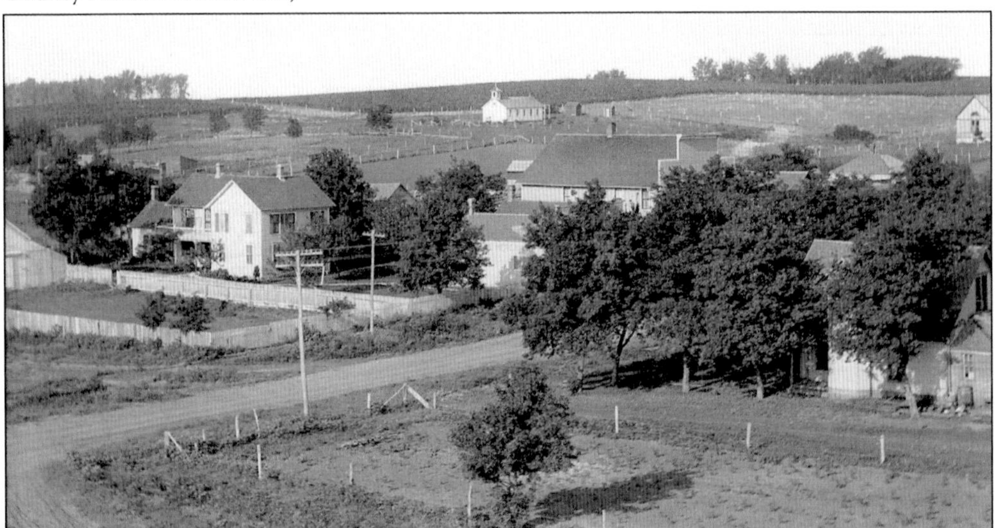

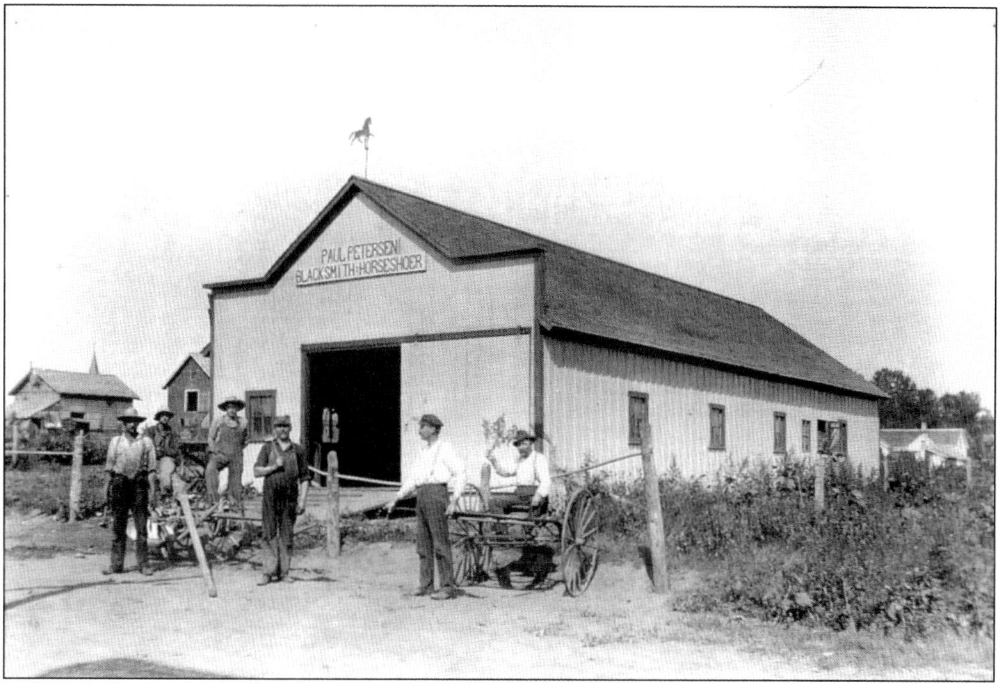

Paul Petersen Blacksmith-Horseshoe Shop in Oyens was one of the busiest establishments in the community for a number of years. Unfortunately, there is no date on this photograph. (Courtesy Plymouth County Historical Museum.)

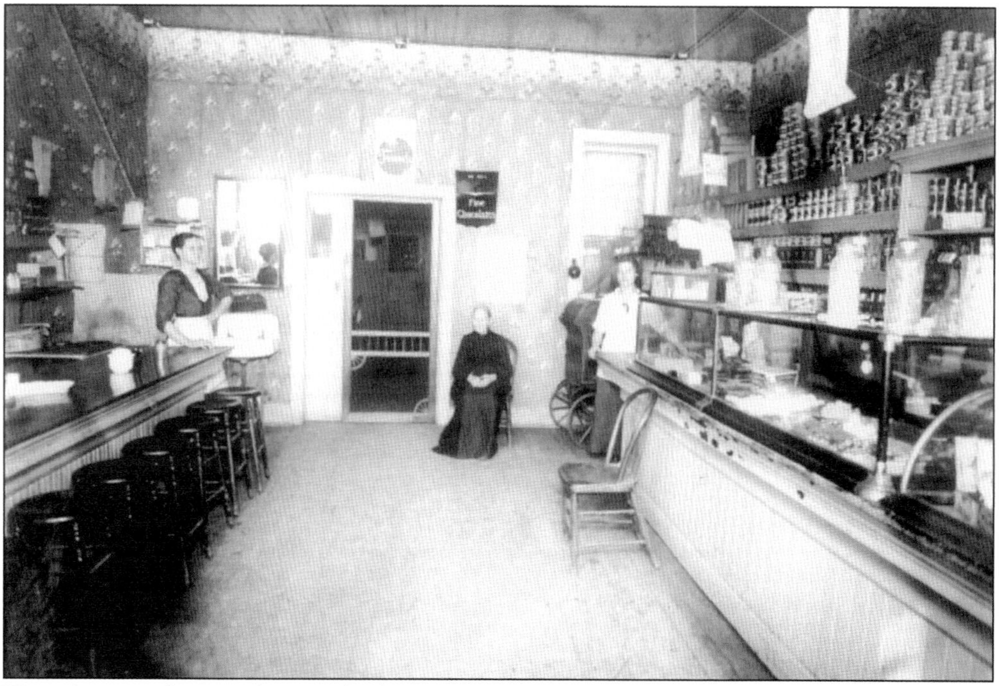

This photograph was taken inside the June Restaurant in Merrill in November 1918. Pictured from left to right are, owner Jennie (House) June, her mother Eda Ann (Boyd) House, and Jennie's youngest daughter, Geneva (June) Dierking. (Courtesy Justin Herbst)

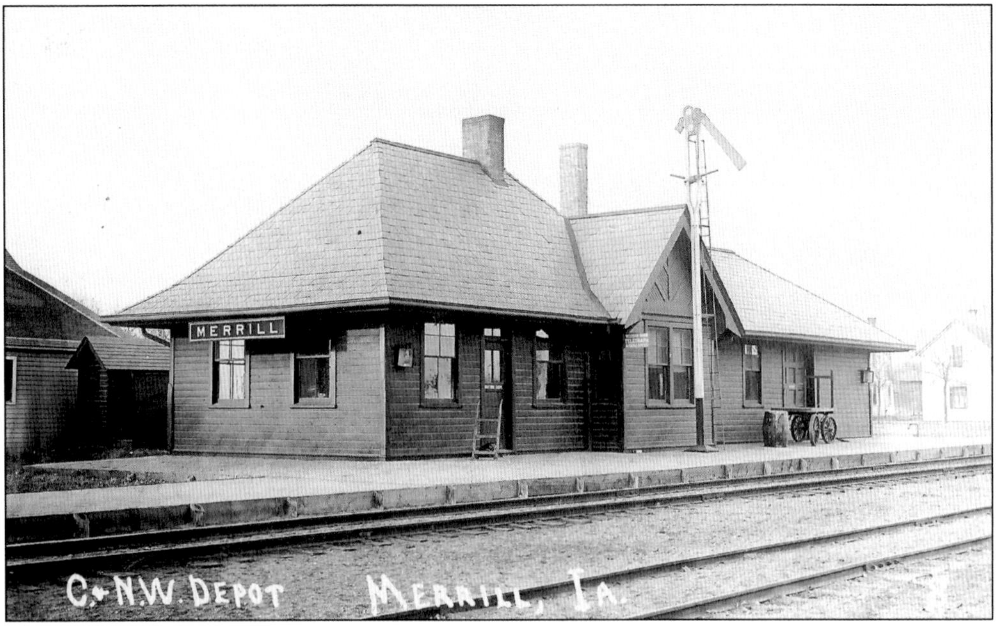

The depot location in every town was the scene of much activity throughout the day. The Chicago and North Western Railway depot at Merrill was no exception. (Courtesy Judy Forgos.)

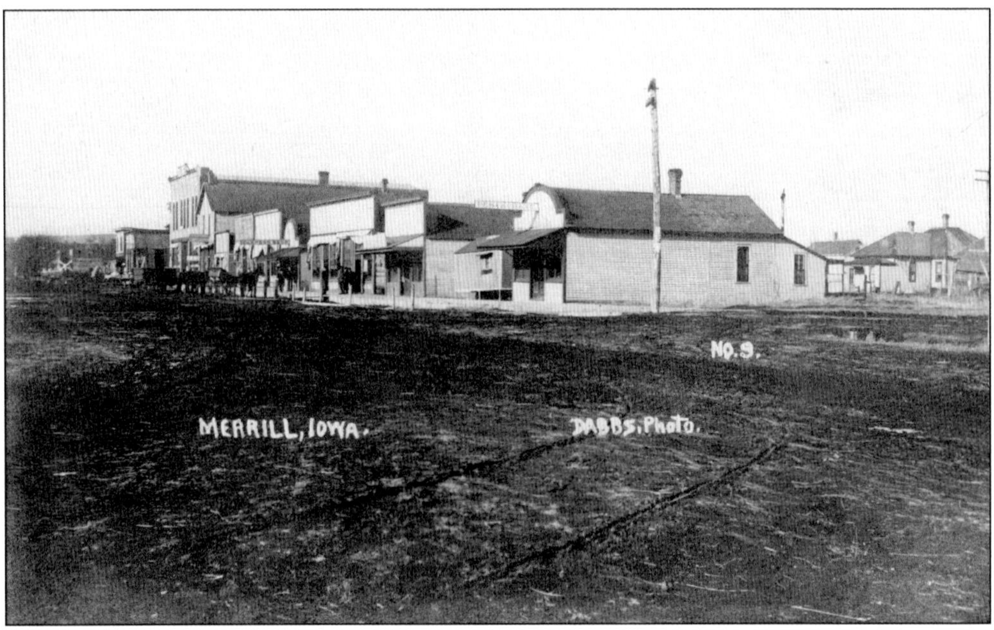

Dabbs Photo Studio made the rounds throughout the county shooting pictures of the small towns. This is a photograph of the street scene at Merrill. (Courtesy Plymouth County Historical Museum.)

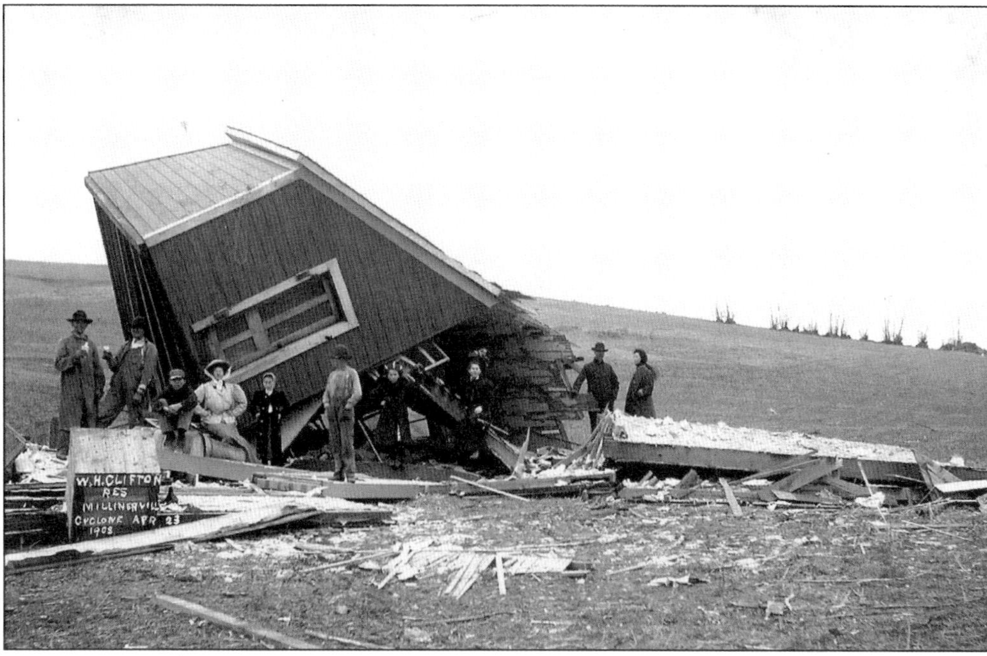

A cyclone at Millnerville happened on April 23, 1908. Photographs of the aftermath were taken of the Pullen and Clifton residences. The *Merrill Record* newspaper gave details of the disaster. The George Milner house, occupied by Doc Clifton, was demolished, and Clifton was slightly hurt. Dick Pullen's house was moved 40 feet from its foundation. Fifteen people hid in the cellar and were unhurt. The Pullen barn was blown to pieces. (Courtesy Plymouth County Historical Museum.)

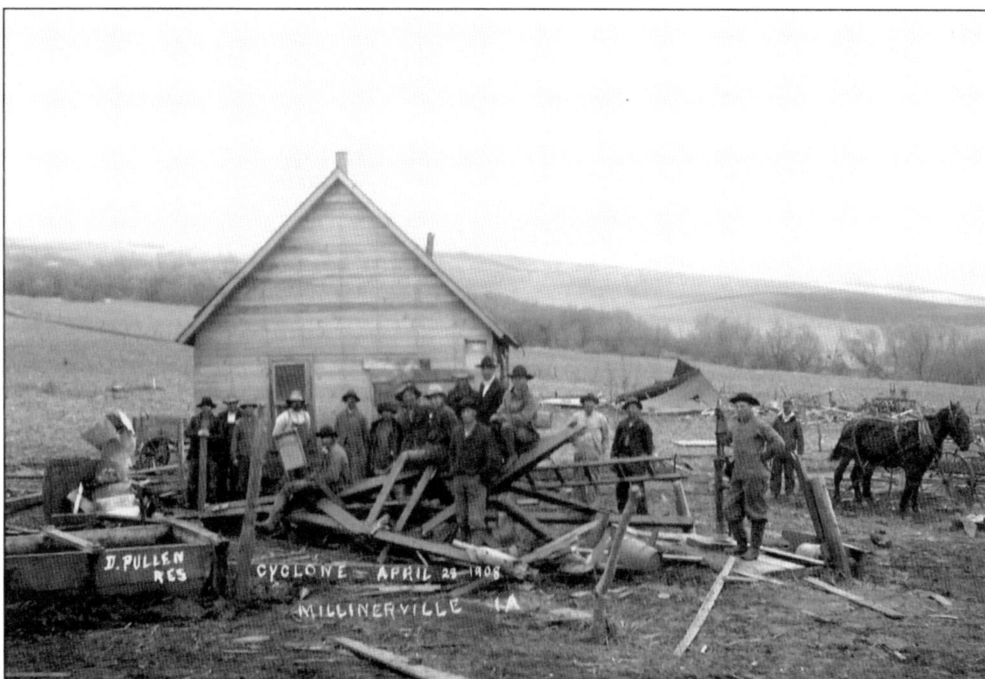

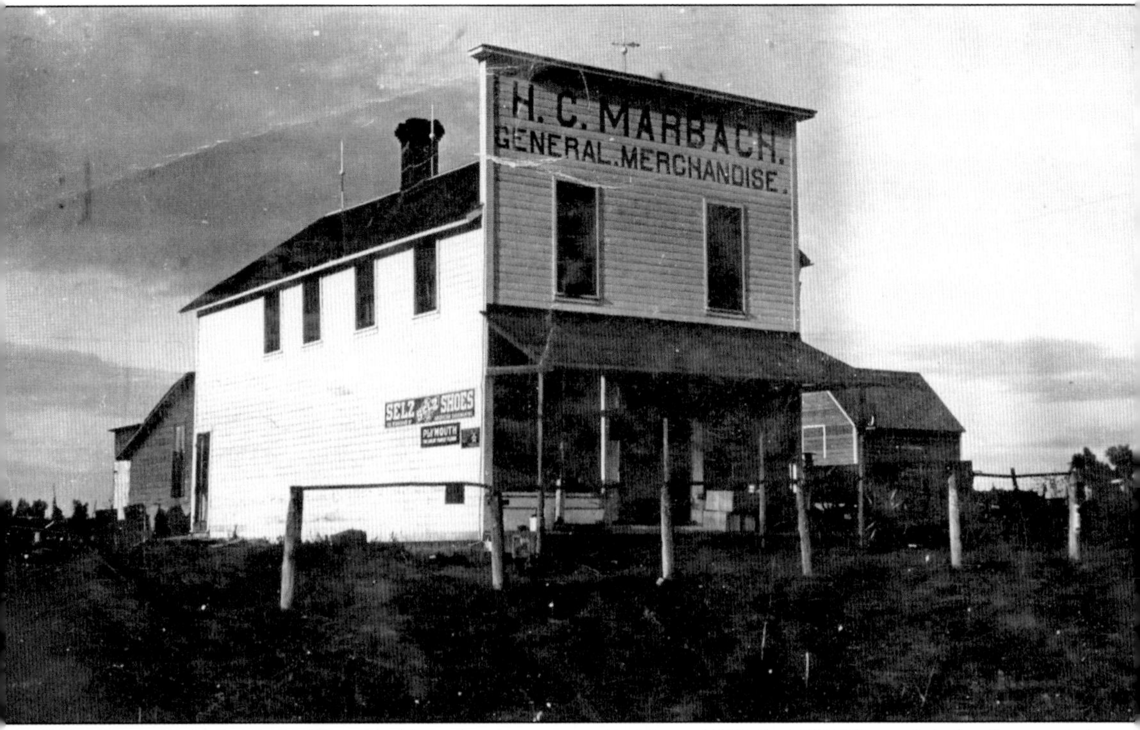

Henry Marbach and Ben Toel bought the store at Ruble in 1909. In 1910, Henry Marbach married Madie Johnson. Ben Toel then sold his partnership share to Marbach. The Marbachs ran the store with the help of his brother, Bernard Marbach. Following the death of her husband, Henry Marbach, on December 18, 1918, and left with five young children and the care of the store, Madie successfully conducted the business. She gained a widespread popularity and enjoyed the confidence of patrons and customers to the fullest degree. Under her direction, the store afforded accommodation to the countryside and was a general place of meeting. Her many acts of kindness, her willingness to do a favor on any and every occasion, and her generous disposition and unfailing courtesy endeared her to countless friends and neighbors. Notice the hitching posts located outside the front door of the store building. (Courtesy Mary Lamoureux.)

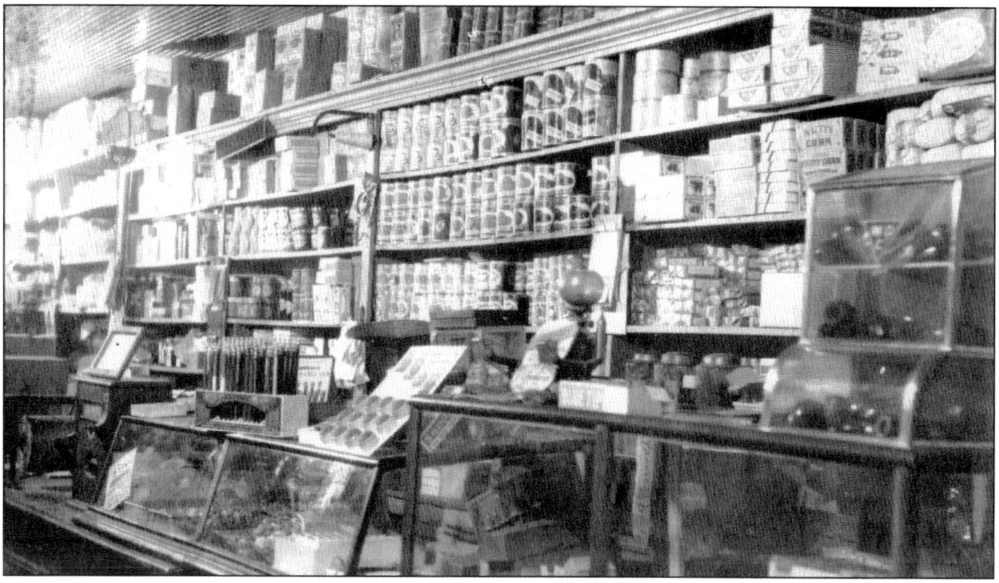

This photograph shows the many items for sale inside the Marbach Store at Ruble. (Courtesy Mary Lamoureux.)

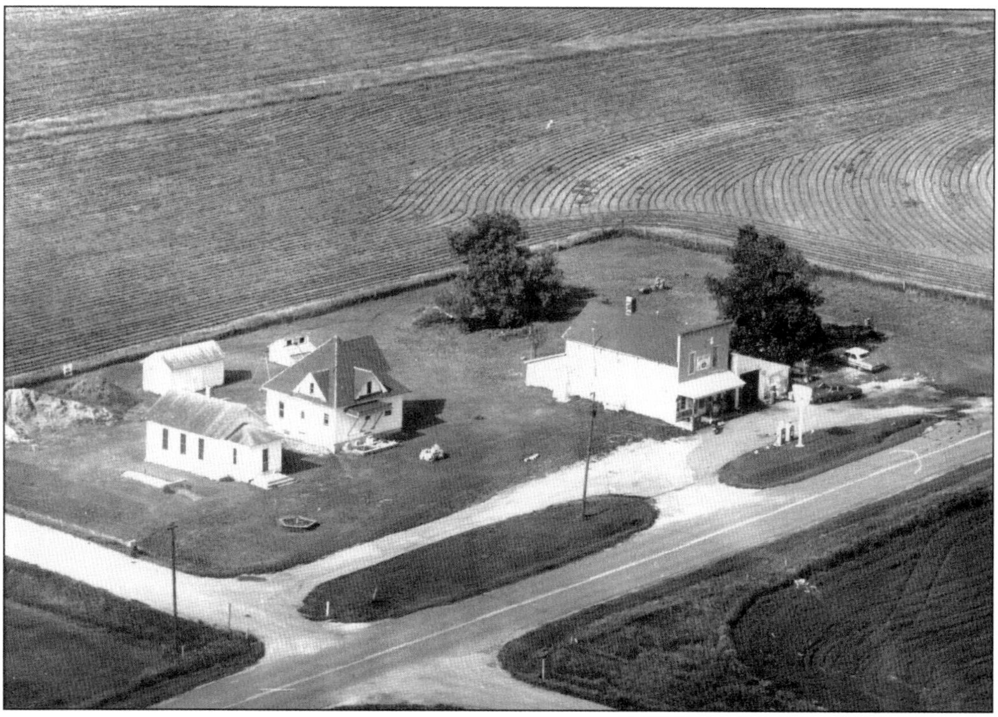

This aerial view of the entire town of Ruble includes the school, backhouse, general store, and one house dwelling. (Courtesy Mary Lamoureux.)

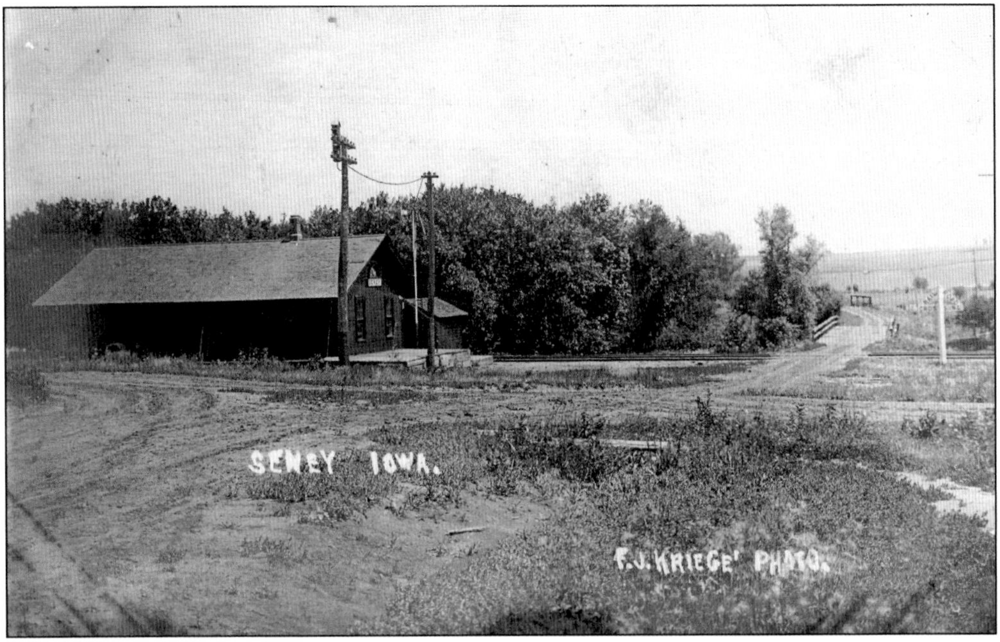

This photograph shows the Seney depot building, located next to the railroad track. The Floyd River bridge can be seen in the background. (Courtesy Linda Ewin Ziemann.)

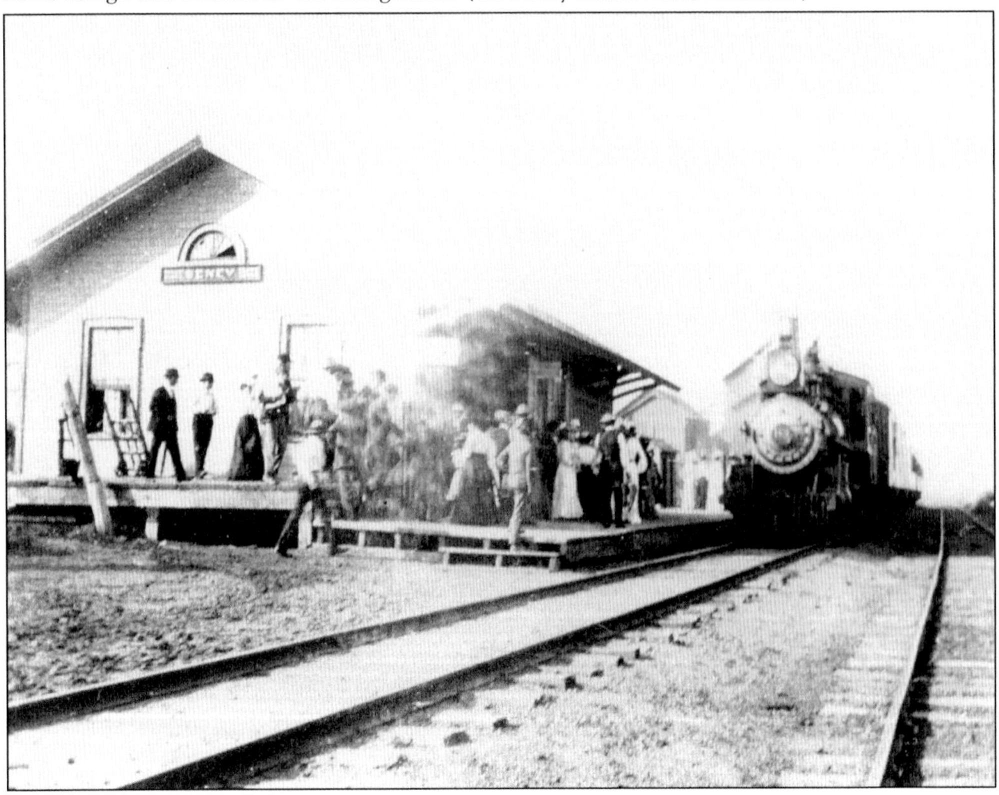

The train depot at Seney drew large crowds, with several trains stopping daily before the dawn of the 20th century. (Courtesy Janice Albert.)

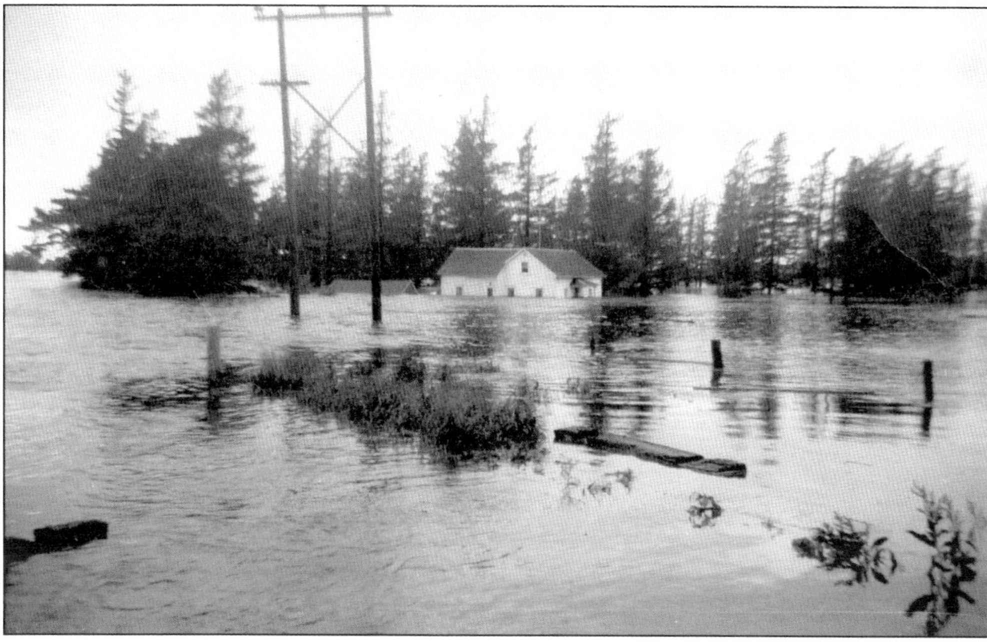

The massive rains, resulting in a devastating flood on Sunday, June 7 and 8, 1953, left several homes and buildings in the Seney area underwater. The *Le Mars Sentinel* reported that the Floyd River was at least 10 feet or more higher than it had ever been in history. Hundreds of livestock perished, which was a total loss to all owners. Mr. and Mrs. Mitchell Zoerink and family lived in the house that is shown submerged in the floodwater. The water was over five feet deep on the first floor. They escaped in time but lost all household goods, clothing, and everything in the house. (Courtesy Linda Ewin Ziemann.)

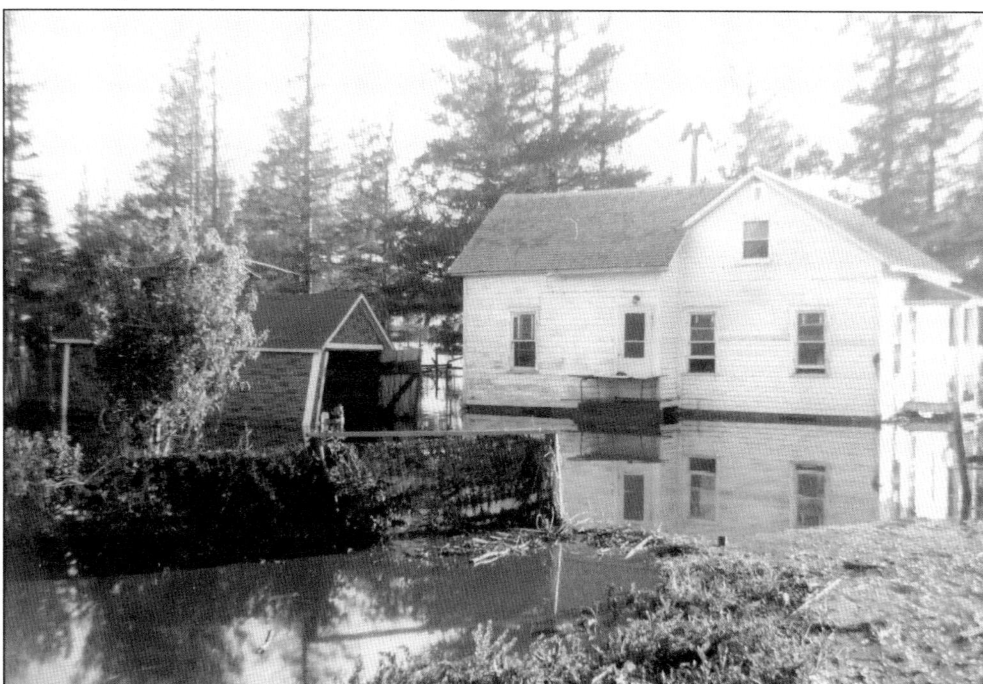

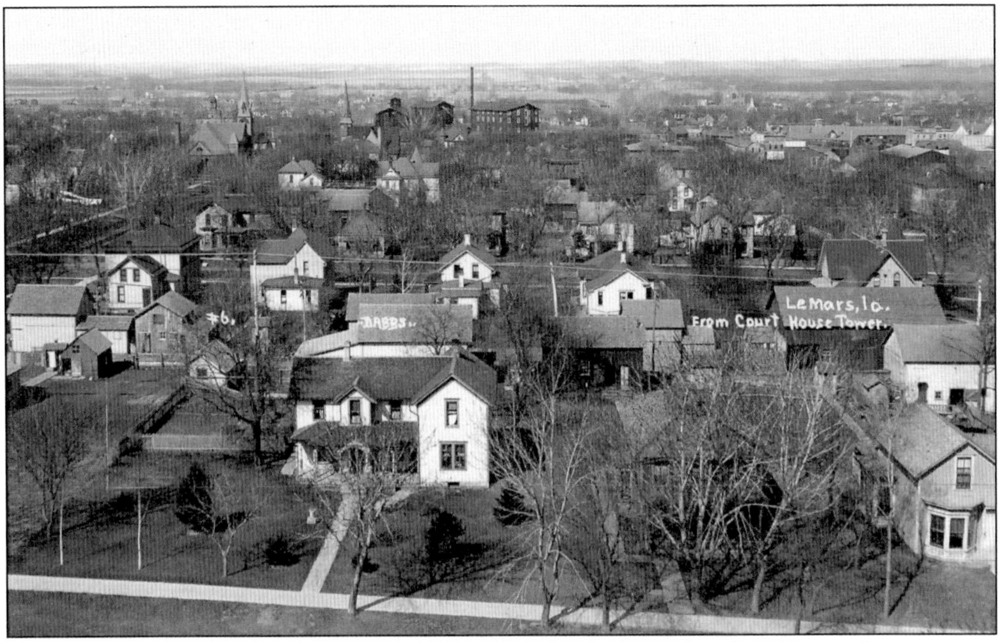

This photograph shows a great aerial view of Le Mars taken from the old courthouse tower. (Courtesy Plymouth County Historical Museum.)

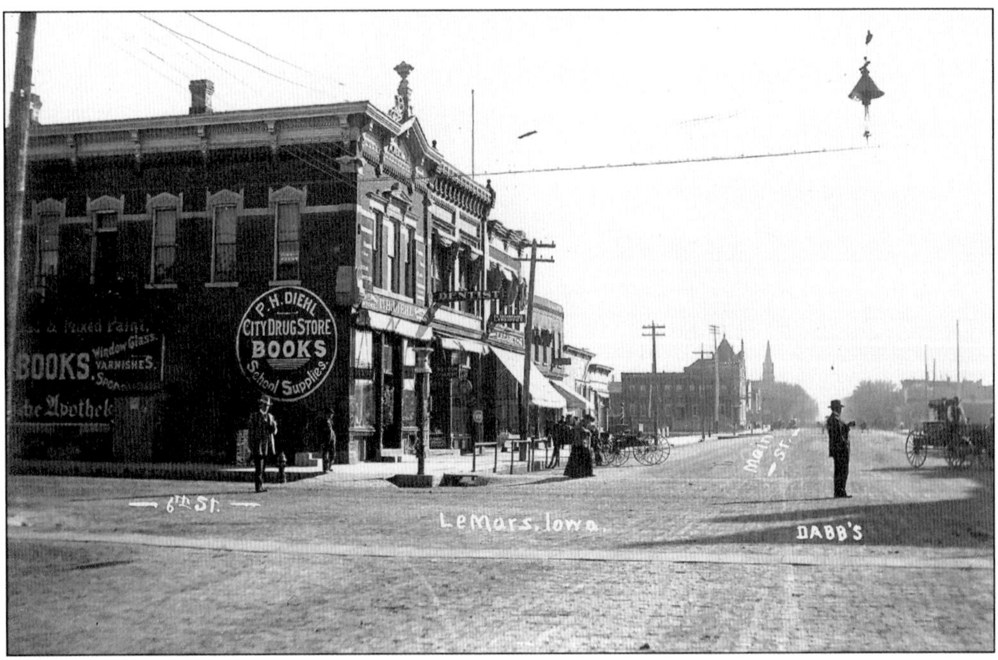

The Dabbs photographer shot this Le Mars street scene at the intersection of Sixth and Main Streets. The P. H. Diehl City Drug Store building is on the corner, advertising books and school supplies. There is also a dentist and land office in this block. At the end of the street, there is the silhouette of a church steeple. (Courtesy Plymouth County Historical Museum.)

Six

MILITARILY COMMITTED

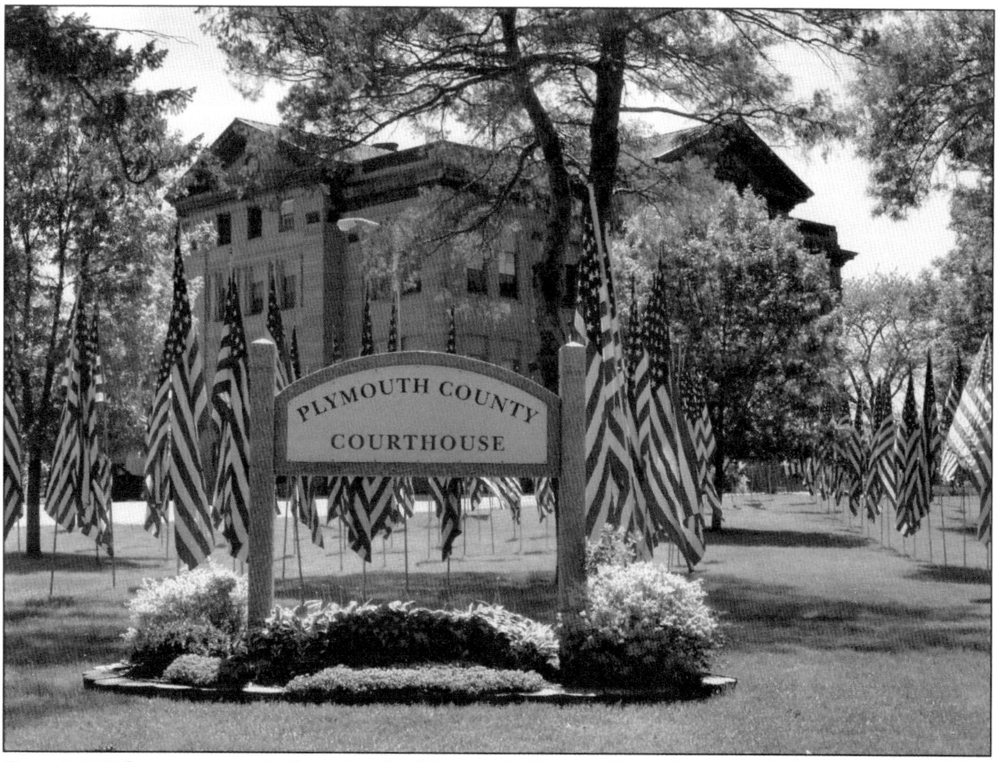

Over 1,000 flags are now displayed at the Plymouth County Courthouse each Memorial Day. This ceremonial tradition, displaying burial flags of men and women who have served from Plymouth County in the military, began in May 1965. Then Wasmer post adjutant, Fred Riter was the man with the idea and vision. His vision has brought to Plymouth County honorable merit and significance, which has been continued from year to year. (Courtesy Linda Ewin Ziemann.)

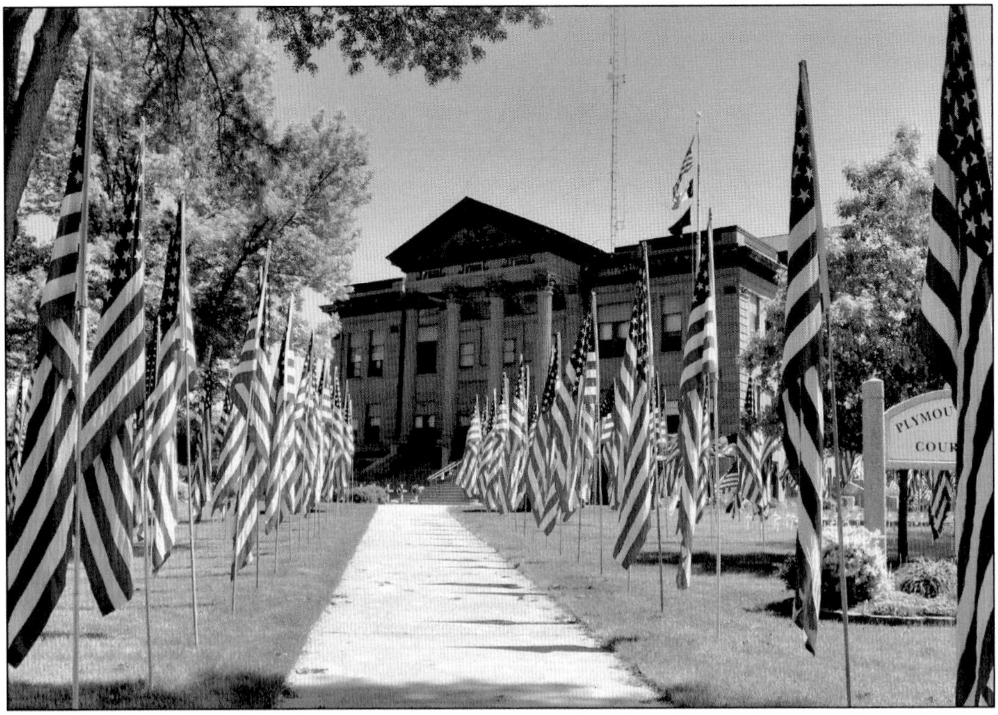

The Avenue of Flags tradition at the Plymouth County Courthouse began with 91 flags on Memorial Day in 1965. That day there were only five avenues of flags. Each year, as more flags come in, the roll call of names has continued on Memorial Day. The newly donated flags each year are given special mention and honor, with family members presenting the flags during the ceremony. (Courtesy Linda Ewin Ziemann.)

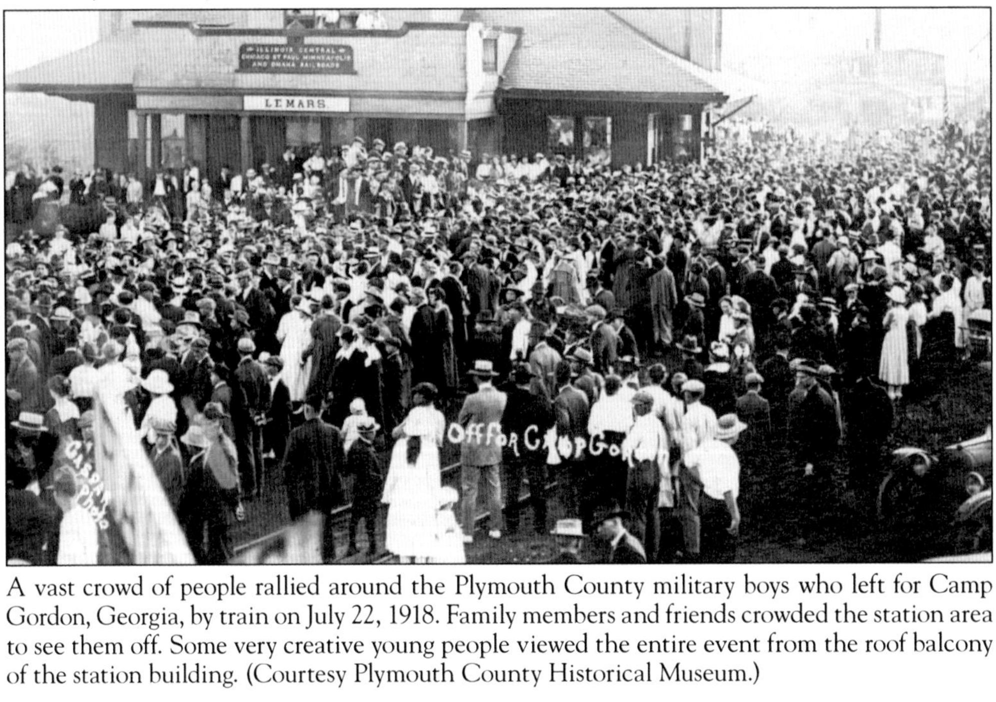

A vast crowd of people rallied around the Plymouth County military boys who left for Camp Gordon, Georgia, by train on July 22, 1918. Family members and friends crowded the station area to see them off. Some very creative young people viewed the entire event from the roof balcony of the station building. (Courtesy Plymouth County Historical Museum.)

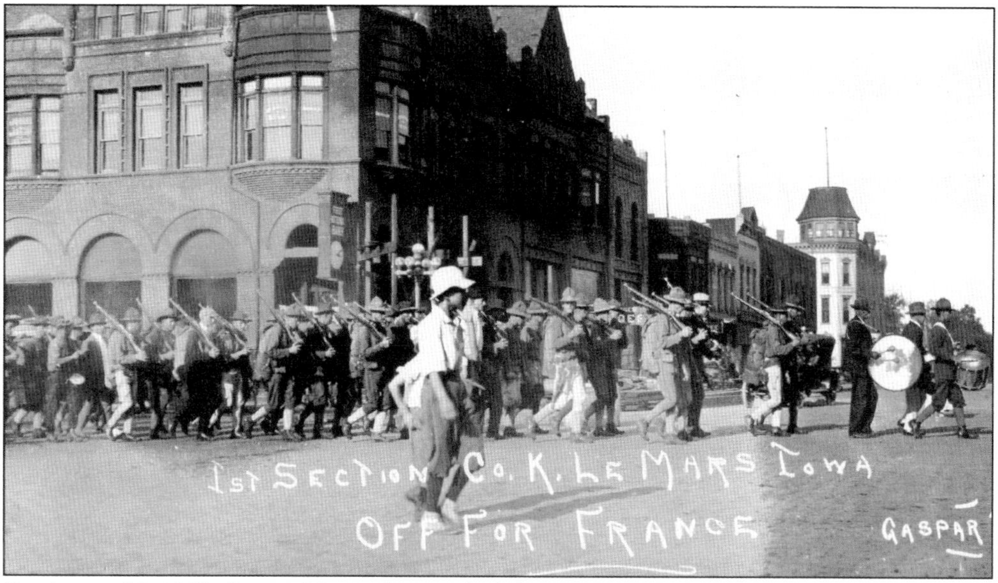

On August 20, 1917, 68 men (chosen by number) from Company K were called to Des Moines to become a part of the 3rd Regiment, 168th Infantry, 84th Brigade, later to be known as a part of the famous Rainbow Division. There was a parade through the streets of Le Mars to the depot. The local band and several thousand people saw the contingent off at the station. (Courtesy Linda Ewin Ziemann.)

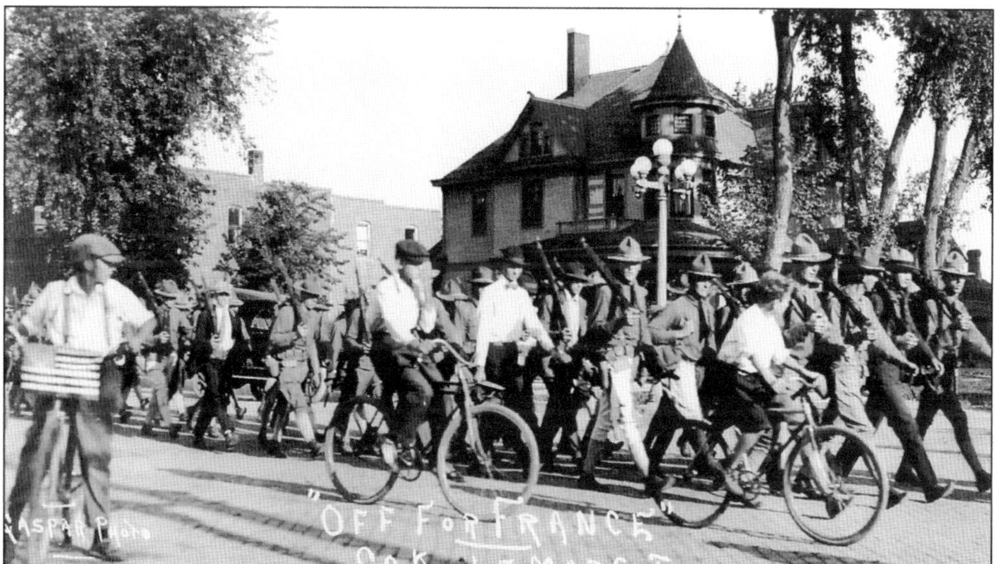

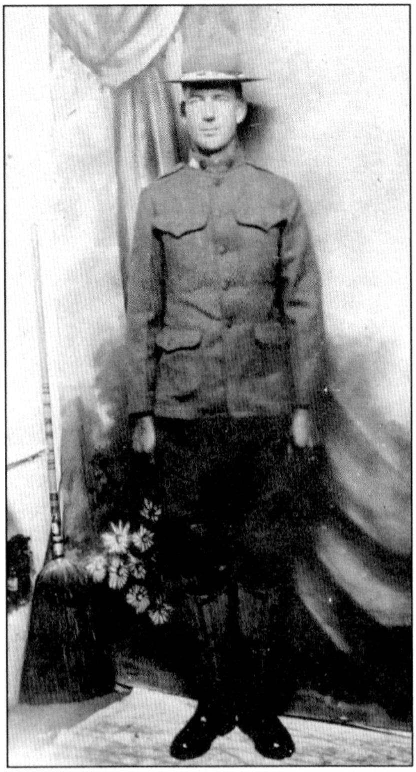

Charles E. Ewin of Seney was one of the original members of Company K. He saw his first active service duty on the Mexican border in 1916 as a member of the Punitive Expedition. Ewin was sent to France in 1917 with the famous Rainbow Division. He survived World War I, returning home to Seney, where he met and married Gladys Kennedy in 1921. (Courtesy Linda Ewin Ziemann.)

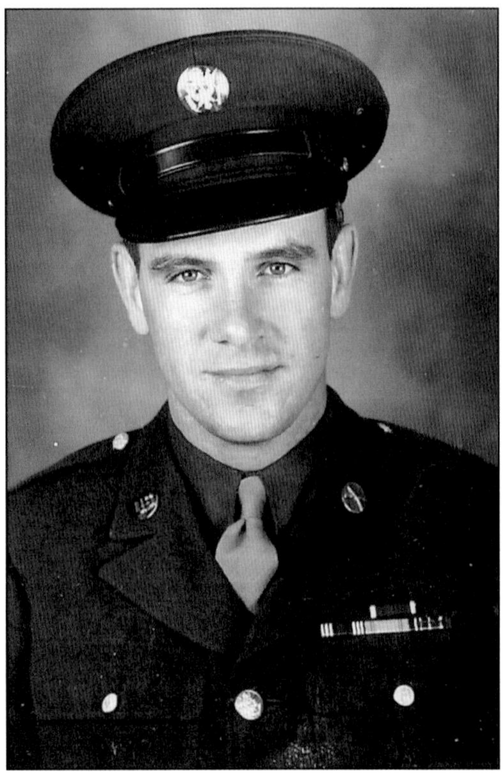

Jay Robertson was the son of John and Ruth Robertson, who farmed northeast of Akron. Originally with the National Guard in Company K, he fought in World War II in North Africa and was captured by the Germans during the Tunisia battle. He escaped from an Axis prison ship in the harbor at Brizerte. His unit fought up the boot of Italy, where Robertson earned several citations. Surviving the war, he returned to Plymouth County and married Opal Sommervold. (Courtesy Tim Tone.)

Seven

TRANSPORTATION THROUGH THE YEARS

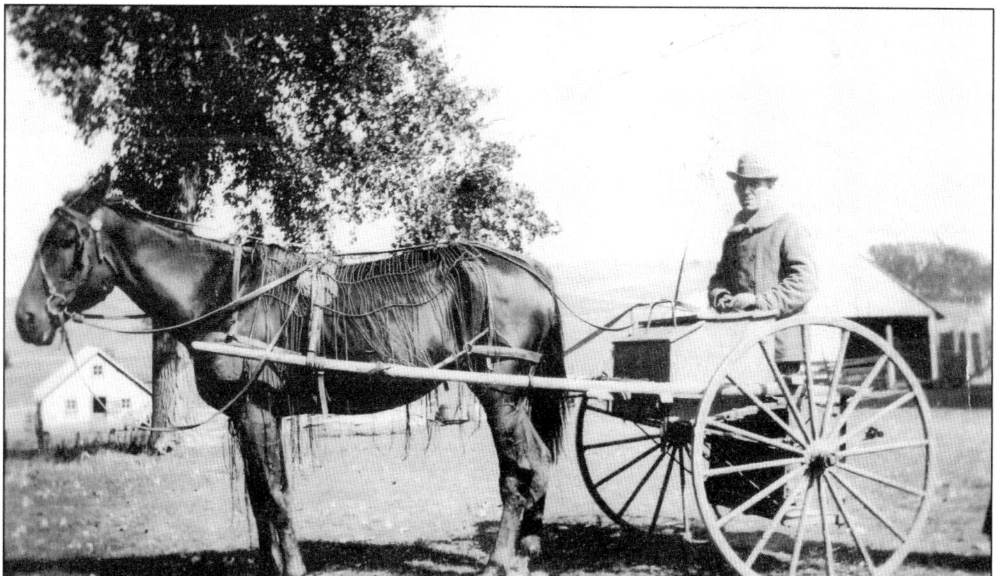

Grant Brown stands on his horse-drawn cart for this photograph. The horse is sporting its fly netting attire. A good team of horses was crucial to the early farming industry. Grant Brown farmed near Adaville on the same place for 44 years. (Courtesy Susan Hunter Miller.)

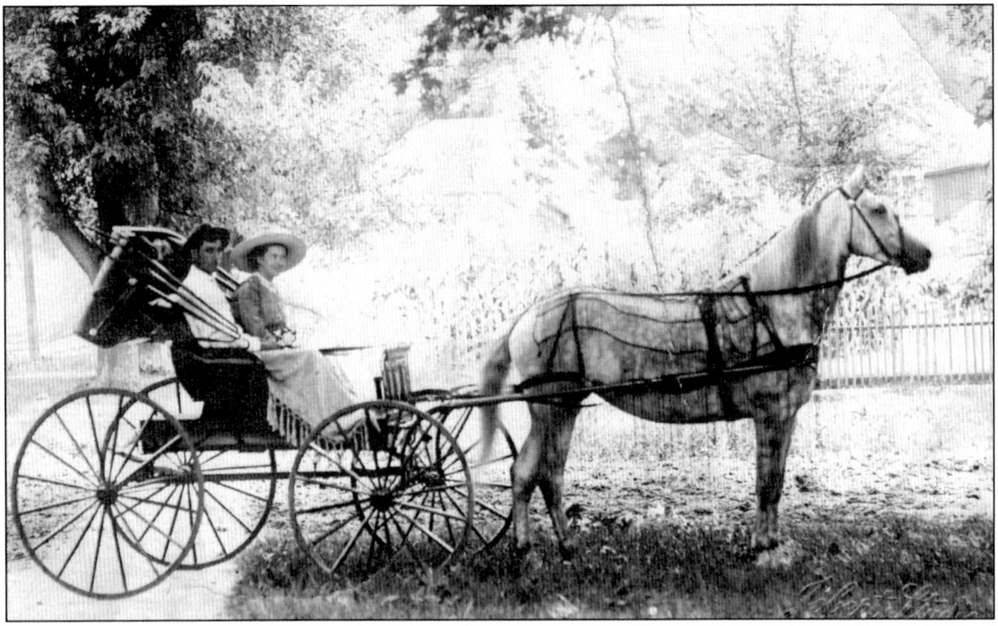

This is a lovely photograph of newlyweds Walter Grebner and his bride Pearl Irene Burrill seated in their horse and buggy. They were married in Adaville on March 27, 1912. Walter was a young farmer with splendid ability, and Pearl was a successful rural schoolteacher. After their marriage, they farmed on the Grebner home place in Johnson Township. (Courtesy Duane and Vivien Reeves.)

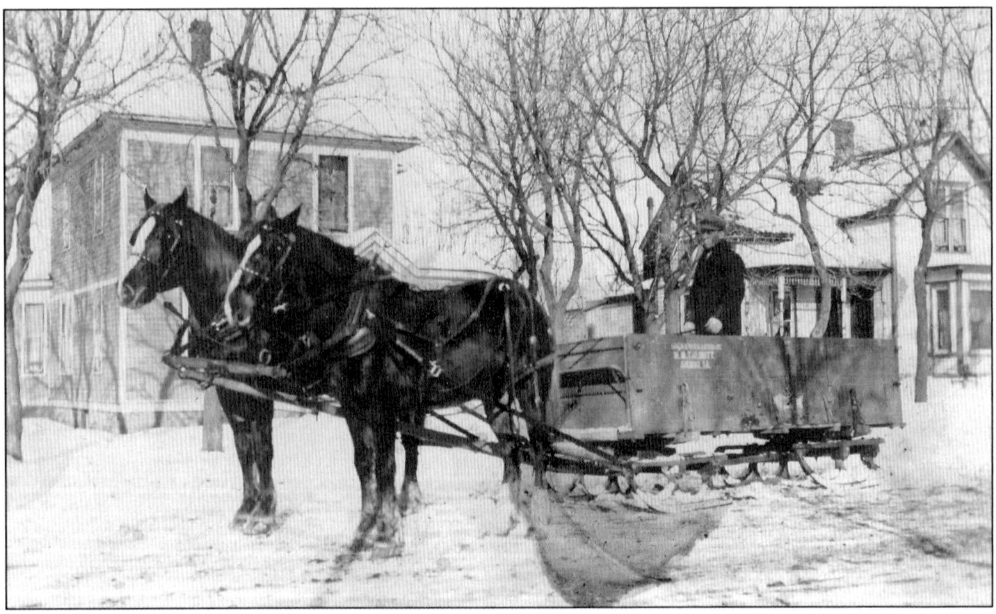

Adam Tindall stands proudly in the wagon sleigh while holding the horses' reins. On the side of the wagon is stamped the name M. M. Talbott, Akron, Iowa. The 1897 Plymouth County directory lists M. M. Talbott of Adaville with the occupation of well driller. (Courtesy Claire and Phyllis Allen.)

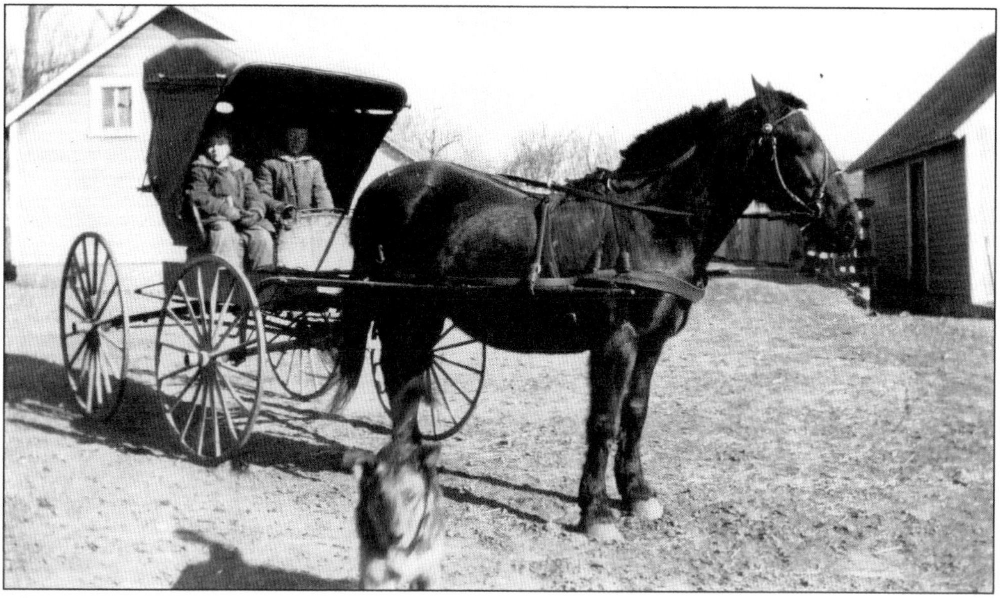

This is a photograph of a horse-drawn buggy with an unidentified couple at the reins. (Courtesy Plymouth County Historical Museum.)

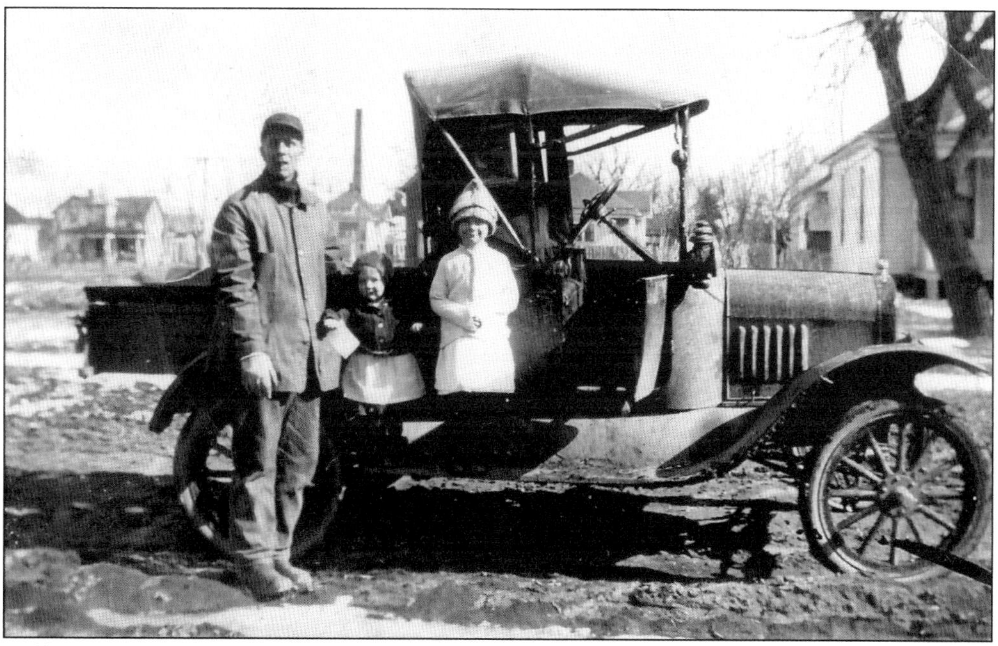

William C. Kern and his two young daughters stop for a photograph, standing by his company pickup. The two young ones are Helen (left) and June. William was employed for a number of years by the Northwestern Bell Telephone Company. (Courtesy Nancy Tindall Yoder.)

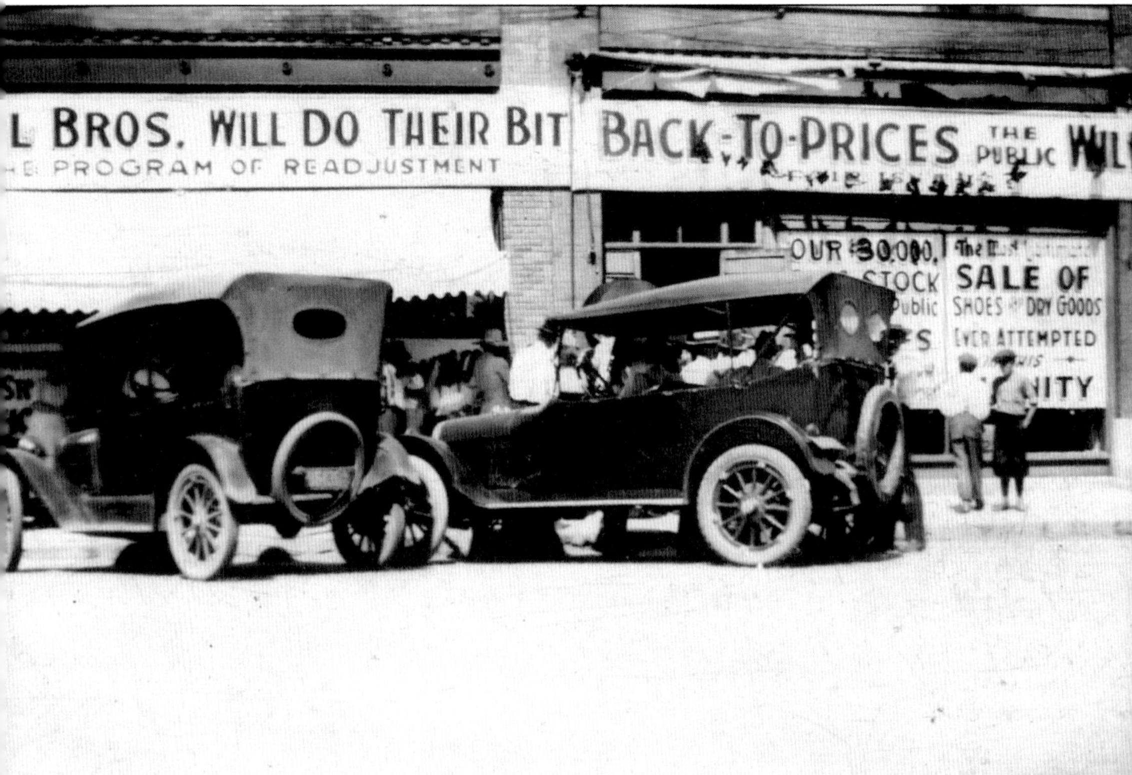

Le Mars shoppers in the 1920s have parked their automobiles in front of the Nuebel Brothers Grocery store. (Courtesy Plymouth County Historical Museum.)

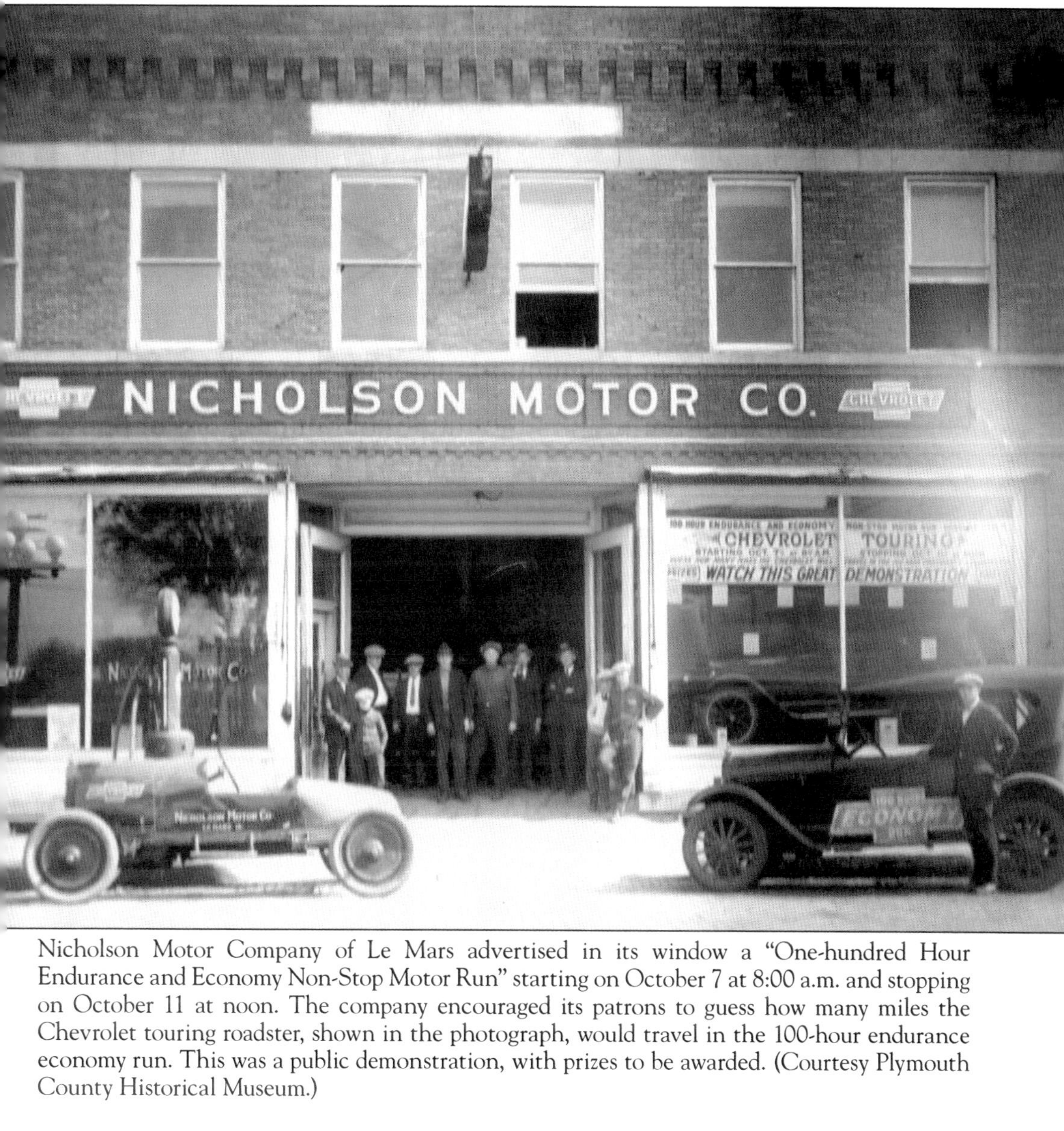

Nicholson Motor Company of Le Mars advertised in its window a "One-hundred Hour Endurance and Economy Non-Stop Motor Run" starting on October 7 at 8:00 a.m. and stopping on October 11 at noon. The company encouraged its patrons to guess how many miles the Chevrolet touring roadster, shown in the photograph, would travel in the 100-hour endurance economy run. This was a public demonstration, with prizes to be awarded. (Courtesy Plymouth County Historical Museum.)

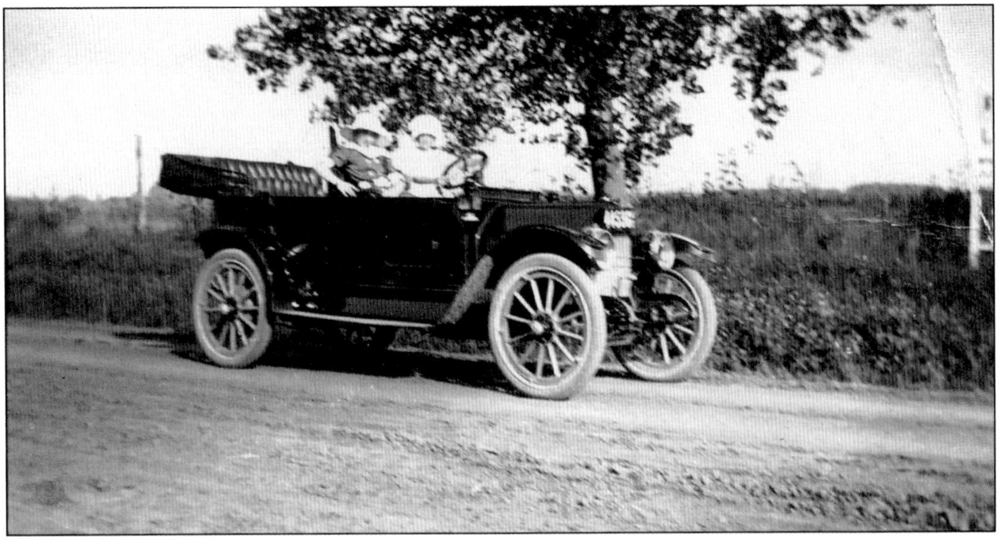

Two unidentified women are enjoying a Sunday drive in the country. (Courtesy Plymouth County Historical Museum.)

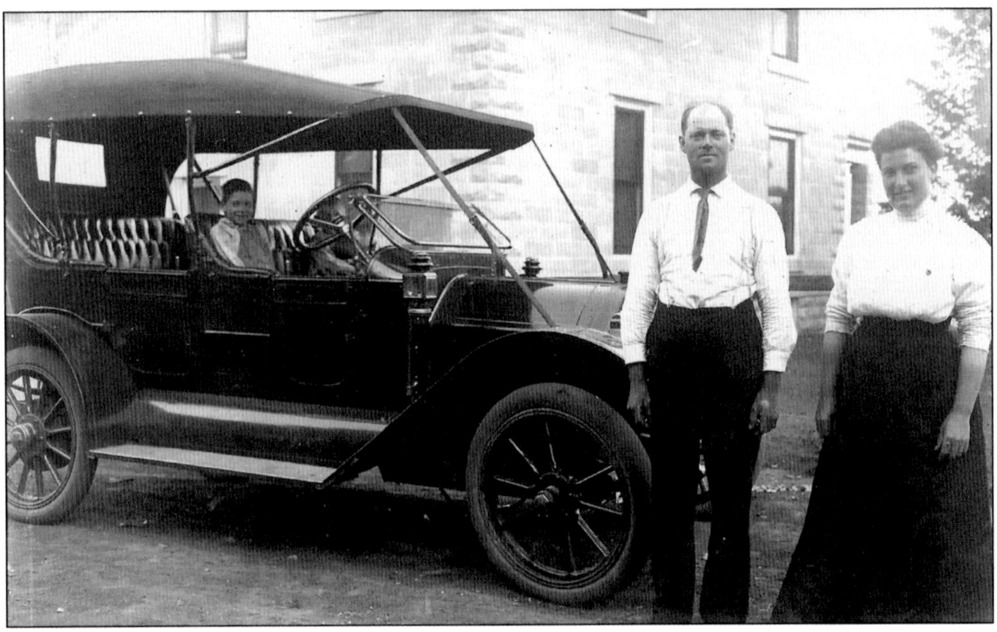

The car in this photograph appears to be foreign-made. The distinguished-looking couple is standing proudly in front of their car, which has the steering wheel on the right front side. Two young boys are seated in the front seat. Unfortunately, there was no identification on this photograph. (Courtesy Plymouth County Historical Museum.)

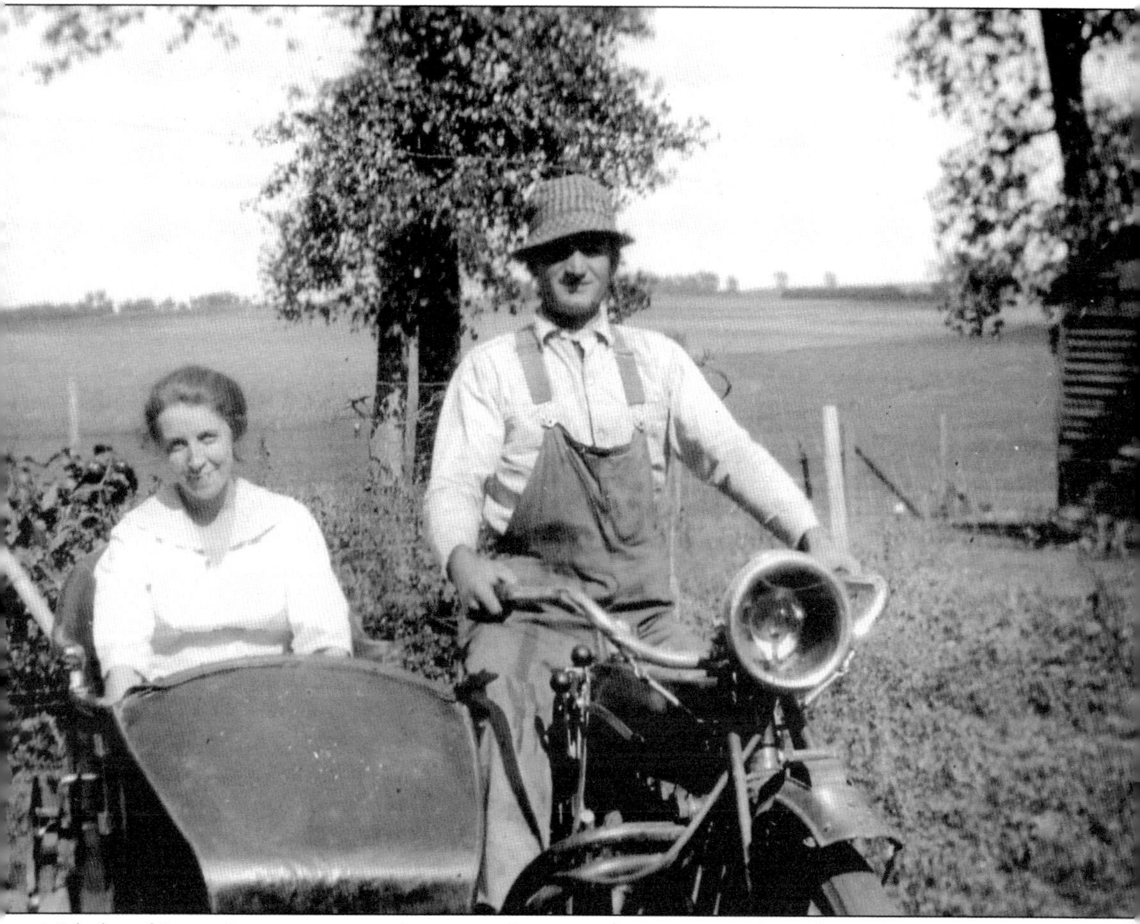

Mabel and Leroy Jennings enjoyed touring about on their motorcycle with a sidecar attached. (Courtesy Nancy Tindall Yoder.)

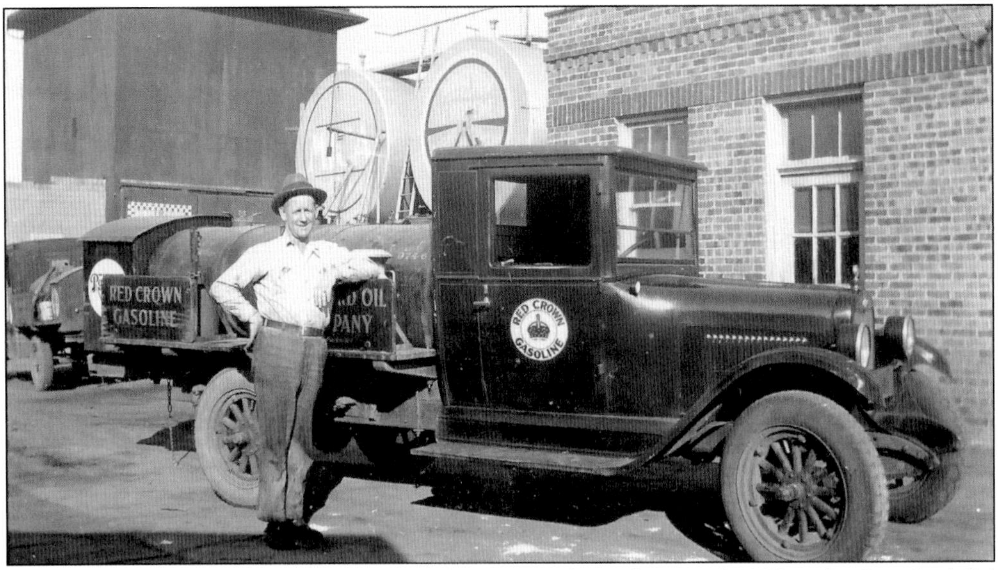

Standard Oil agent Sid Locer stands with his new tank truck around 1927 at the Standard Oil bulk plant near the train depot in Le Mars. (Courtesy Tim Tone.)

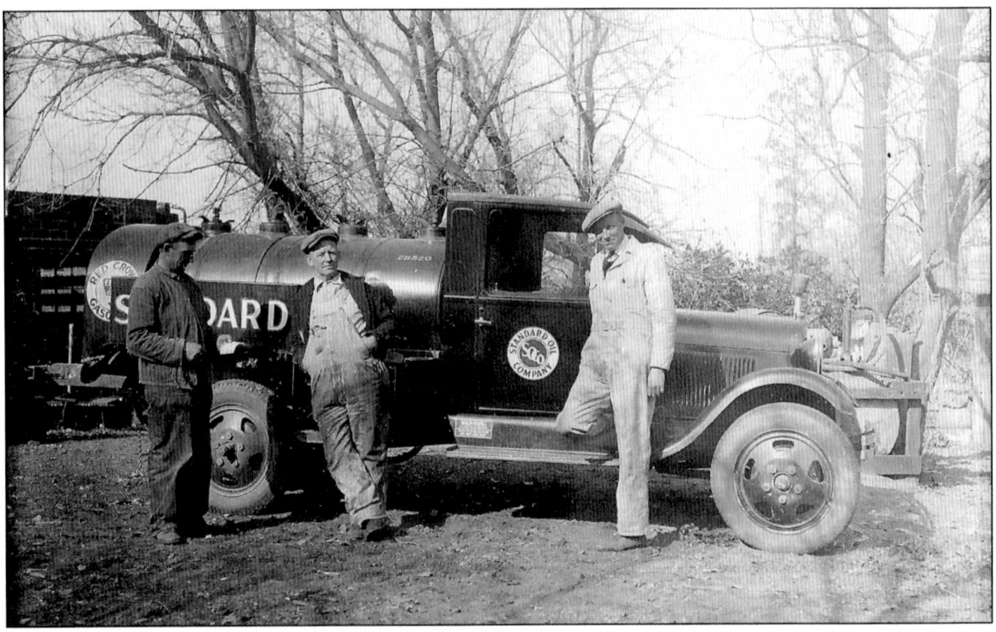

The Standard Oil bulk plant was located on the east edge of Le Mars near the train depot. Agent Sid Locer leans on one of his trucks, and Verle Moorehead rests his foot on the running board. A customer looks over a gasoline invoice. (Courtesy Tim Tone.)

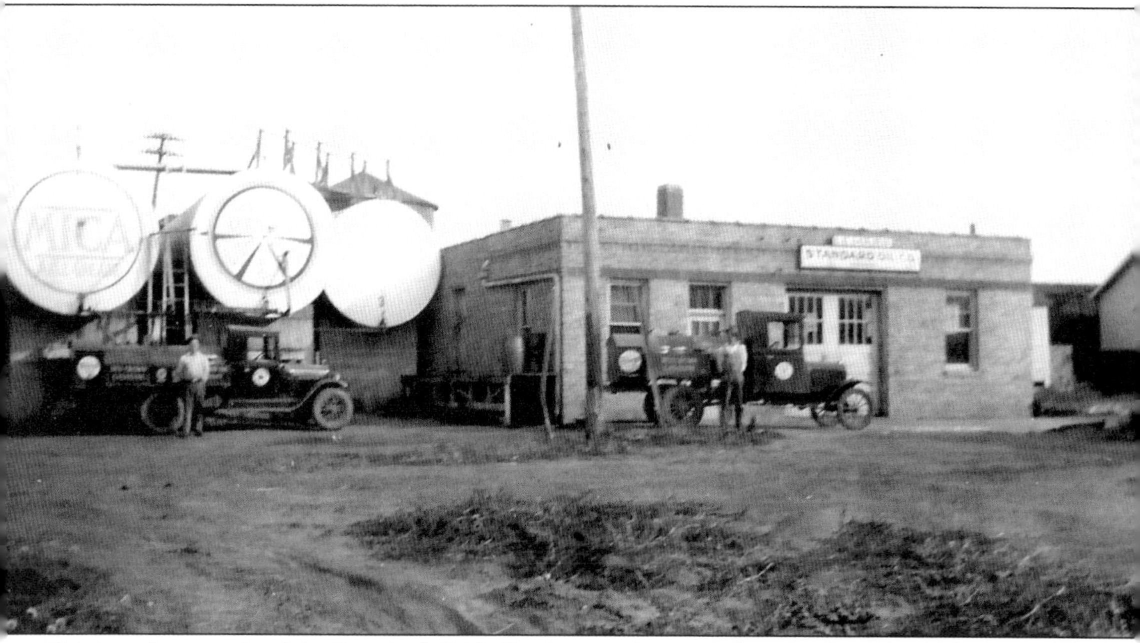

This is a photograph of the Standard Oil bulk plant on the east edge of Le Mars near the train depot. Standard Oil agent Sid Locer, wearing a white shirt, and Verle Moorehead, wearing coveralls, stand in front of Sid's tank trucks. (Courtesy Tim Tone.)

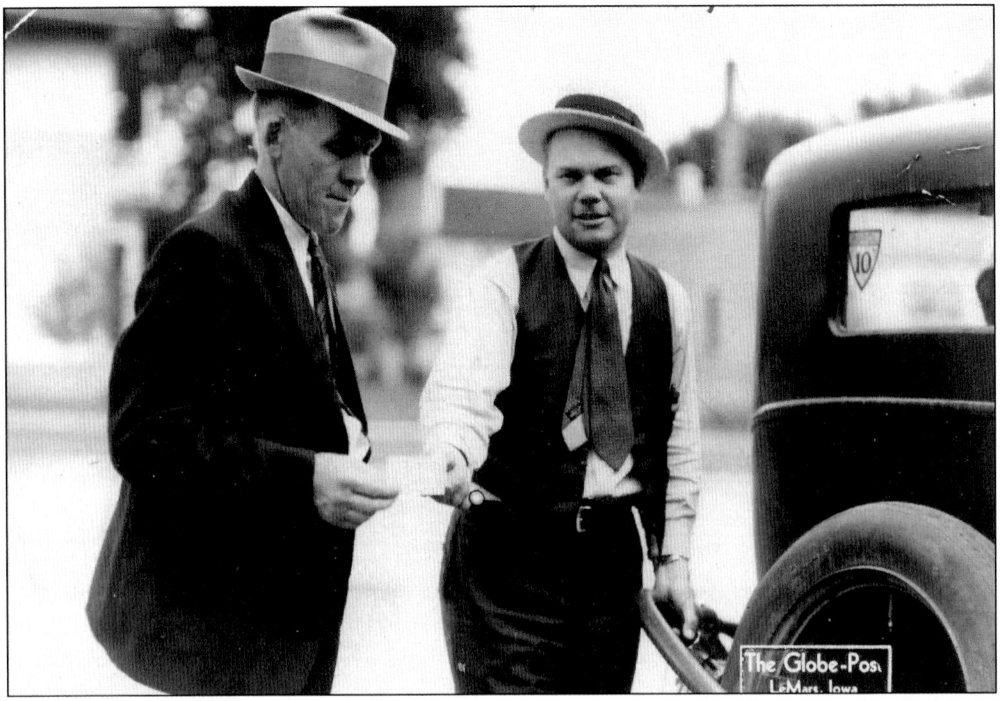

This May 1938 photograph shows Oscar Johnson, a Henry Township farmer, and L. L. Meek, manager of the Plymouth Co-op Oil Company, transacting business. The picture was taken for *Globe-Post* newspaper advertising. The shield sticker on the rear window of the car says Agrol 10, which was the name for corn alcohol gasoline at that time. (Courtesy Plymouth County Historical Museum.)

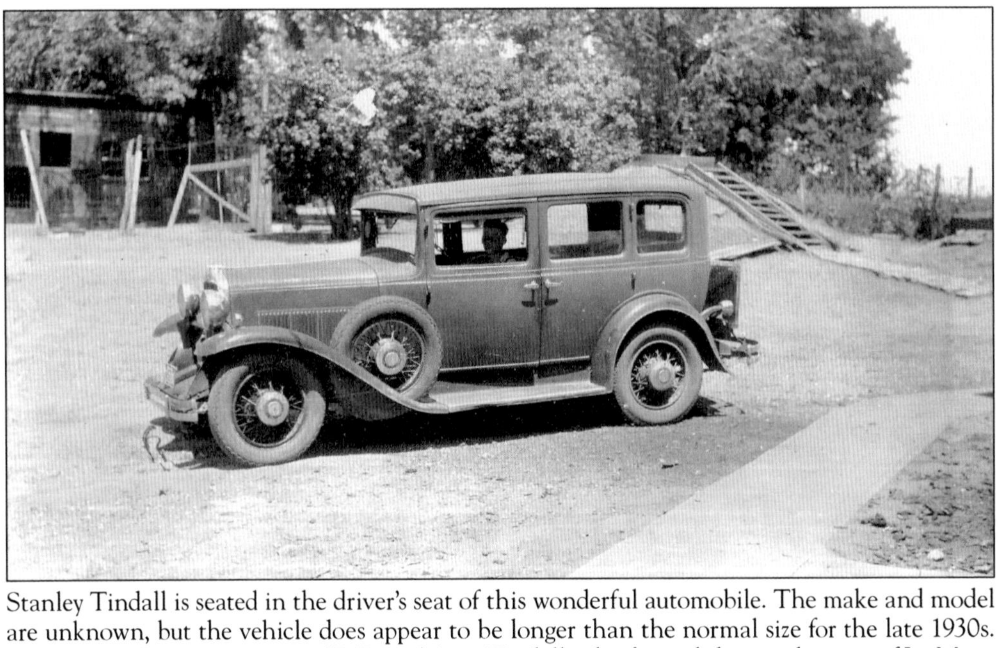

Stanley Tindall is seated in the driver's seat of this wonderful automobile. The make and model are unknown, but the vehicle does appear to be longer than the normal size for the late 1930s. Stanley was the youngest son of J. D. and Amy Tindall, who farmed three miles west of Le Mars. (Courtesy Nancy Tindall Yoder.)

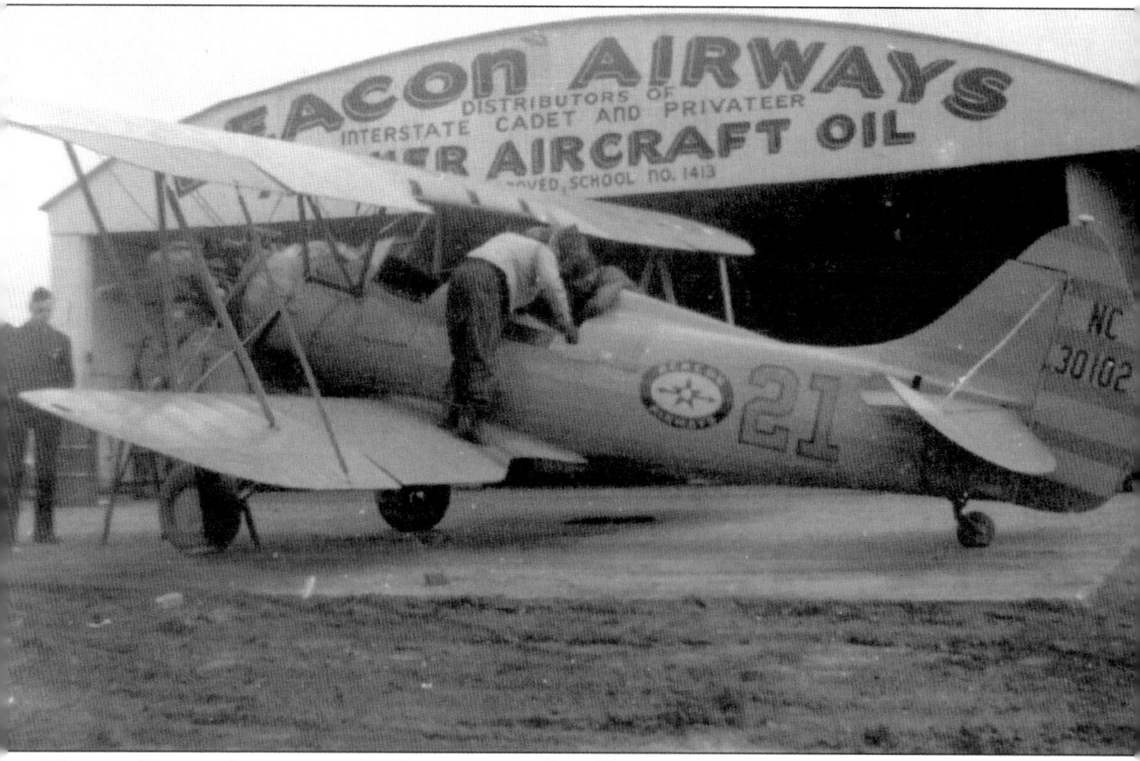

The new Beacon Airways, renting hangar space from Western Union College, began use in May 1941, situated about a mile south of Le Mars on Highway 75. L. W. Duvon was chief instructor at the airport. An agreement with the U.S. government provided pre-cadet flight training and housing for U.S. Army and Navy air cadet candidates. In January 1943, this arrangement was changed to apply to U.S. Navy air cadets only. Civil pilot training was given in Le Mars, from which the candidates would go to U.S. Navy flight school. While in Le Mars, the cadets were housed in Wernli Hall, at the college. This training situation ended when the U.S. Navy withdrew its planes and men, in August 1944. The college and Beacon Airways continued to provide civilian flight training until after the war. (Courtesy Plymouth County Historical Museum.)

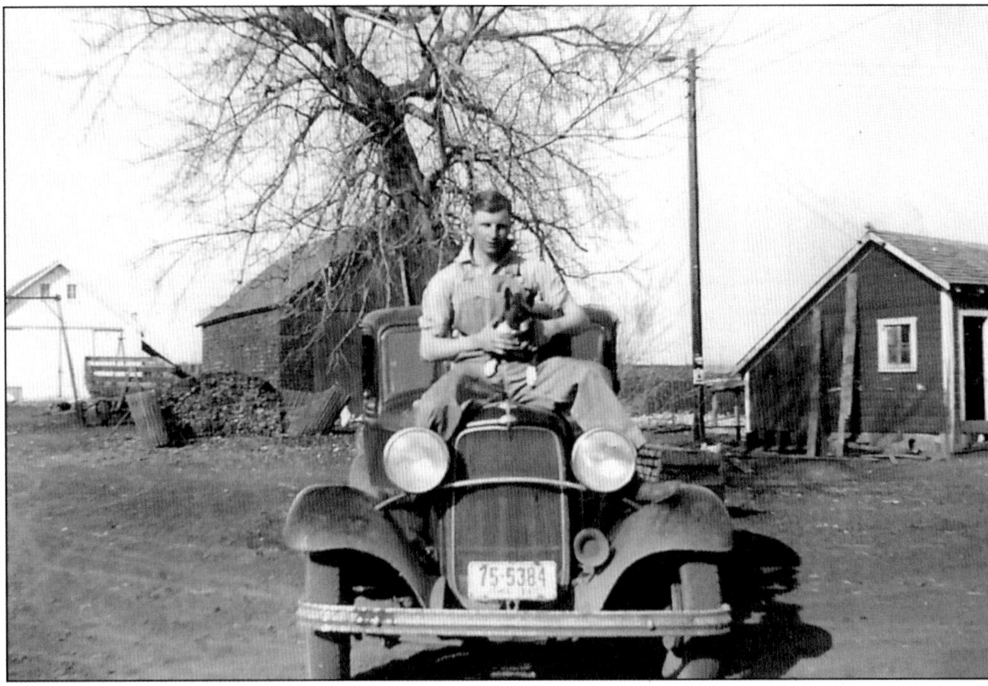

Seated on his 1934 Ford pickup with his dog is Donald "Bud" Lucken. He is the son of state senator J. Henry Lucken and Cecilia (Woll) Lucken, who farmed southeast of Akron. Bud later married Darlene Robertson. (Courtesy Tim Tone.)

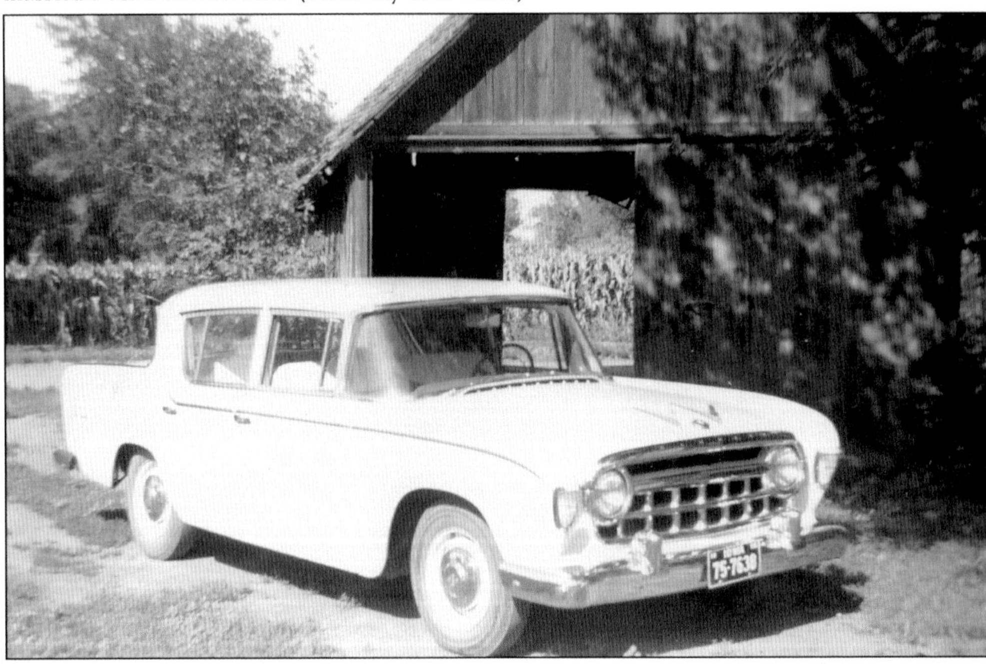

A new 1956 Rambler automobile was purchased at Grau Company in Le Mars by Vernon Ewin. The new car is parked at the Ewin home in Seney. Notice the corn growing in the field next to the alleyway beyond the garage. Knee high by the Fourth of July was the sign of a good yield to come. (Courtesy Linda Ewin Ziemann.)

Eight

TRAINING TOMORROW'S LEADERS

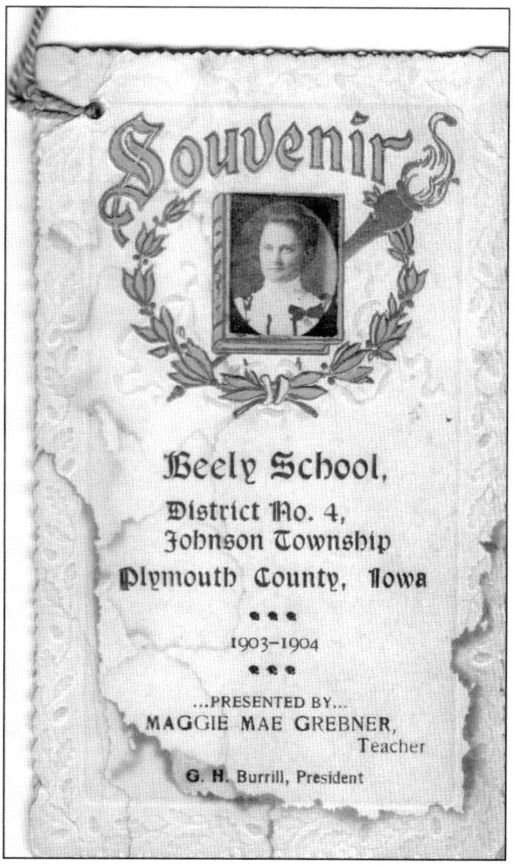

It was common practice for the early teachers to present end-of-the-year school souvenir booklets to their students. This 1903–1904 souvenir booklet was presented to the students of Beely School, District No. 4, Johnson Township, by their teacher, Maggie Mae Grebner. A photograph of the teacher is located on the booklet cover. George H. Burrill was president of the school board at that time. (Courtesy Duane and Vivien Reeves.)

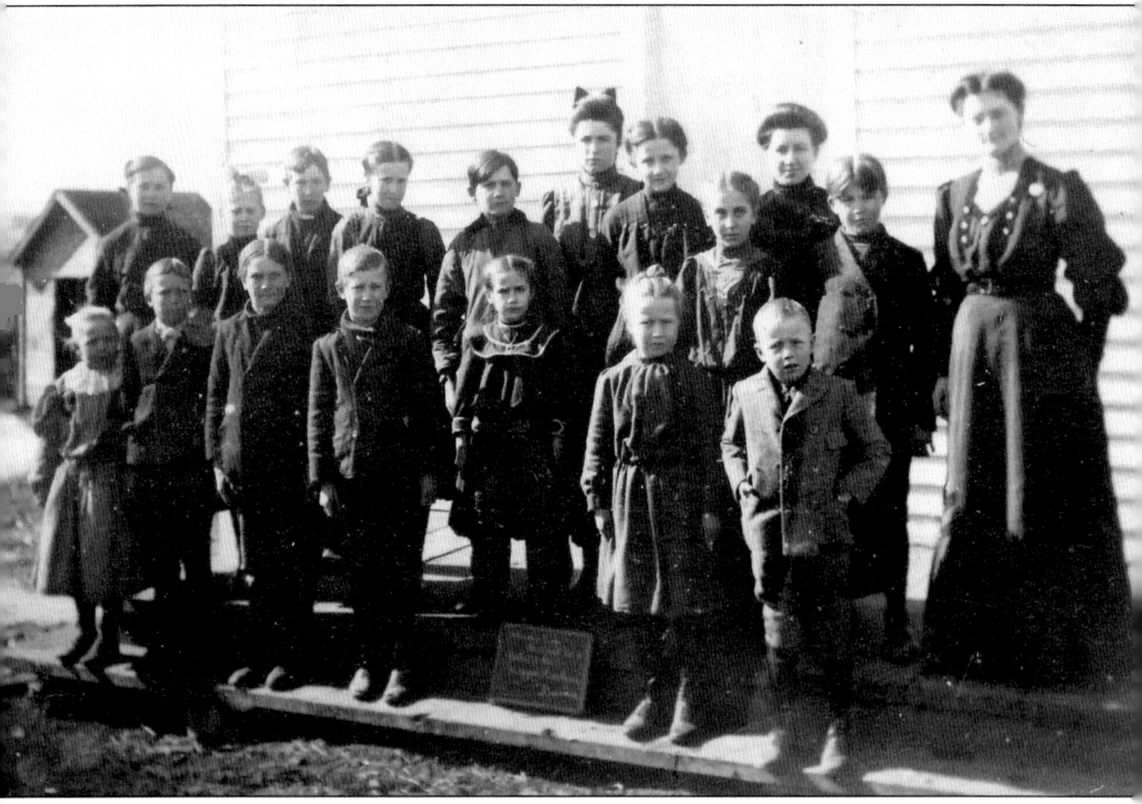

This wonderful photograph of Maggie Grebner and her students from the year 1903–1904 has survived time. The students are, from left to right, (first row) Anna Lucken, J. Henry Lucken, Jake Ruedy, Herman Ohlrichs, Mary Faye Burrill (later married to Henry Dempster, then to Calvin Eyres), and Simon Lucken, (second row) Clara Buehre (later Wetrosky), Tillie Ruedy, and Carl Fletcher; (third row) Pearl Burrill (later married to Walter Grebner), Florence Burrill (later married to Adam Ross Clarke), John Ohlrichs, Eva Burrill (later married to Henry Clarke, then to Butch Hanssen), Clarence Grebner, Emma Buehre (later Susemihl), Clara Grebner, Bertha Draheim (later Feuerhelm), and teacher Maggie Grebner (later Hammond). (Courtesy Duane and Vivien Reeves.)

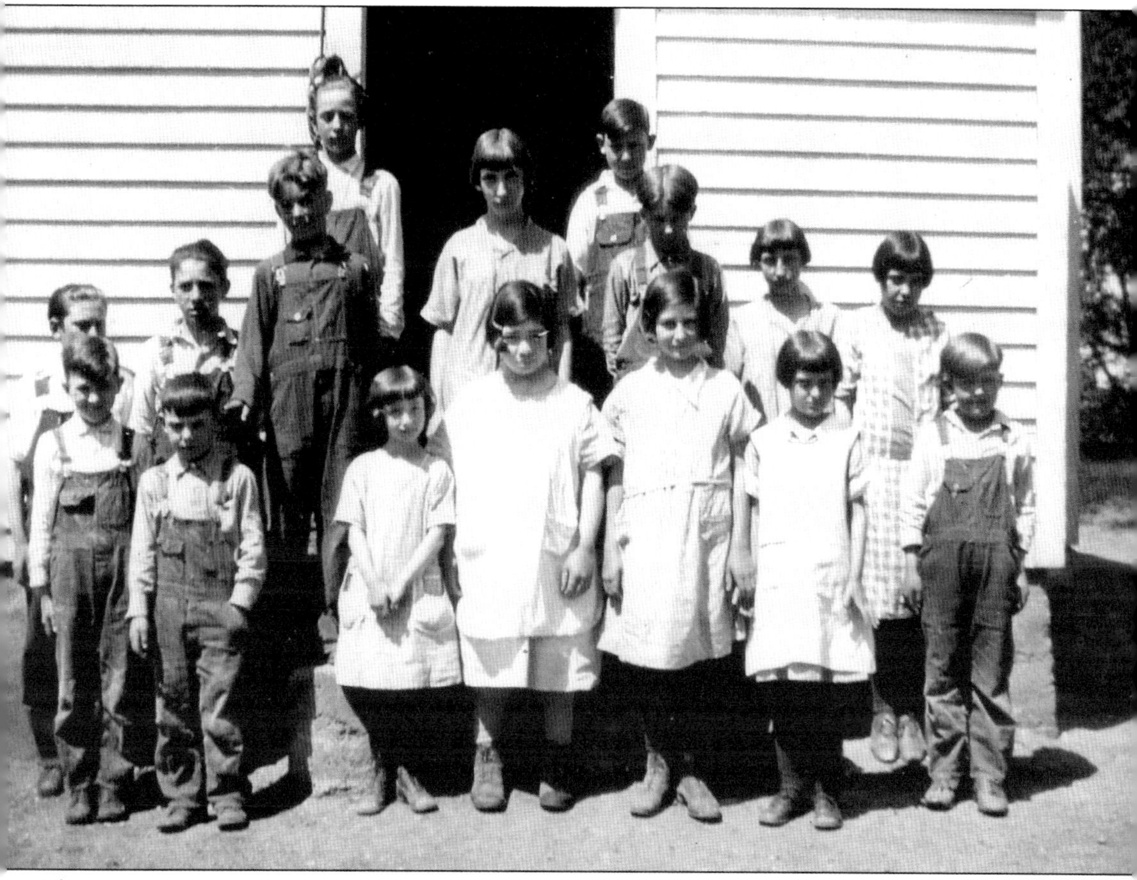

This is a group photograph of the students of Johnson Township No. 5 rural school in the spring of 1927. Their teacher at that time was Miss E. Ferne King, daughter of Warren J. and Birdie King of the Adaville area. Unfortunately, there is no identification of the students on this photograph. This was the teacher's last school assignment, after which she married Rev. S. A. Jones, on June 1, 1927. (Courtesy Linda Ewin Ziemann.)

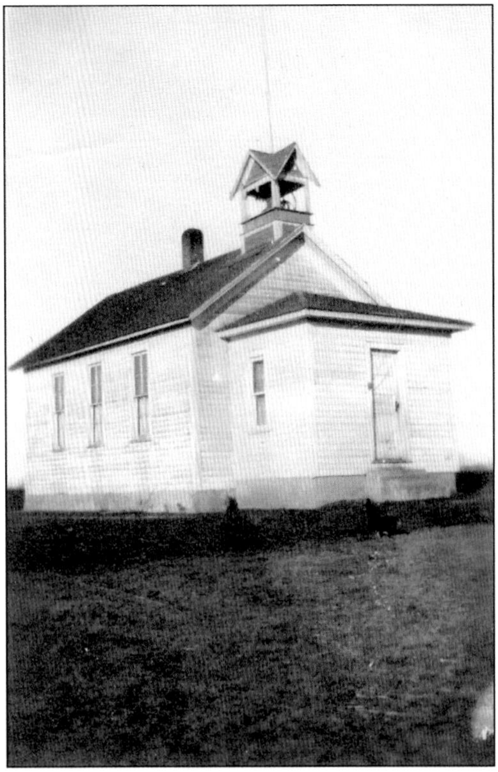

The Ruble school building is still standing in Ruble today. This school was known as the Johnson Township District No. 2 school. School was conducted at Ruble for many years, closing finally in 1959. (Courtesy Mary Lamoureux.)

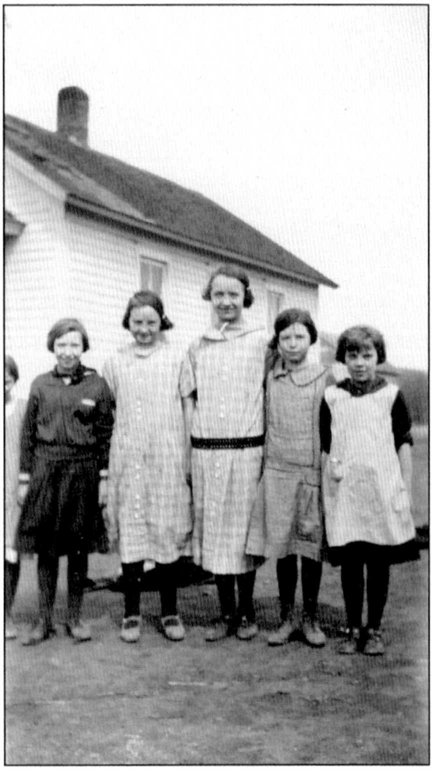

This is a group of Ruble school female students. The girls are identified on the back of the picture, from left to right, as Carolyn J., Henrietta Meins, Helen Marbach, Ruth Marbach, Mildred Miller, and Lucille J. The date of the photograph is supposed to be after 1912. (Courtesy Mary Lamoureux.)

Minnie Lilly was an early rural schoolteacher. This lovely lady was photographed by J. M. Dwight studio in Remsen. (Courtesy Plymouth County Historical Museum.)

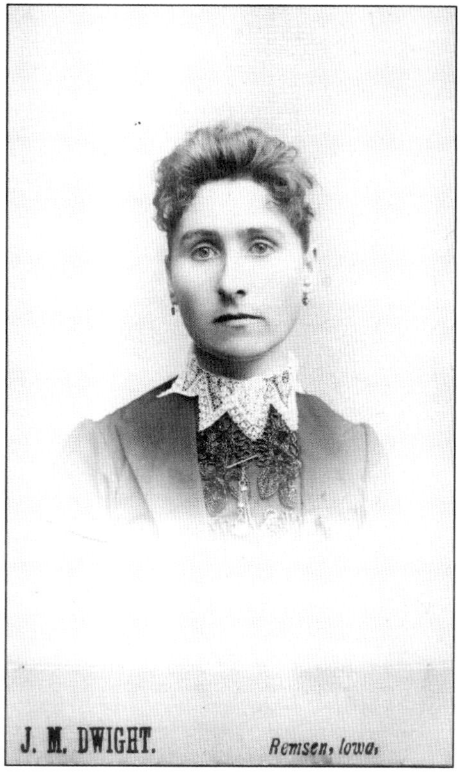

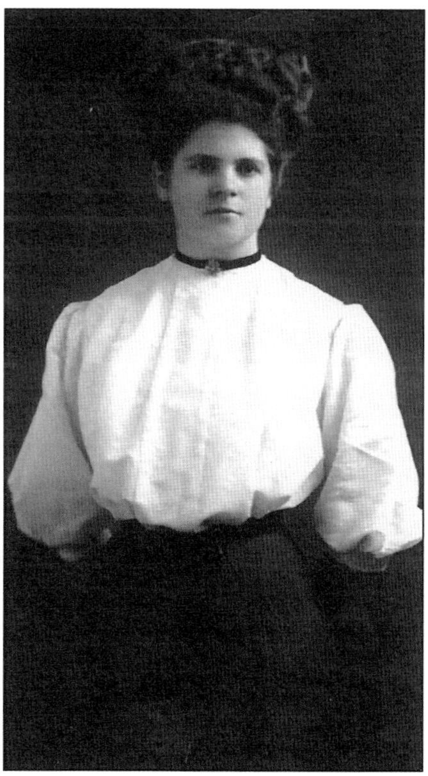

Bessie Robertson was a country schoolteacher in Plymouth County in 1910. Since teachers could not be married, she had to quit when she married Sid Locer in 1911. Bessie was the daughter of early Plymouth County settlers Duncan and Belle Robertson. (Courtesy Tim Tone.)

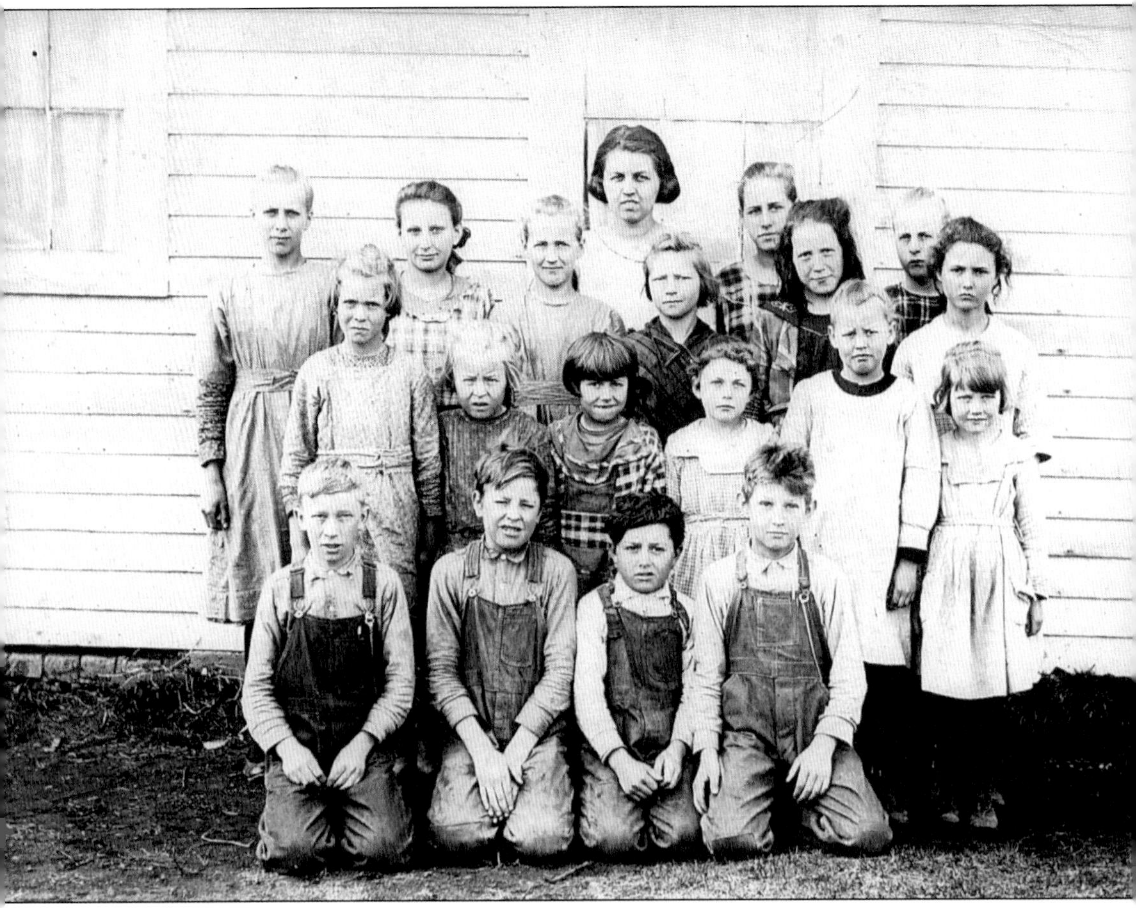

Grant No. 9 pupils and their teacher in 1921 are, from left to right, (first row) Elmer Osterbuhr, George Kruse, Laurence Euken, and Carl Mammen; (second row) Della Popken, Hilda Popken, Margaret Botsford, Dorothy Euken, Edna Kruse, and Margaret Euken; (third row) Clara Popken, Minnie Mammen, Emma Popken, teacher Florence Luiken, Anna Osterbuhr, Mary Botsford, Evelyn Boyting, Alma Popken, and Doretta Pecks. (Courtesy Plymouth County Historical Museum.)

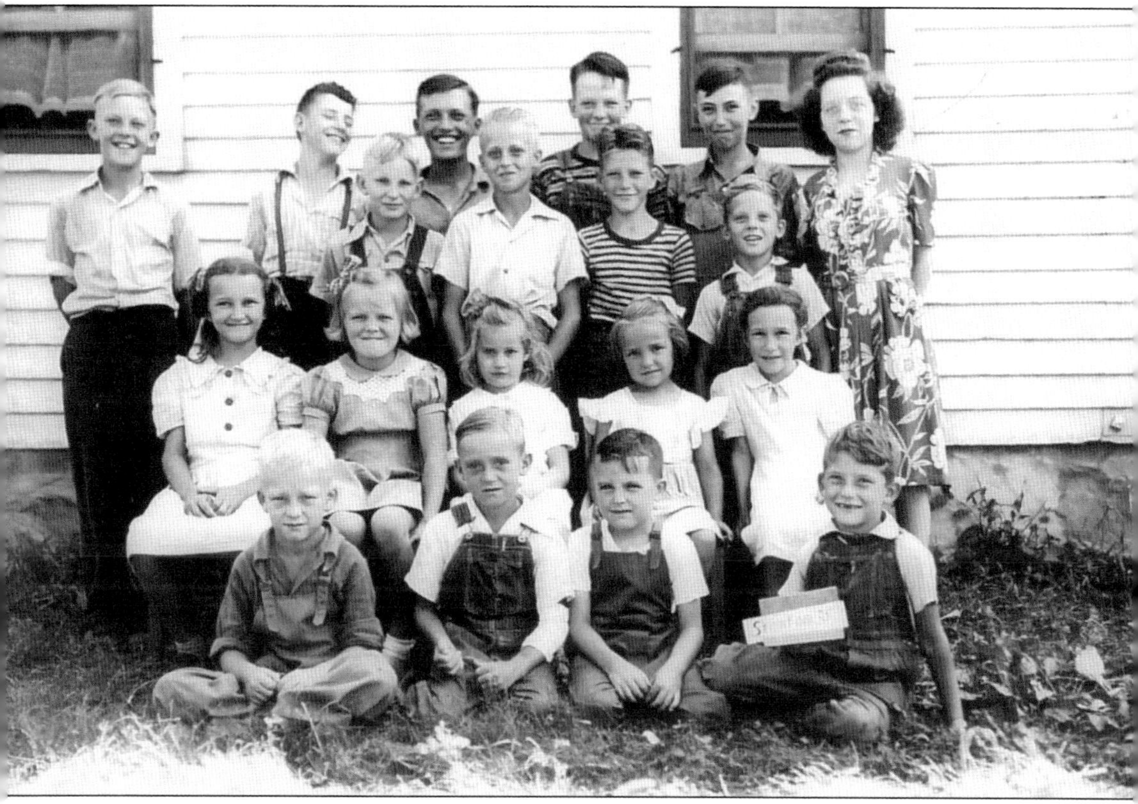

Stanton No. 5 pupils and their teacher are photographed in the spring of 1945. They are, from left to right, (first row) Gerald Luken, Jim Hodgson, Dan Kehrberg, and Keith Kounkel; (second row) Dorothy Rolfes, Norma Jean Kehrberg, Anita Schwartz, Margaret Rolfes, and Norma Rolfes; (third row) Charles Kehrberg, Clayton Hodgson, Norman Kehrberg, and Blaine Kounkel; (fourth row) Harold Luken, Duane Heidbrink, Wesley Heidbrink, Bill Kehrberg, Francis Rolfes, and teacher Gladys Fischer. (Courtesy Plymouth County Historical Museum.)

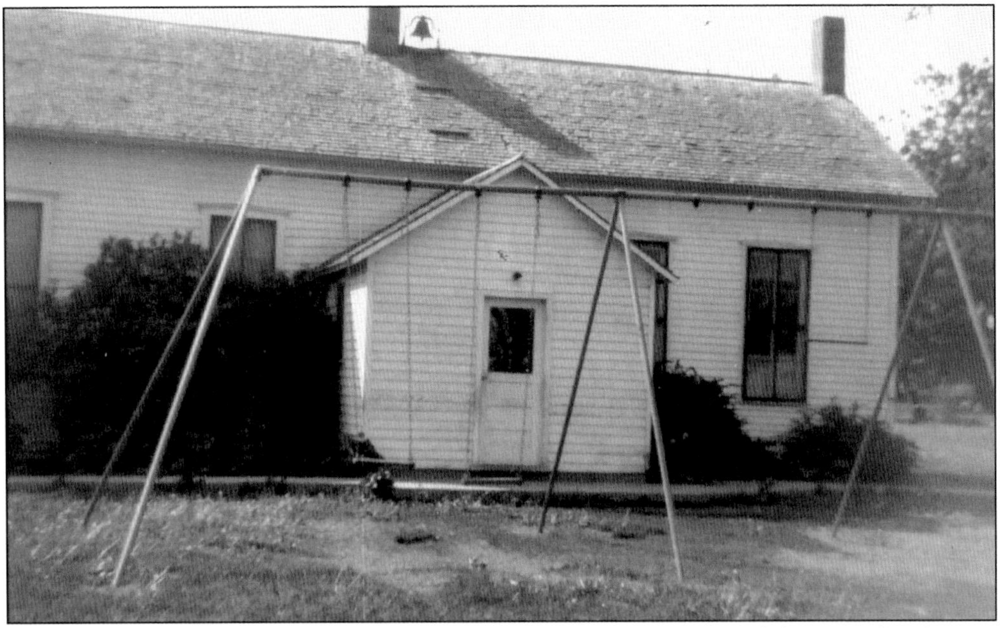

Seney rural school was opened in the late 1800s. Several generations of the same family were taught in the two-room school through the years. Every year the students performed for their parents and friends during the school Christmas program. In May, the teachers sponsored an end-of-the-year school picnic on the school grounds. The entire town would turn out and share in the bountiful potluck meal. (Courtesy Linda Ewin Ziemann.)

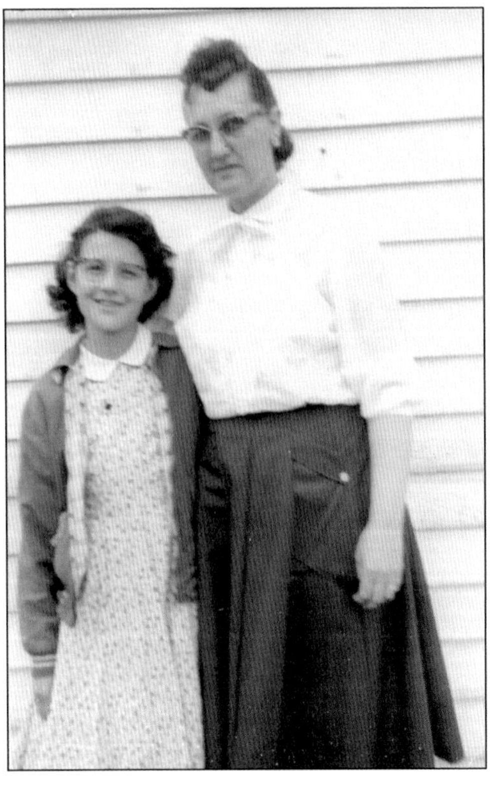

Dorothea DeBoer taught the students in the "Big Room" (fourth through sixth grade) at the Seney school from 1957 to 1960. DeBoer is pictured in this photograph with student Linda Ewin in May 1959. (Courtesy Linda Ewin Ziemann.)

Mrs. Arie Bomgaars taught the younger students (kindergarten through third grade) in the "Little Room" at the Seney school, spanning the years of 1953–1962. Bomgaars is pictured with students Diana Ewin (left) and David Ewin. (Courtesy Linda Ewin Ziemann.)

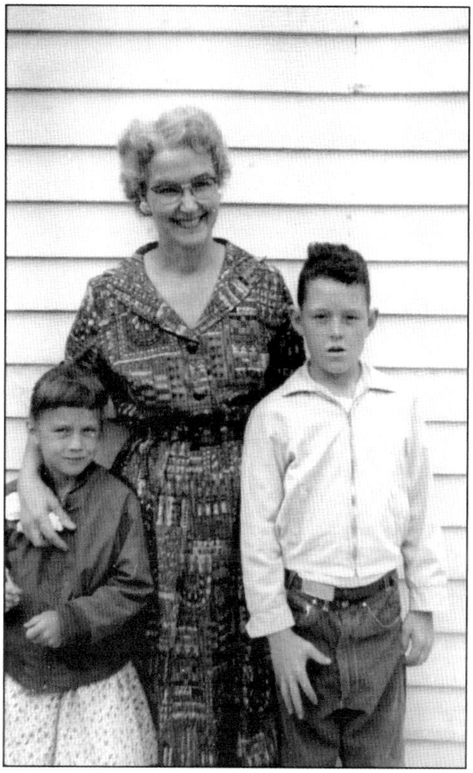

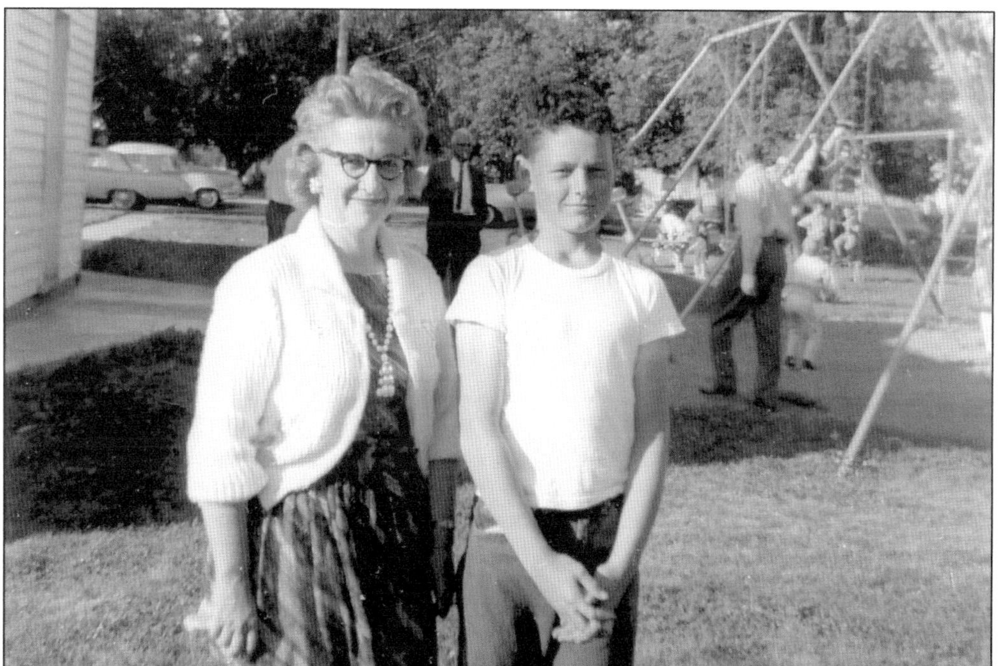

Luella Siege taught the Big Room students the last school year before the Seney school closed in May 1962. Siege is pictured in this photograph with student David Ewin. (Courtesy Linda Ewin Ziemann.)

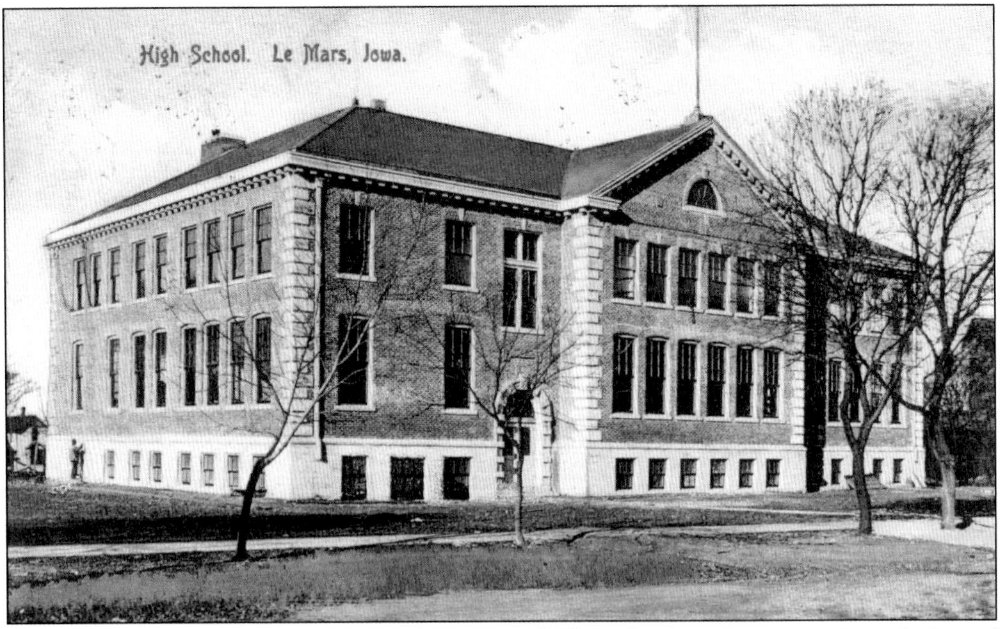

The Le Mars High School building was built in 1905. The school was known in the early days of its history as Le Mars Central High School. (Courtesy Plymouth County Historical Museum.)

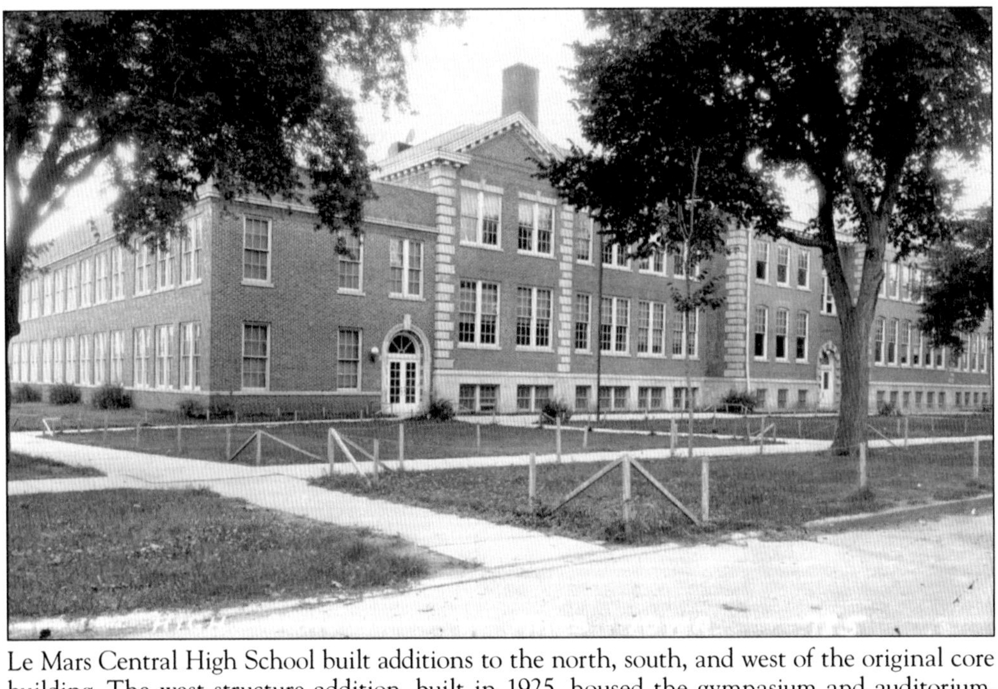

Le Mars Central High School built additions to the north, south, and west of the original core building. The west structure addition, built in 1925, housed the gymnasium and auditorium. By the 1960s, a brand-new gymnasium was built near the football stadium in south Le Mars. (Courtesy Plymouth County Historical Museum.)

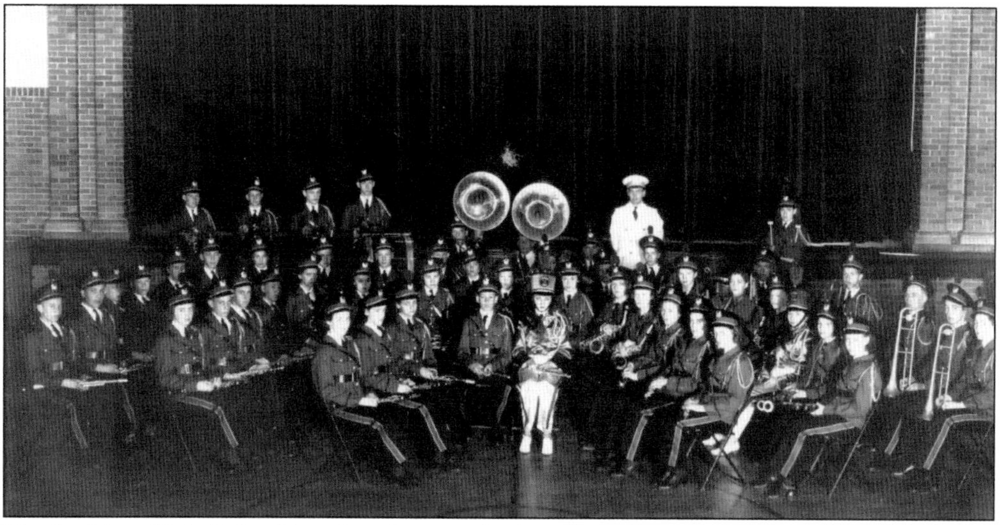

The Le Mars High School band is photographed in the school gymnasium in the late 1930s. Only one student is identified. The young boy, flutist, seated just to the left of the girl wearing white pants, is Vernon Ewin. (Courtesy Linda Ewin Ziemann.)

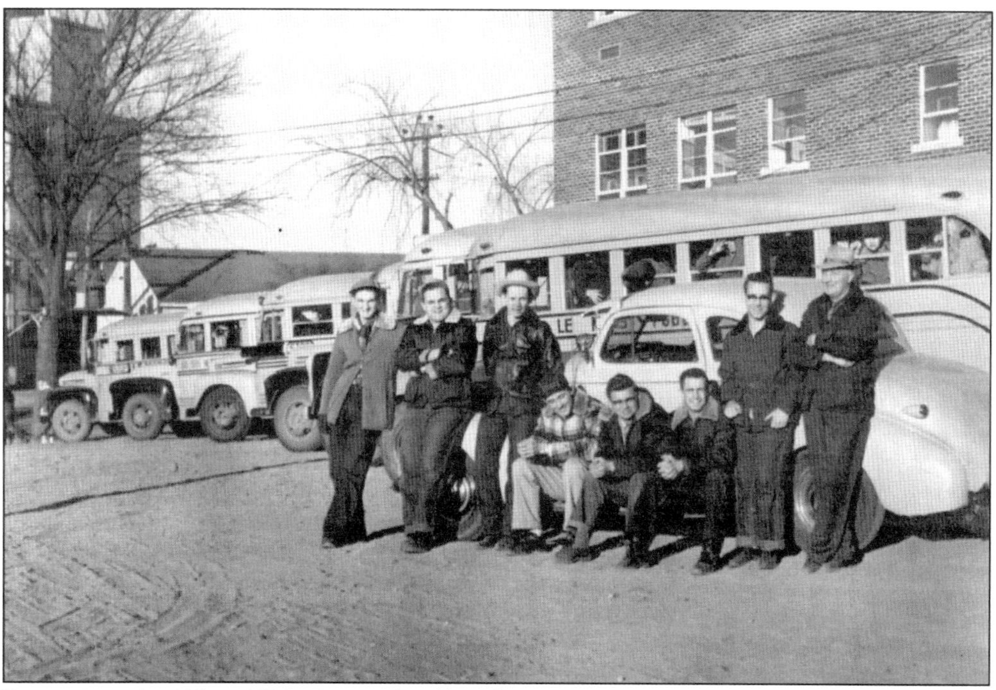

Pictured are the 1954–1955 Le Mars school bus drivers. They are, from left to right, Leland Eyres, Norman Crotsen, Max Scott, Carroll "Butch" Marty, Frank Yeager, Cliff Ellerbeck, Rolland Baehringer, and supervisor Herman Juffers. (Courtesy Plymouth County Historical Museum.)

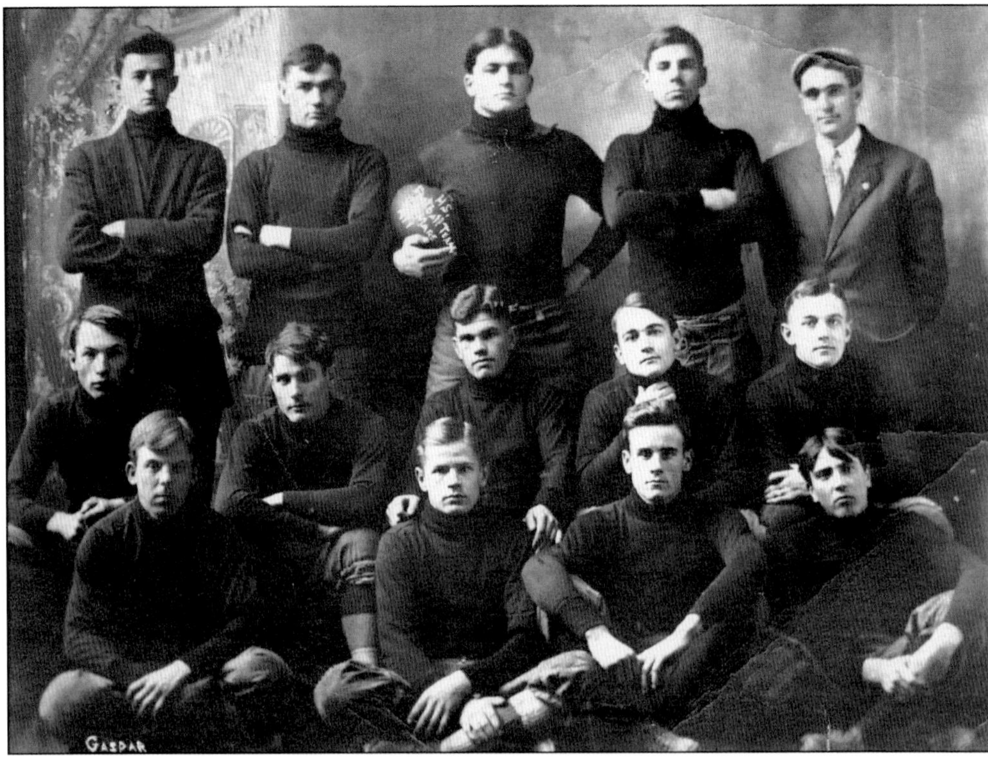

The Le Mars Central High School football players pose for a picture with a football. The year 1911 is written on the football. There is no identification of the players on this photograph. (Courtesy Plymouth County Historical Museum.)

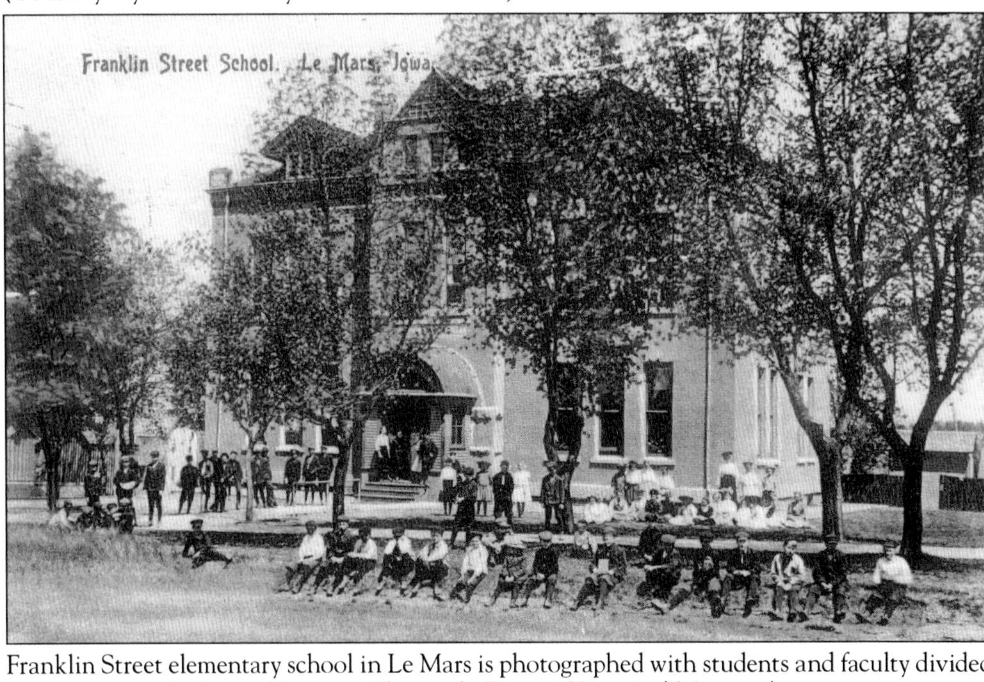

Franklin Street elementary school in Le Mars is photographed with students and faculty divided into groups on the lawn. (Courtesy Plymouth County Historical Museum.)

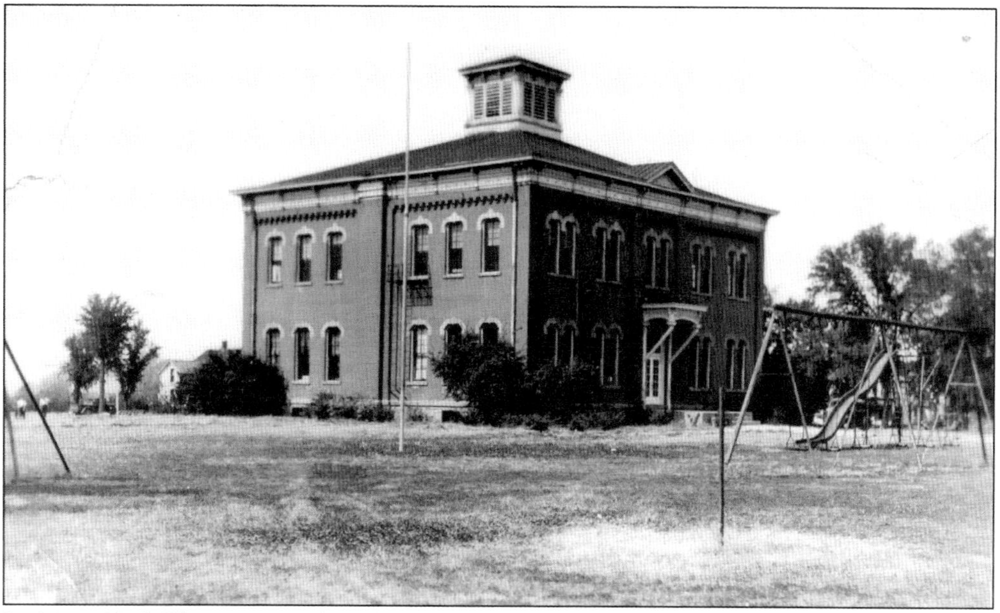

Le Mars Clark Elementary School building is shown in this photograph. (Courtesy Plymouth County Historical Museum.)

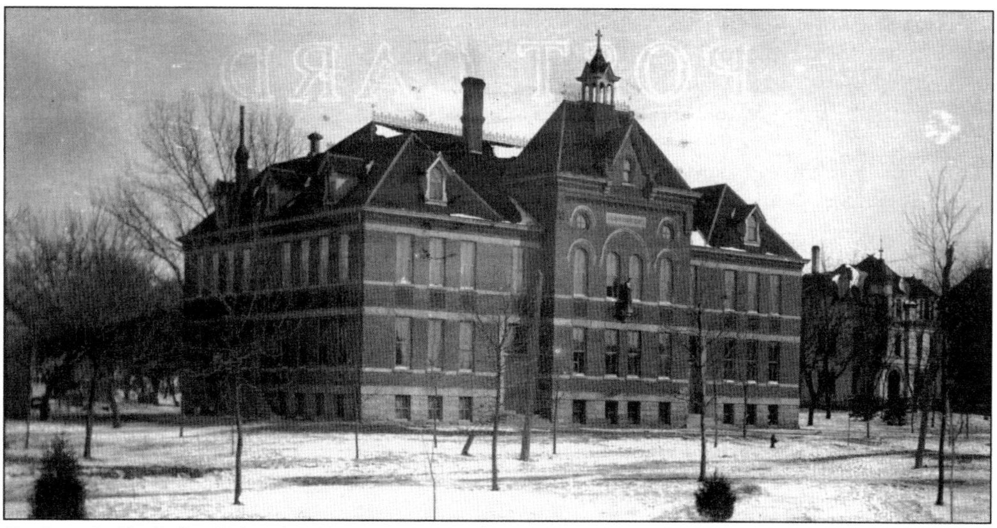

St. Joseph Catholic School in Le Mars served many years as an excellent educational facility. (Courtesy Plymouth County Historical Museum.)

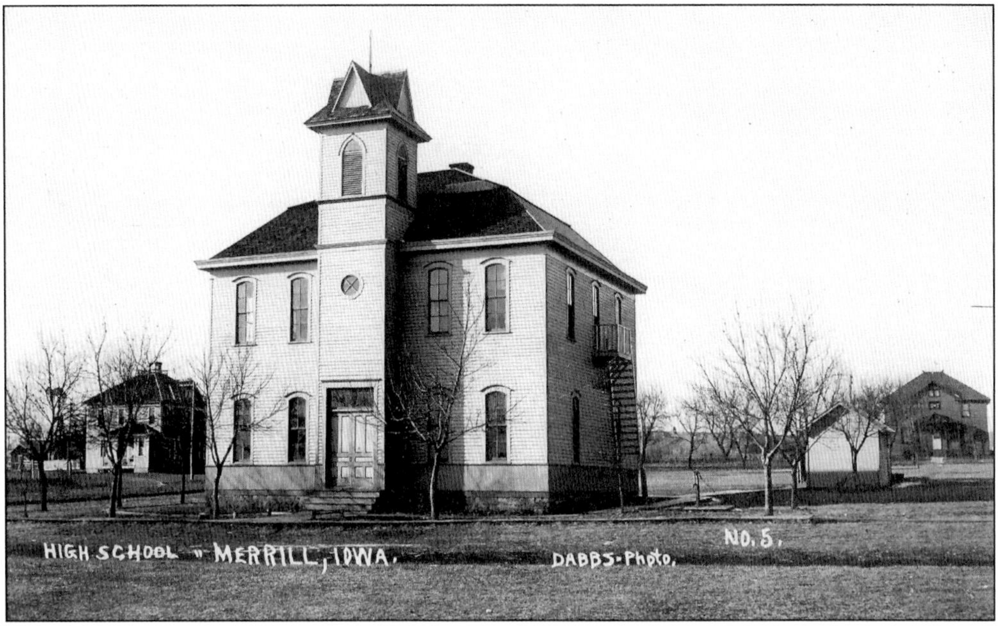

Dabbs Photo Studio took this wonderful picture of the early Merrill High School. The photographer also captured some of the residences on nearby streets. (Courtesy Judy Forgos.)

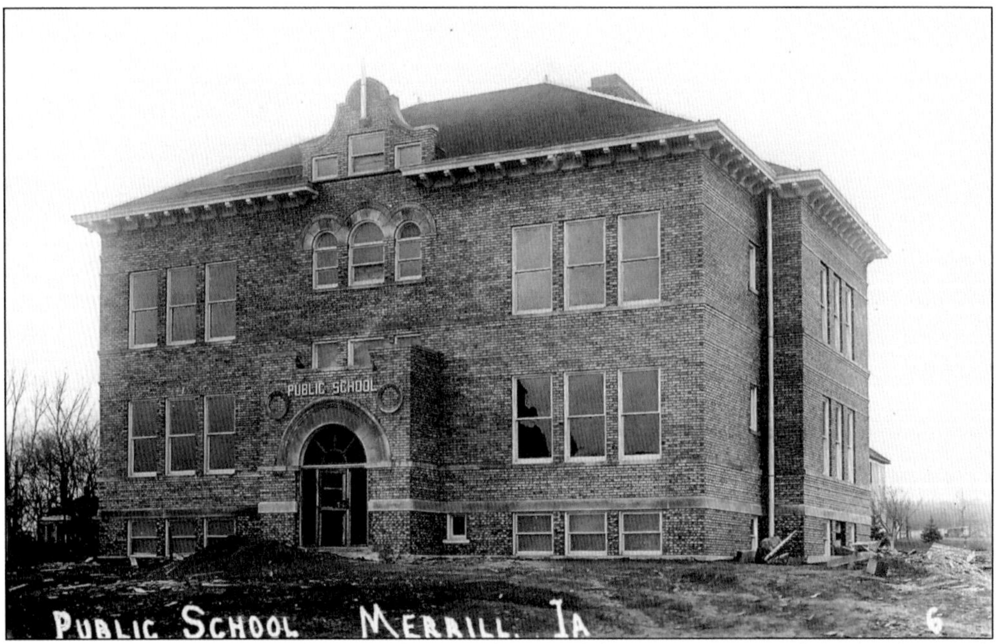

This is a later photograph showing the completion of the construction of the brick Merrill Public School building. The construction cleanup needs to be done, along with landscaping. (Courtesy Judy Forgos.)

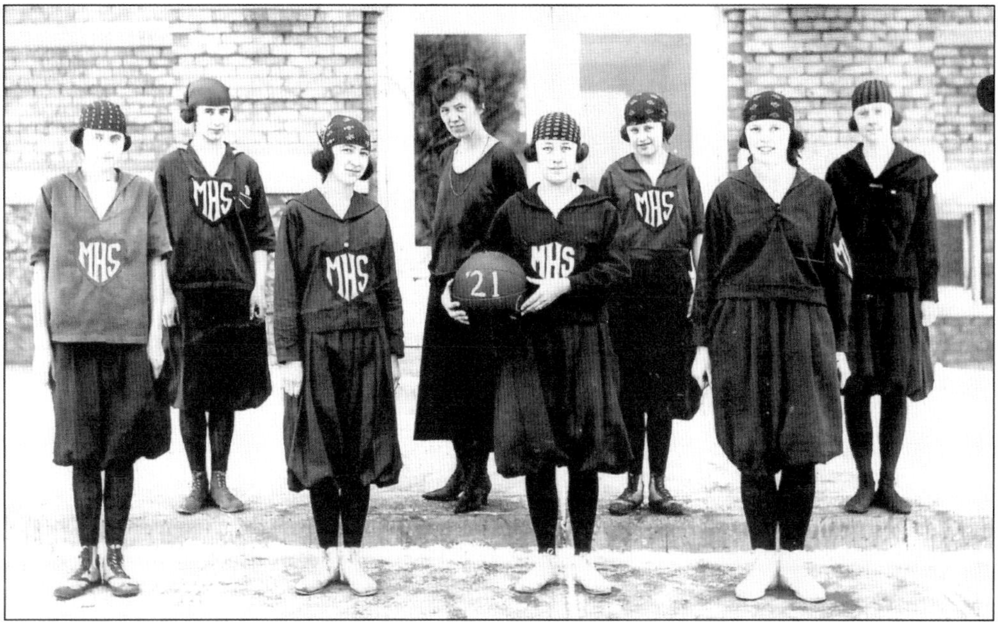

The 1921 Merrill girls' basketball team poses for this wonderful photograph. Ferne King, first row on the far right, is the only player identified. King told stories about how she would ride the family horse from their farm near Adaville into Merrill to attend girls' practice sessions. (Courtesy Plymouth County Historical Museum.)

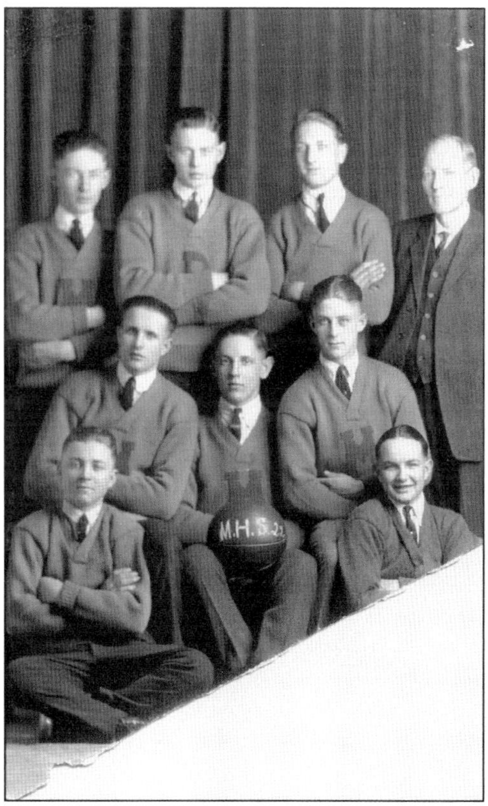

The 1922 Merrill boys' basketball team members are, from left to right, (first row) Wilfred Harris and Clarence Hemphill; (second row) Harold Bauerly, Alvin Hancer, and Fred Kling; (third row) Dwight Hauff, Bill Murphy, Dale Tooker, and Prof. C. F. Clark. (Courtesy Linda Ewin Ziemann.)

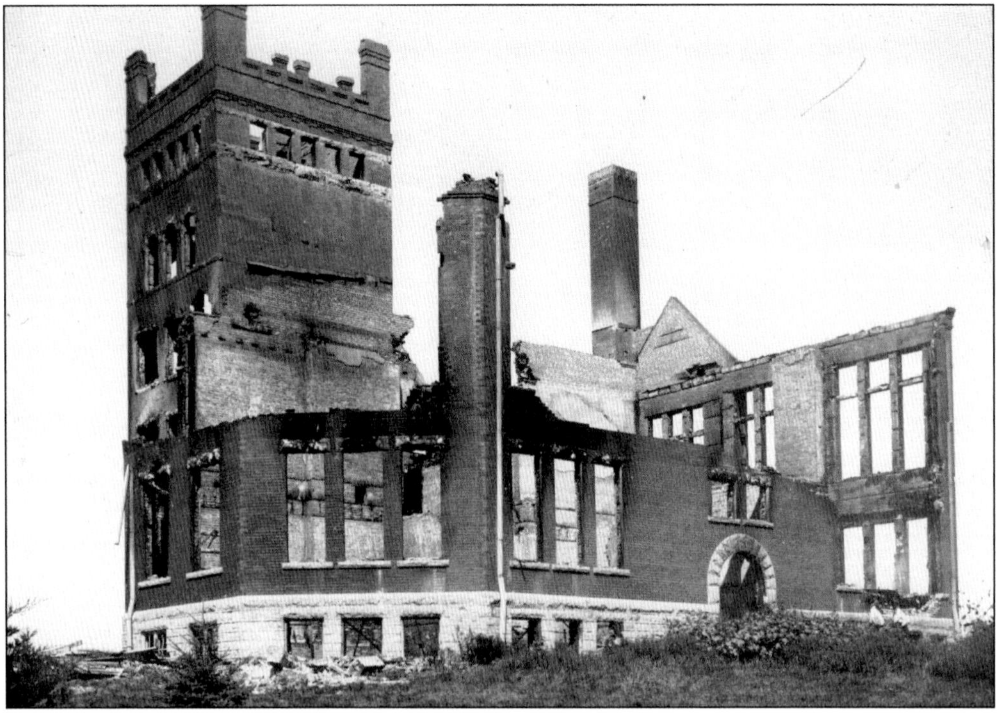

This is a photograph of the remains of the first Western Union College building, which was struck by lightning and destroyed by fire on August 24, 1900. (Courtesy Plymouth County Historical Museum.)

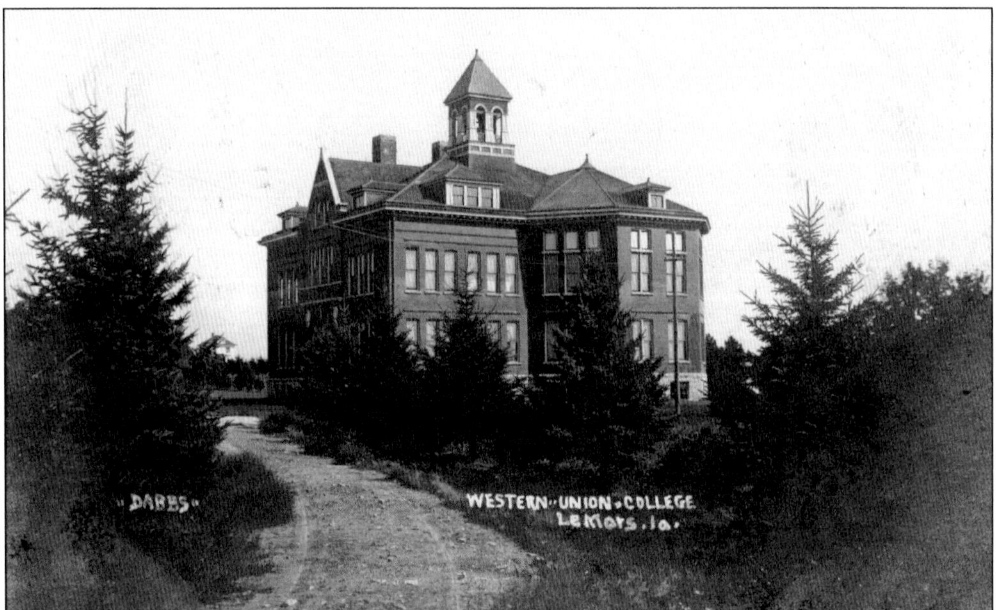

Western Union College was to have opened in September 1900. But when a lightning strike burned the building, it was not until September 1901 that the college officially opened. (Courtesy Plymouth County Historical Museum.)

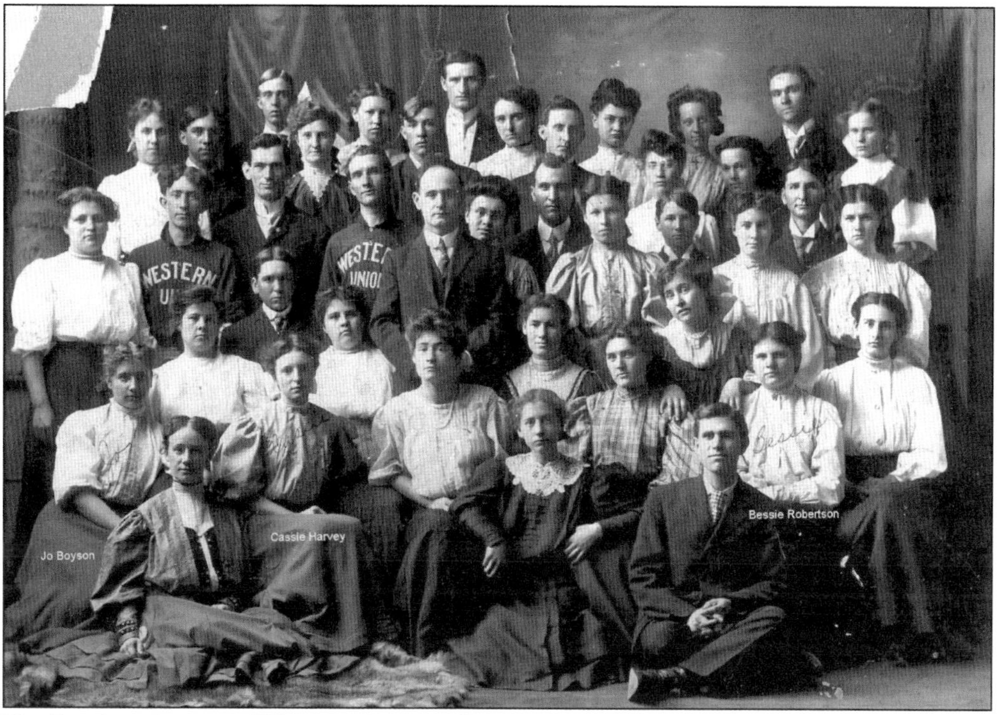

The Excelsior Society of Western Union College poses for this group photograph in 1907. There are three young ladies identified on the photograph in the first row. (Courtesy Tim Tone.)

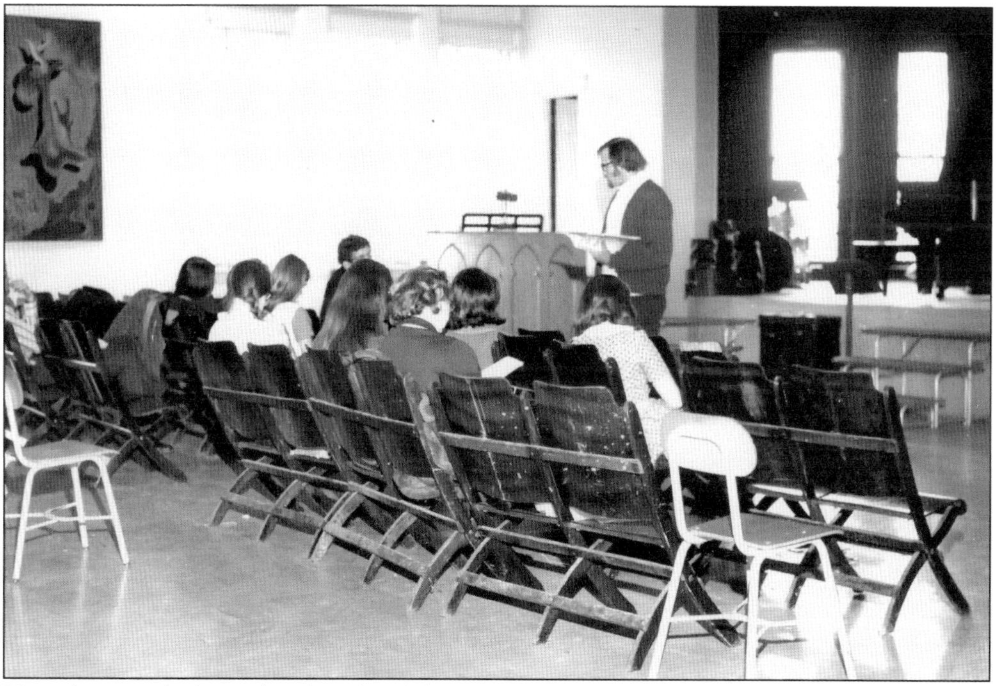

This photograph shows the chapel and theater room on the upper level of Thoren Hall on the Westmar campus, picturing a class of students. Westmar College was the former Western Union College of Le Mars. (Courtesy Plymouth County Historical Museum.)

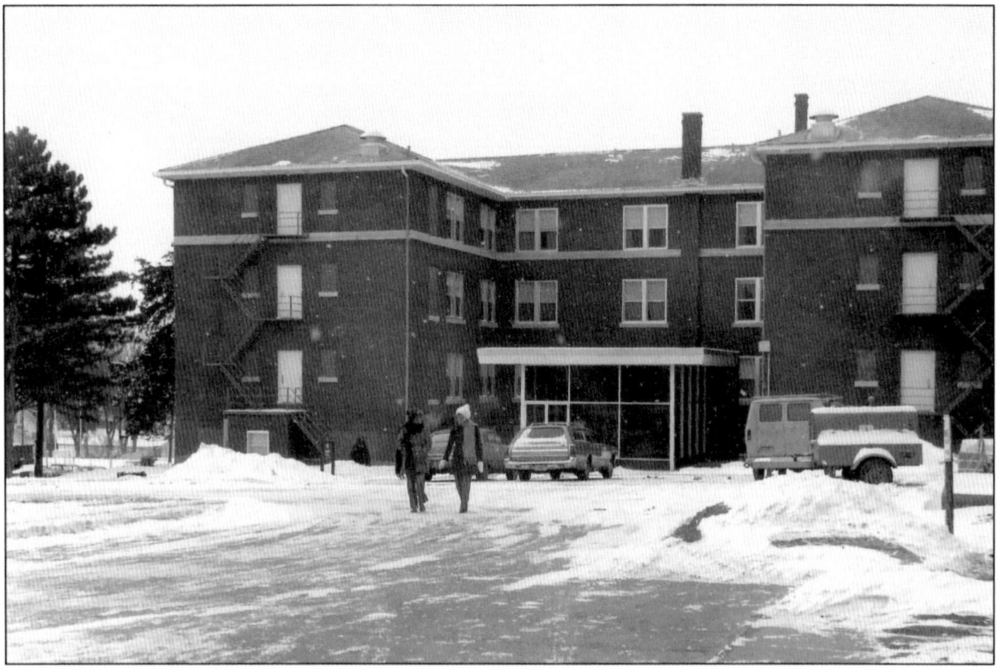

The north side of Bonebrake Hall at Westmar College in Le Mars is seen here. (Courtesy Plymouth County Historical Museum.)

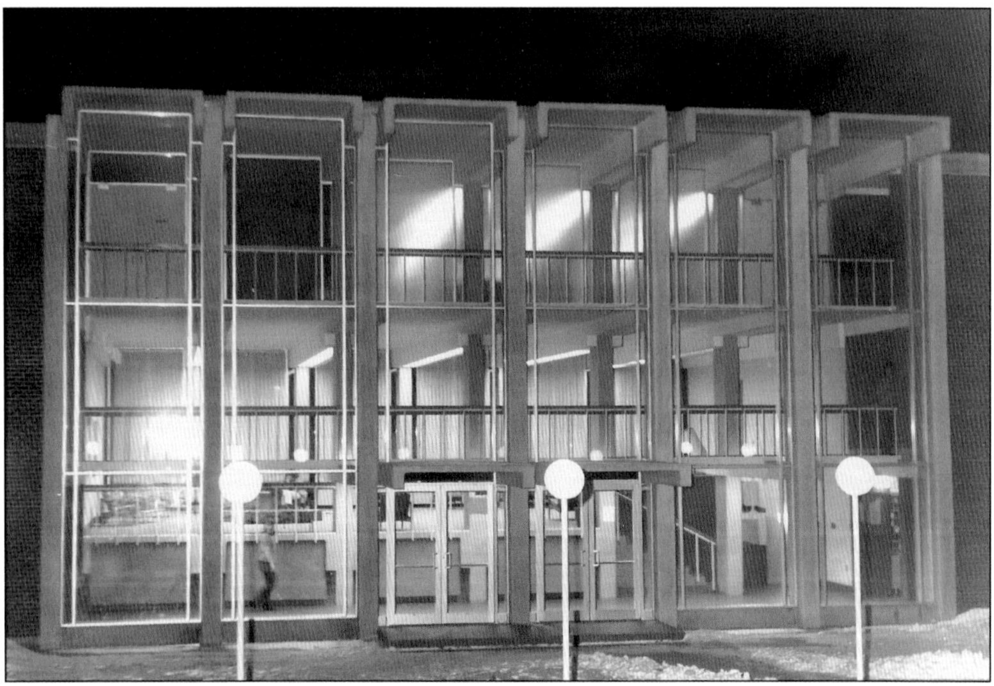

The east side of Wernli Hall, known as the "Fish Bowl," on the former Westmar campus earned its nickname from the glass-windowed walls. Wernli Hall was demolished on March 12, 2002. (Courtesy Plymouth County Historical Museum.)

Nine

A Smattering of County Photographs

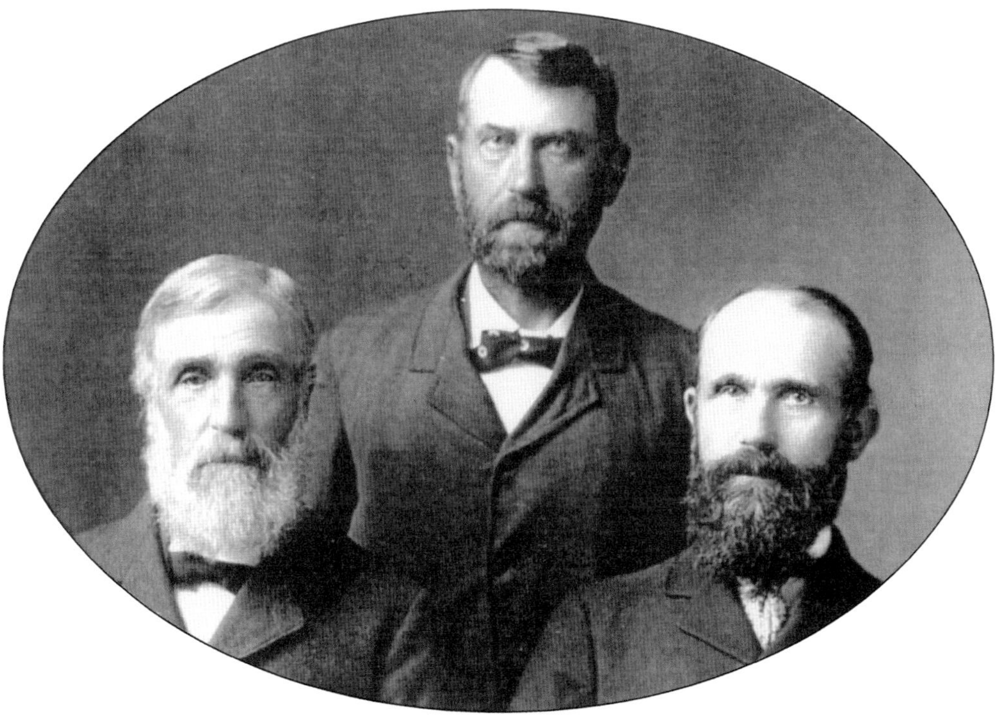

This is a terrific photograph of the three Hentges brothers. John and Nicolas lived and thrived in Le Mars. John opened a clothing store in Le Mars, and Nicolas pursued a career as a plasterer. The third brother, Theodore, also lived in Le Mars for a time but then moved to farm some land near Sheldon and Alton in Sioux County. (Courtesy Duane Biever.)

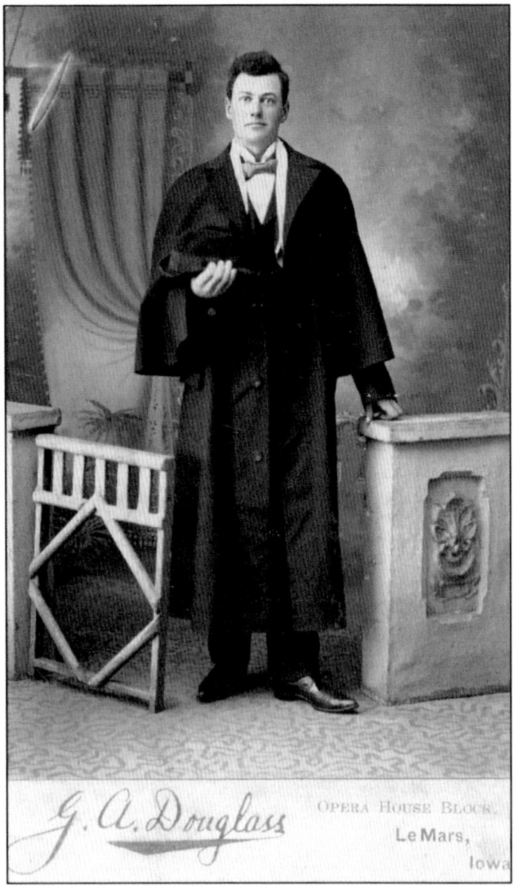

This dapper young man is Ernest Kennedy, son of Watson Moses Kennedy. He was born in November 1876. The G. A. Douglass Studio, located in the Opera House Block in Le Mars, took this photograph. Ernest's uncle Miles Kennedy farmed near Seney. (Courtesy Linda Ewin Ziemann.)

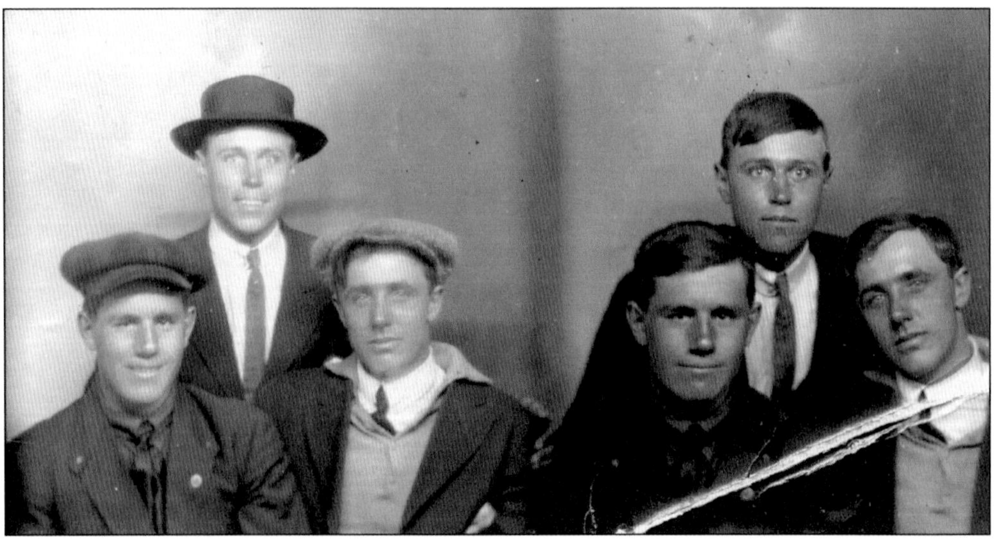

These three friends—Willie Jeffers, Earl Chapman, and Jack Lancaster—all from near Seney, traveled to Sioux City to have this photograph taken. The young men crowded into one of those photo booths with a curtain, each wearing a hat, putting a coin in the machine to get their picture taken several times in rapid succession. (Courtesy Linda Ewin Ziemann.)

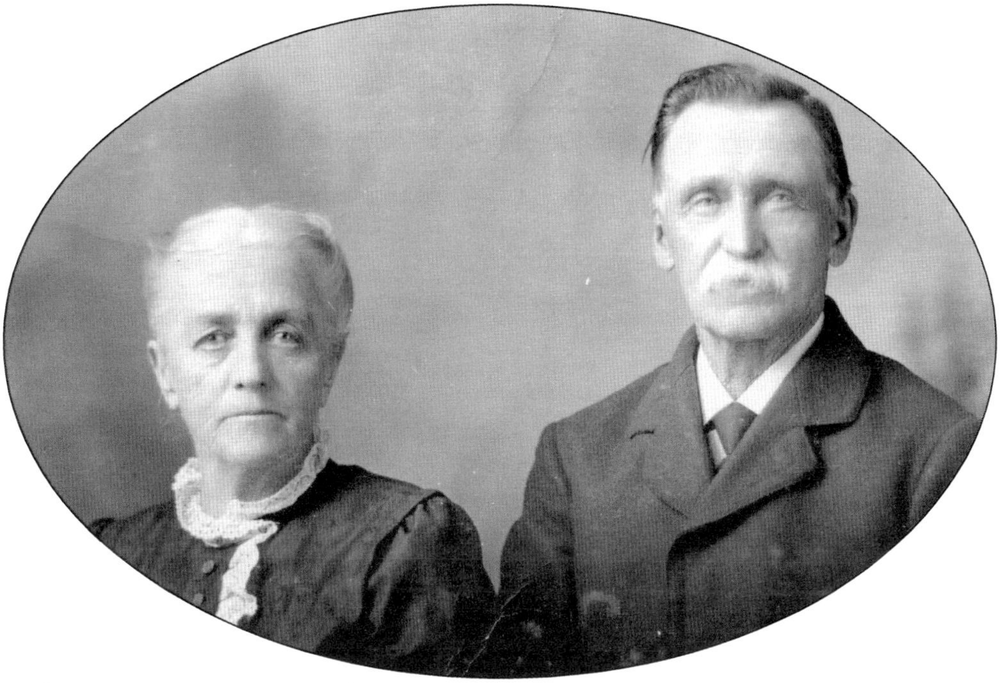

William C. (W. C.) Lancaster and Margaret (Knewstubb) Lancaster, from near Seney, celebrated their 50th wedding anniversary in 1916 and had this photograph done for the occasion. W. C. and Margaret Lancaster were married on August 26, 1866. (Courtesy Linda Ewin Ziemann.)

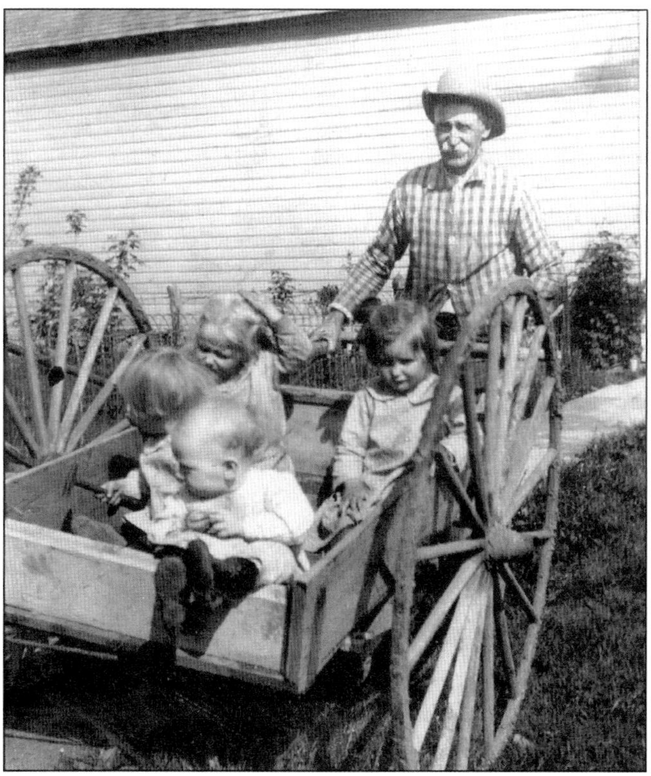

W. C. Lancaster enjoyed wheeling his grandchildren in a wooden cart on his farm. The children are Kenneth Rees in the front, Florence Penning at center, Margaret Moore in the back left with her hand up, and Mabel Penning in the back on the right. Margaret has grabbed her head with a stressed expression on her face. Her cousin, Florence, seated just in front of her, is turned sideways and holding a mallet. (Courtesy Linda Ewin Ziemann.)

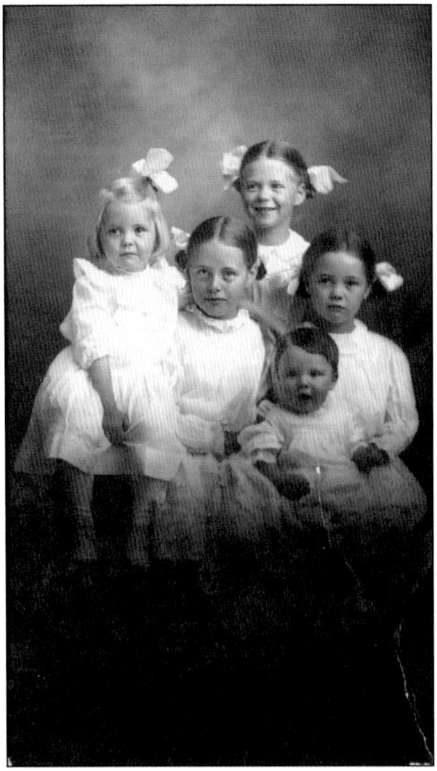

This is a lovely family photograph of the small children of Warren J. and Birdie King of Adaville. The children were born in the early 1900s and raised in Plymouth County. The girls, donning bows in their hair, are, from left to right, Freda, Elva, Ferne, and Ione. The youngest, a son named Stanley, is being held by Ione. (Courtesy Linda Ewin Ziemann.)

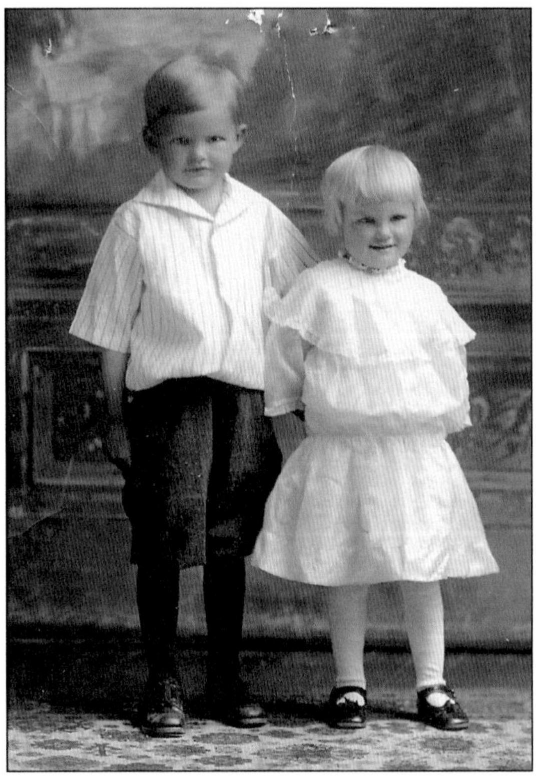

The Doering siblings photographed together are George (born in 1912) and Irene (born in 1914). (Courtesy Plymouth County Historical Museum.)

Alfred Esla, age four, and Albert Gerald (Jerry) Tone, age two, were brothers all dressed up in 1922. They are siblings to Hope, Ransom, Bart, Ruth, Elaine, and Naomi, all children of Grace (Adams) Tone and Esla Alfred Tone who lived near Hawarden. Alfred Tone later farmed in Plymouth County. (Courtesy Tim Tone.)

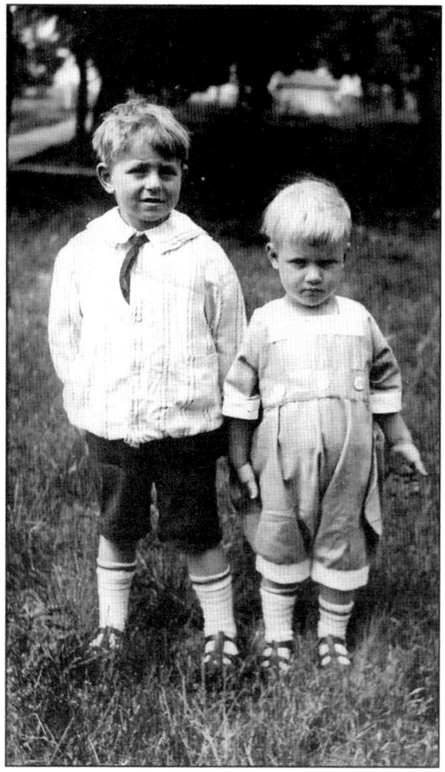

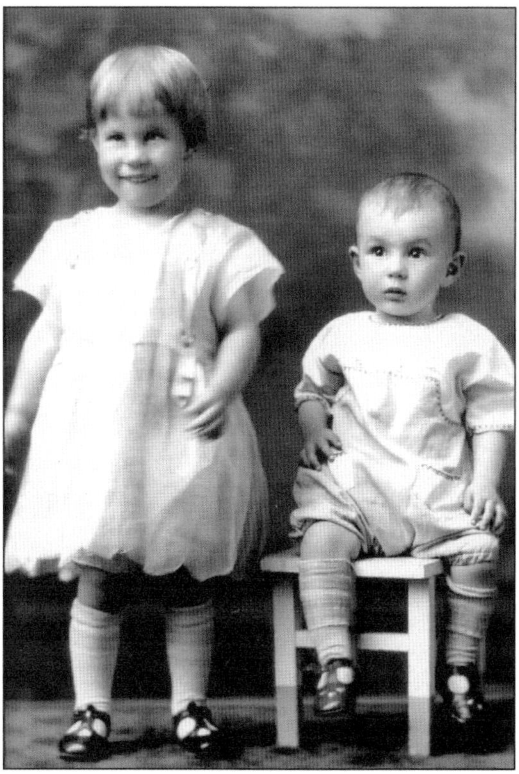

Ethel and Vernon Ewin, the young children of Charles and Gladys Ewin of Seney, are photographed together in 1924. (Courtesy Linda Ewin Ziemann.)

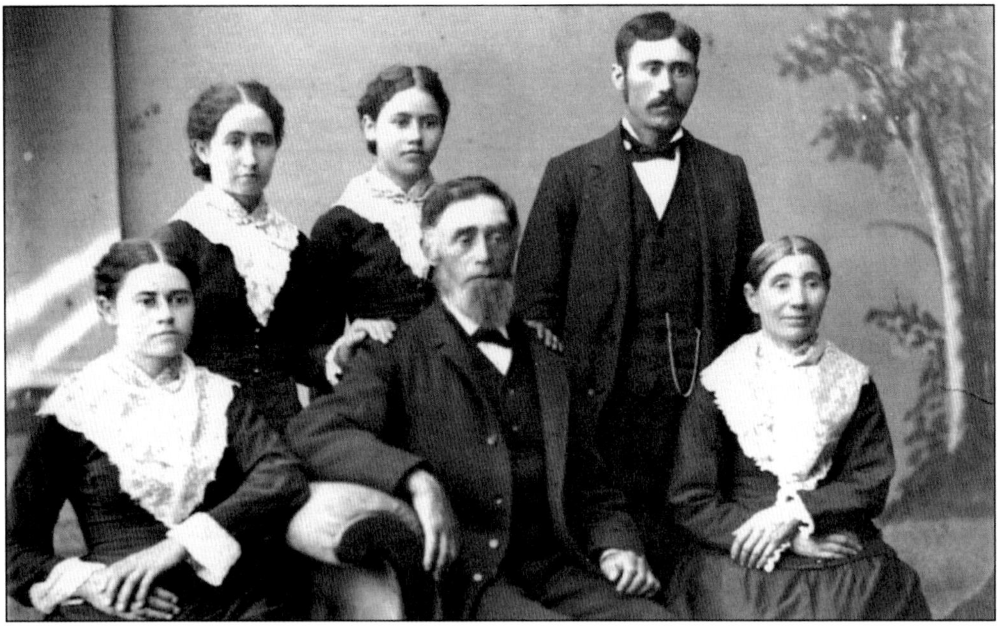

In this *c.* 1885 photograph, John Schneider and his wife, Katharine (Winter) Schneider, seated at the right in the first row, are pictured with their children in birth order, Philip Schneider, Anna M. (Schneider) Bock, Fredericke Schneider, and Mary Martha (Schneider) Koenig. John is decorated as the first permanent settler in Plymouth County. He settled in 1856 on what is now Section 4 of Hungerford Township. (Courtesy Justin Herbst.)

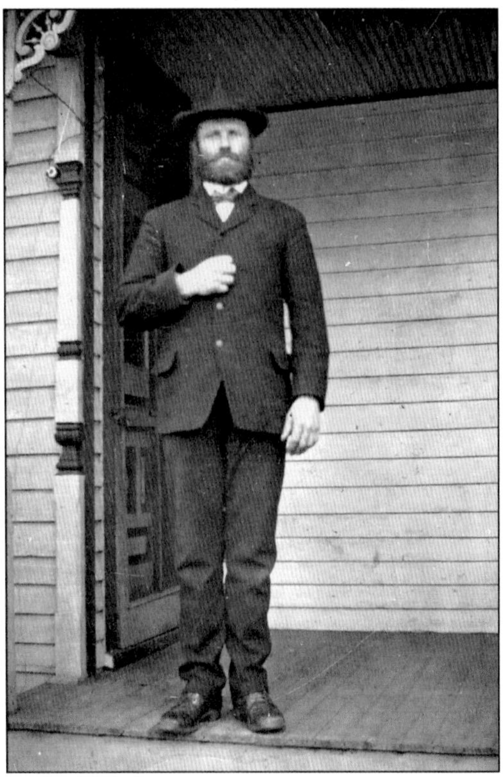

Bert Reeves of Elgin Township posed for this picture on the front porch of his parents' home in Seney shortly after 1900. Bert's parents were Arthur Reeves and Elizabeth (Mercer) Reeves. (Courtesy Duane and Vivien Reeves.)

Watson D. Kennedy and Ida Alderson were married at the home of the bride in Seney on July 22, 1903. They both were members of families that had called Seney home for several years. (Courtesy Linda Ewin Ziemann.)

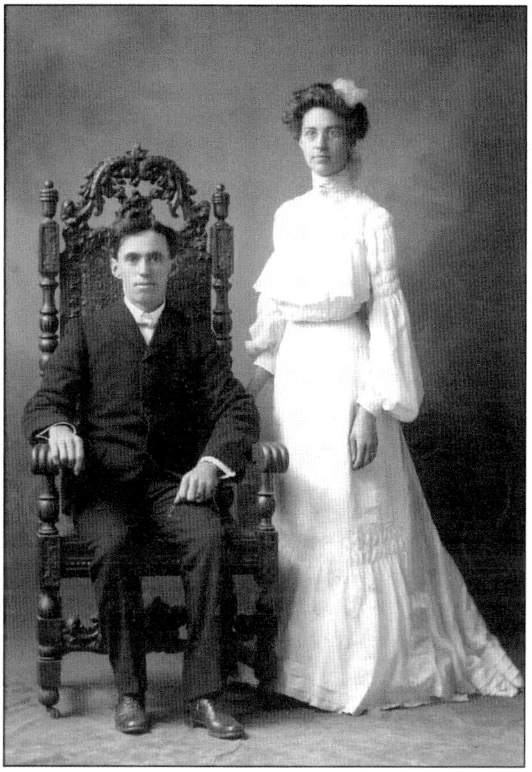

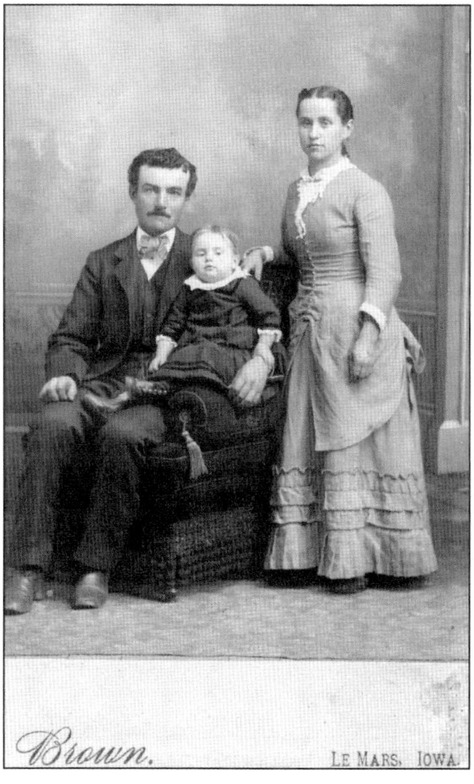

Charles and Edith Brown are photographed with their daughter, Amy, in this early family photograph. This couple farmed near Adaville. (Courtesy Nancy Tindall Yoder.)

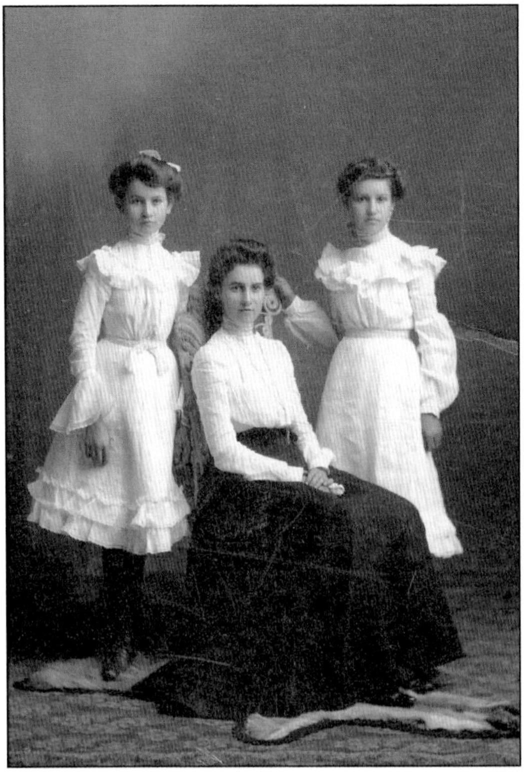

These three lovely sisters are Mary, Amy, and Alice Brown, the daughters of Charles and Edith Brown of near Adaville. Mary became a schoolteacher and suffered a sudden death in 1921. Amy married J. D. Tindall, and they farmed near Dalton, west of Le Mars. Alice married John Bryant and farmed in Plymouth County. (Courtesy Nancy Tindall Yoder.)

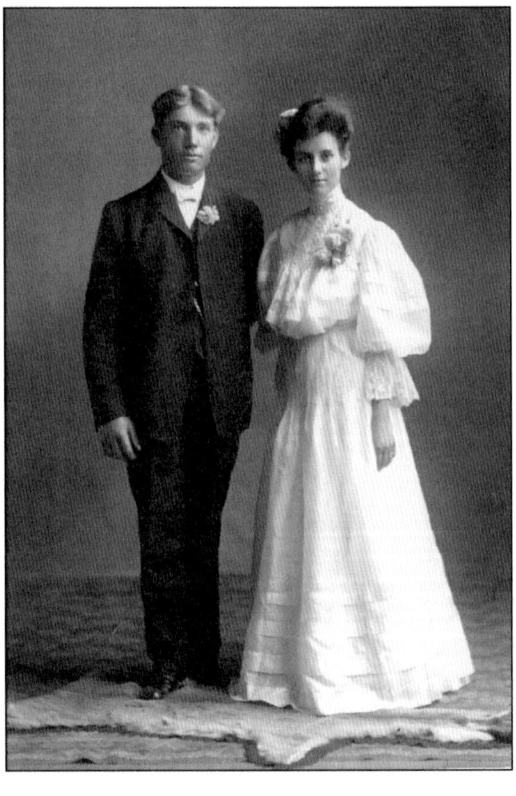

J. D. (Jack) Tindall married Amy Brown at the home of the bride's parents in Johnson Township on June 28, 1905. Jack and Amy raised a family of seven children on their family farm near Dalton. Jack Tindall bought the farm in 1914. (Courtesy Nancy Tindall Yoder.)

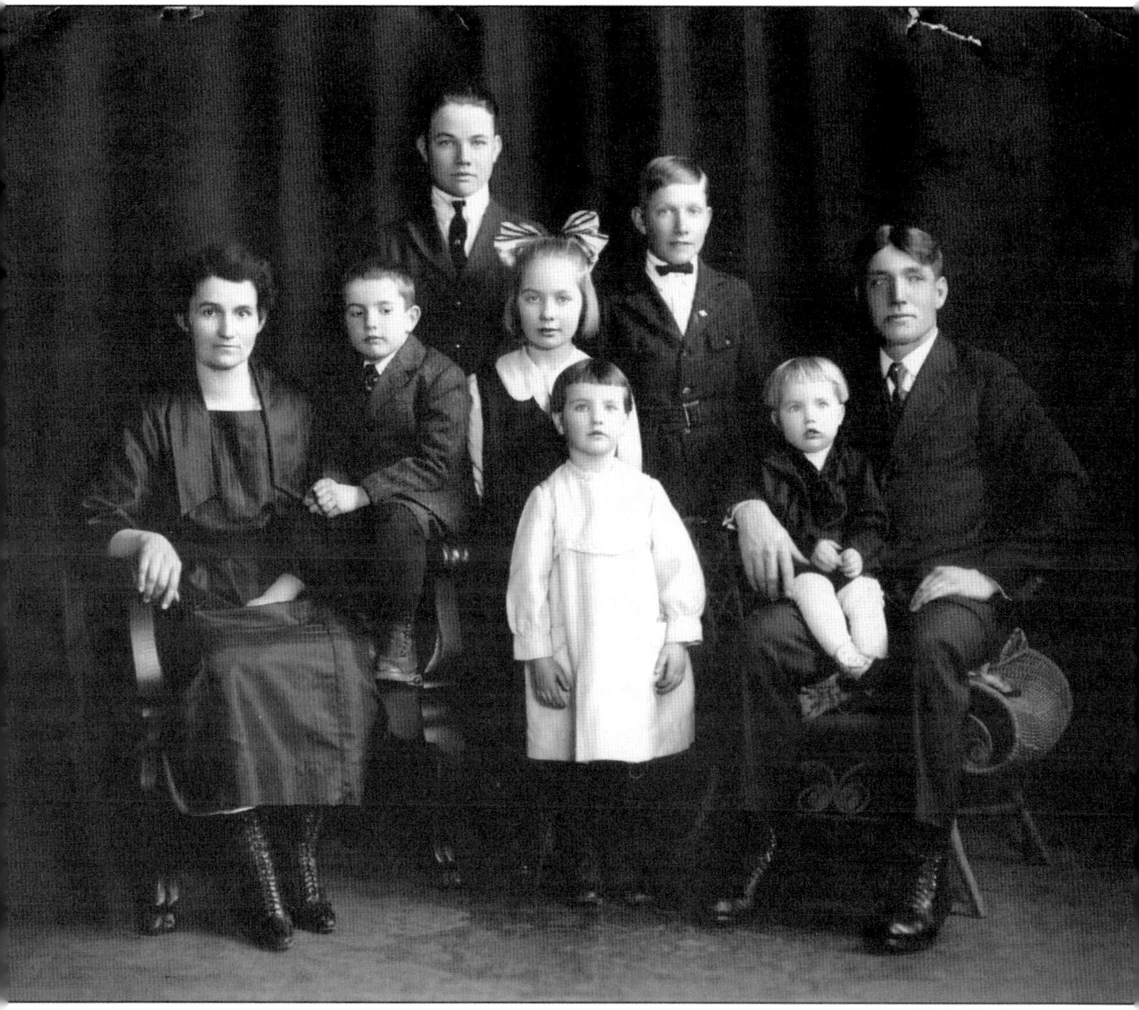

J. D. and Amy Tindall are photographed together with their children. The picture was taken before the birth of their youngest daughter, Mary. Mildred is standing in the front. The other family members are, from left to right, (first row) mother Amy, Robert, Stanley, and father J. D.; (second row) Clark, Florence, and Richard. (Courtesy Nancy Tindall Yoder.)

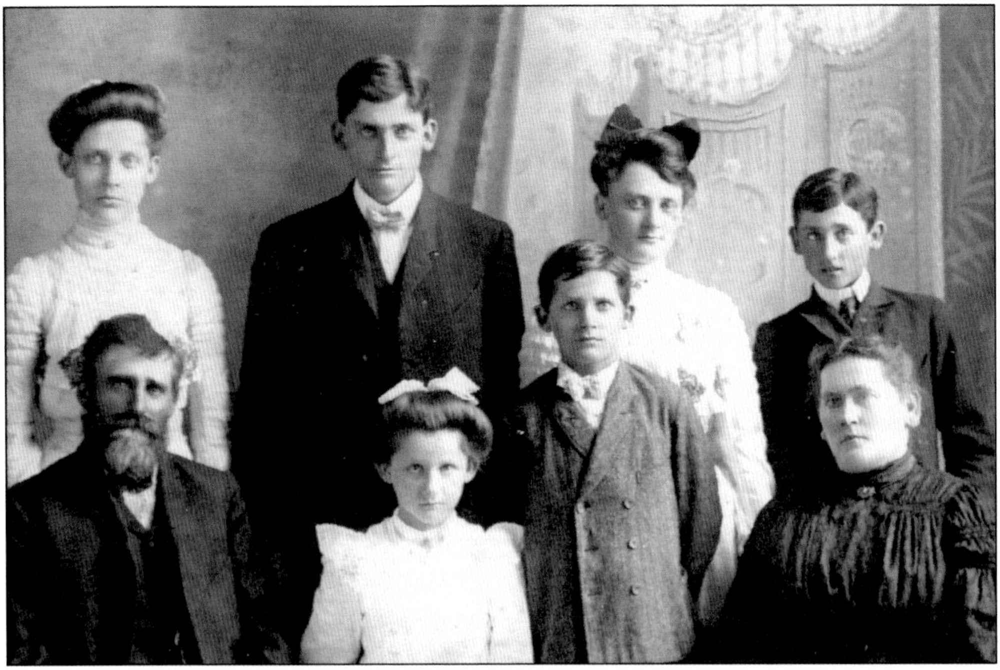

The family of J. G. Grebner of Johnson Township poses for a group photograph. The family members are, from left to right, (first row) George, Clara, Clarence, and Hattie; (second row) Lizzie, John, Maggie, and Walter. (Courtesy Claire and Phyllis Allen.)

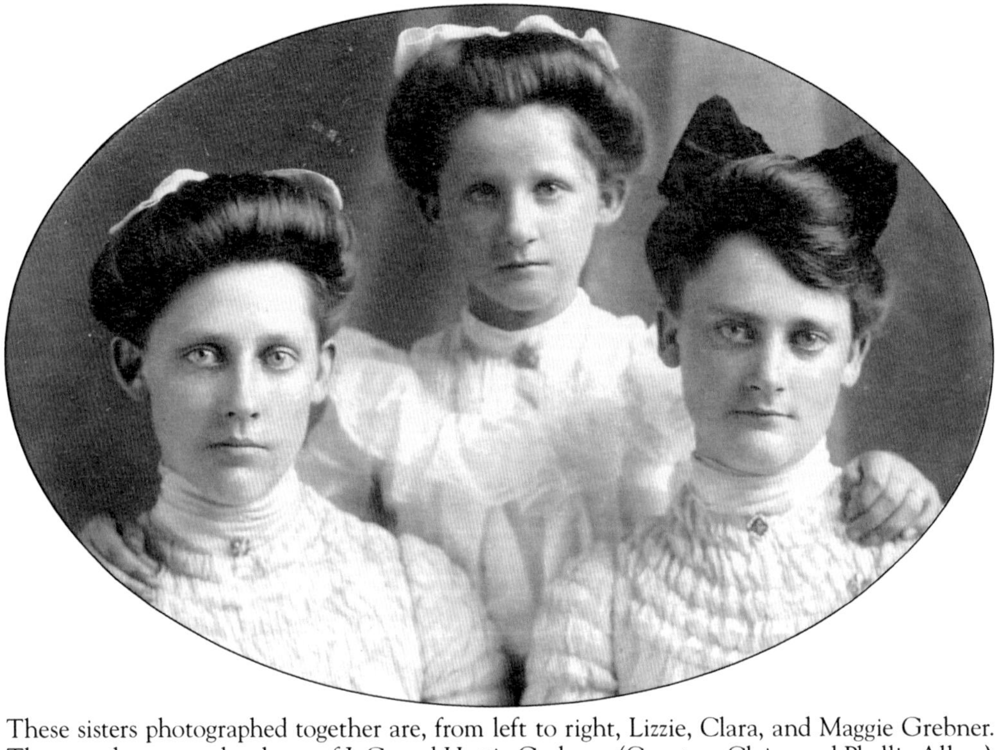

These sisters photographed together are, from left to right, Lizzie, Clara, and Maggie Grebner. They are the young daughters of J. G. and Hattie Grebner. (Courtesy Claire and Phyllis Allen.)

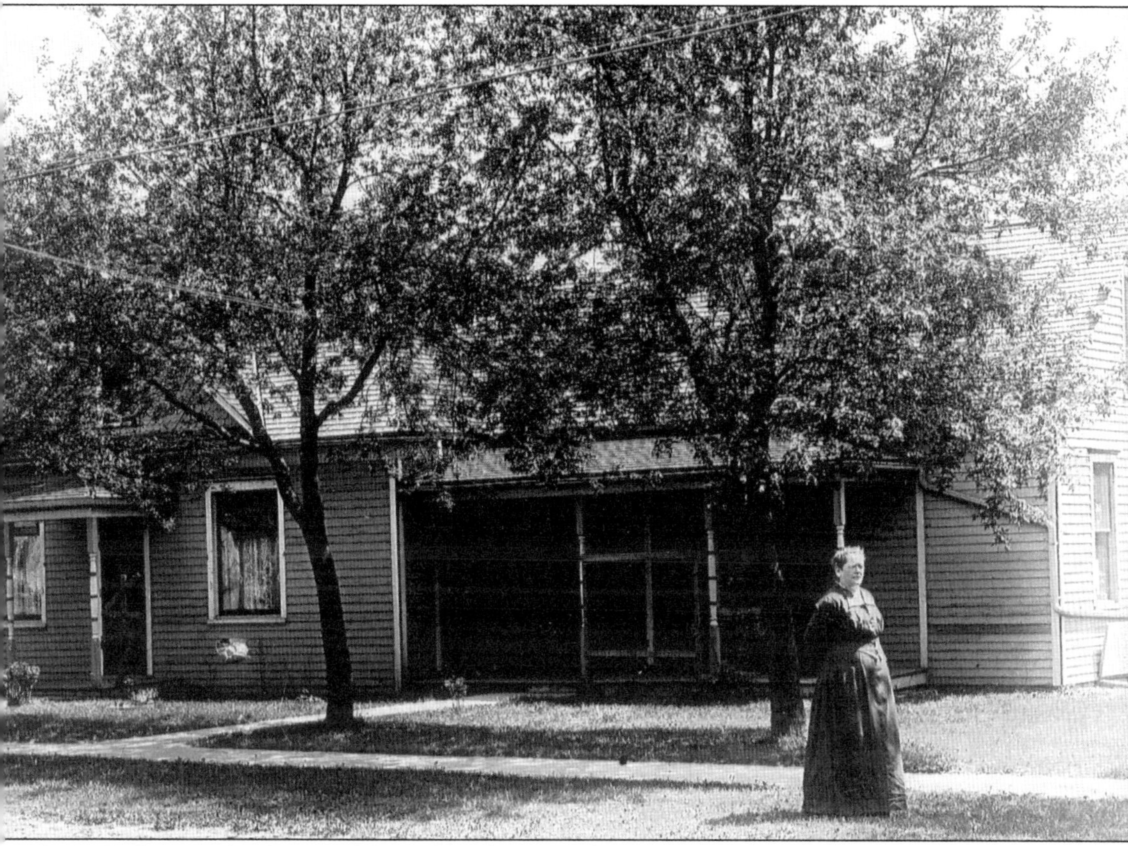

J. G. Grebner and wife moved from their farm in Johnson Township to a residence in Merrill. Hattie Grebner is shown standing in the front yard. (Courtesy Claire and Phyllis Allen.)

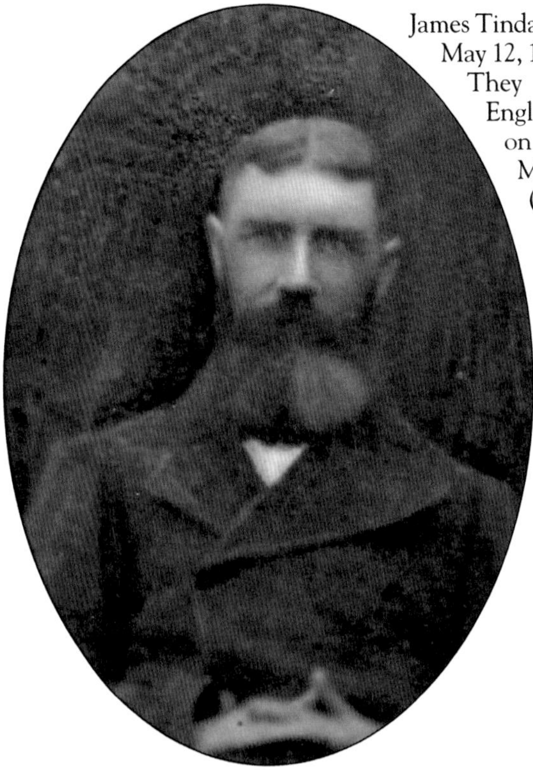

James Tindall started for America on his wedding day on May 12, 1880, with his bride, Agnes Galbraith Currie. They came from Chatton, Northumberland, England. After reaching America, they settled on farmland in Plymouth County. He died on May 7, 1903, leaving Agnes and six children. (Courtesy Nancy Tindall Yoder.)

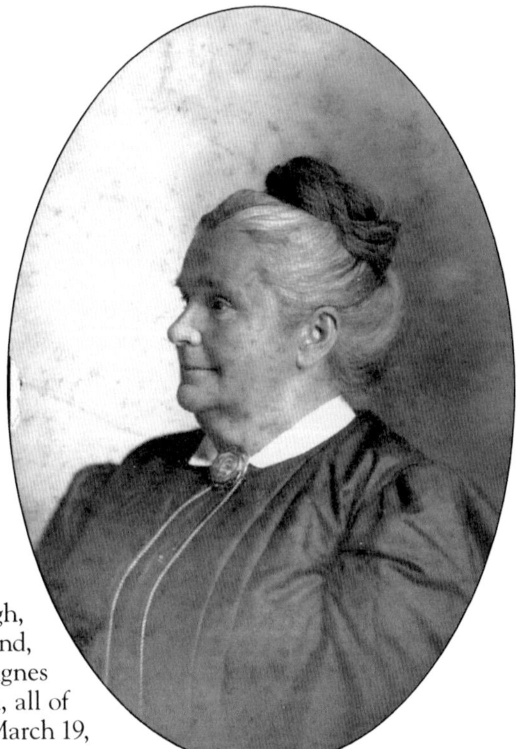

Agnes Galbraith Currie was born in Edinburgh, Scotland, and later settled in Chatton, England, to help her uncle who was a pastor there. Agnes married James Tindall. They had six children, all of them born in Plymouth County. She died on March 19, 1935. (Courtesy Nancy Tindall Yoder.)

Student and teacher are shown in this 1909 photograph. They are M. Faye Burrill (left) and her sister, Pearl Burrill. Pearl was an early Plymouth County schoolteacher before her marriage to Walter Grebner in 1912. (Courtesy Duane and Vivien Reeves.)

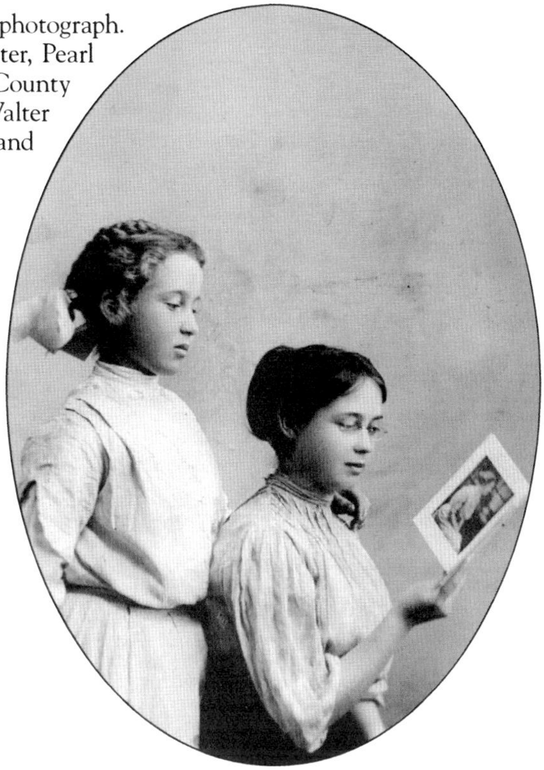

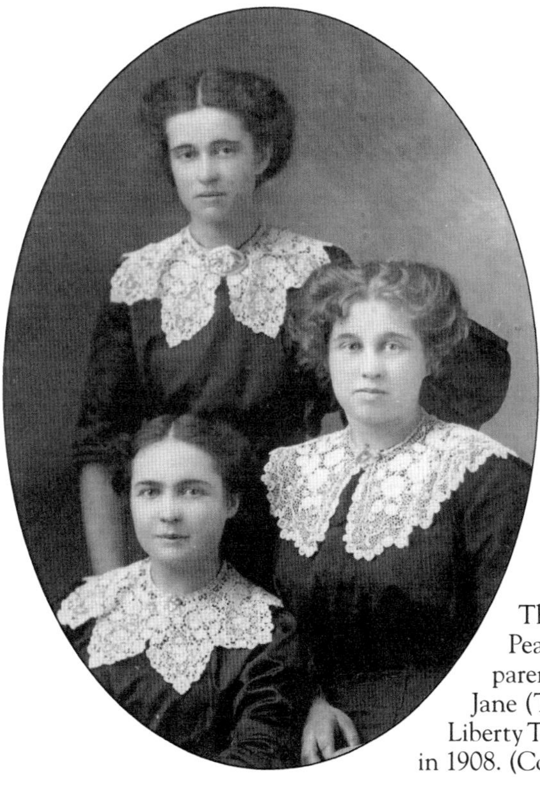

The Burrill sisters are, from left to right, Pearl, Eva (standing), and Florence. Their parents were George Henry Burrill and Mary Jane (Tullis) Burrill. They farmed in Johnson and Liberty Townships before moving to Union Township in 1908. (Courtesy Duane and Vivien Reeves.)

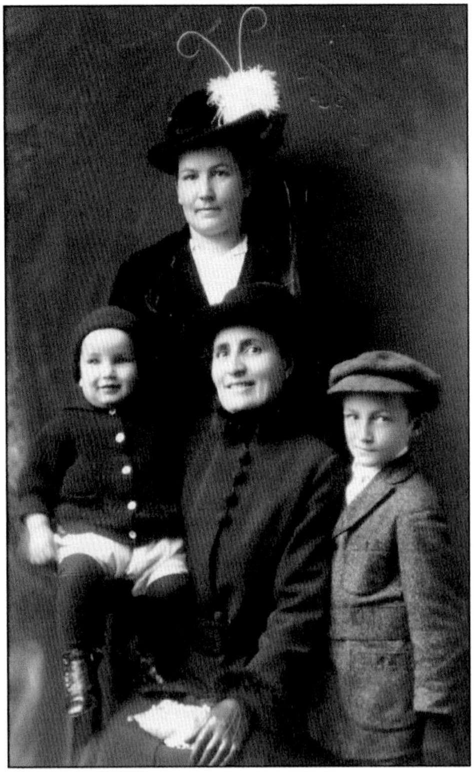

This photograph was taken in Sioux City. Mae Parker Hemphill is the lady in the back. In the first row, from left to right, are Gerald George "Bill" Hemphill, Ida Hemphill (their aunt), and Wallace Kyle (Wally) Hemphill. Wally and Bill were the sons of Mae and Samuel Hemphill. The Hemphill family lived in Merrill for several years. (Courtesy Pat Hemphill.)

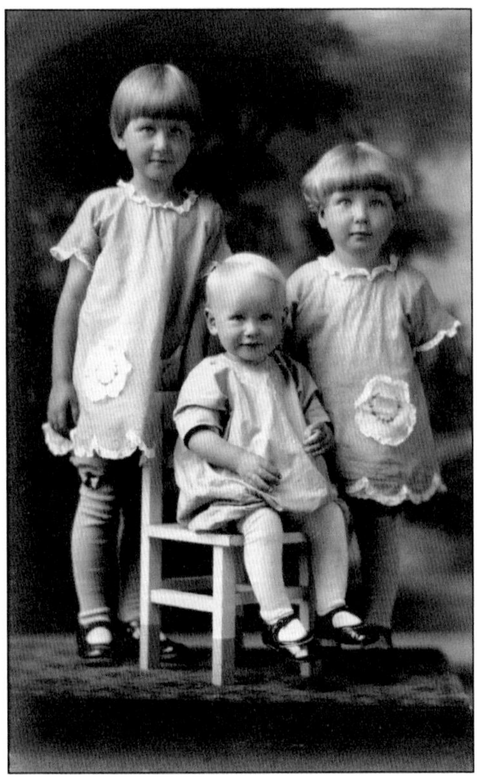

Three Osborne siblings are pictured together in this photograph. They are, from left to right, Georgine and Lois, with their brother Bill seated in the chair. They were the children of George and Agnes Osborne. The photographer was Dickensheets of Le Mars. (Courtesy Marvin Cooper.)

This 1895 family group is the daughters and one granddaughter of Mathew and Ella Ewin of Seney. They are, from left to right, (first row) Iona Ewin and Minnie Mae Witt, who is standing in front of her mother, Nellie; (second row) Mary Effie Ewin and Nellie Witt of Le Mars. (Courtesy Linda Ewin Ziemann.)

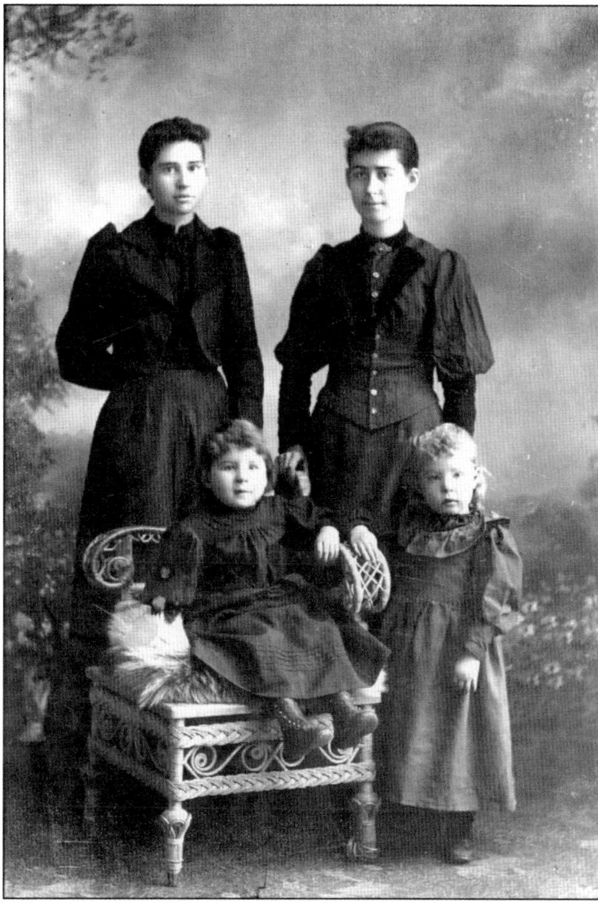

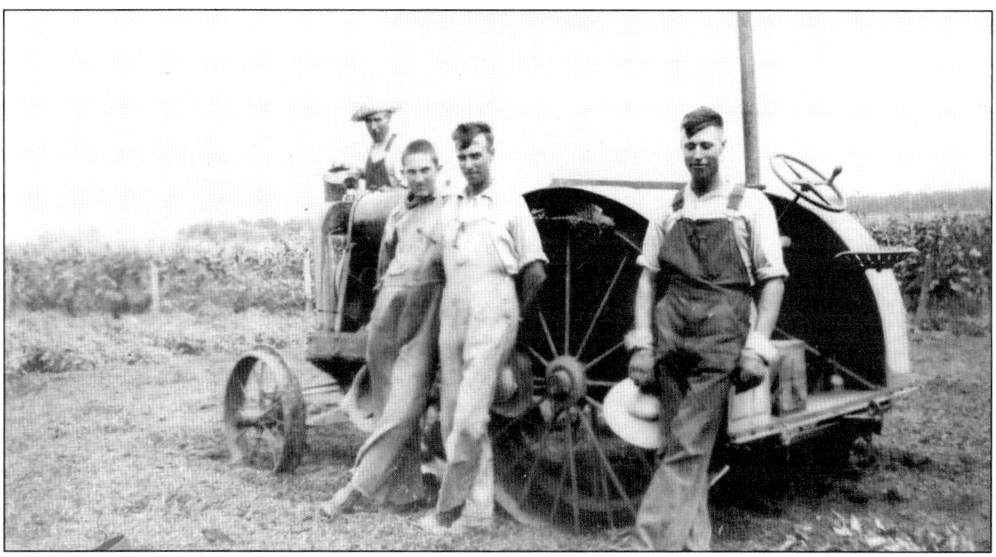

The year is 1921, and it is threshing time at Earl Chapman's farm in Elgin Township, Plymouth County. Chapman is the young man standing at the far right. Earl's father, Elam Chapman, is the older man wearing a straw hat at the far left. (Courtesy Marvin Cooper.)

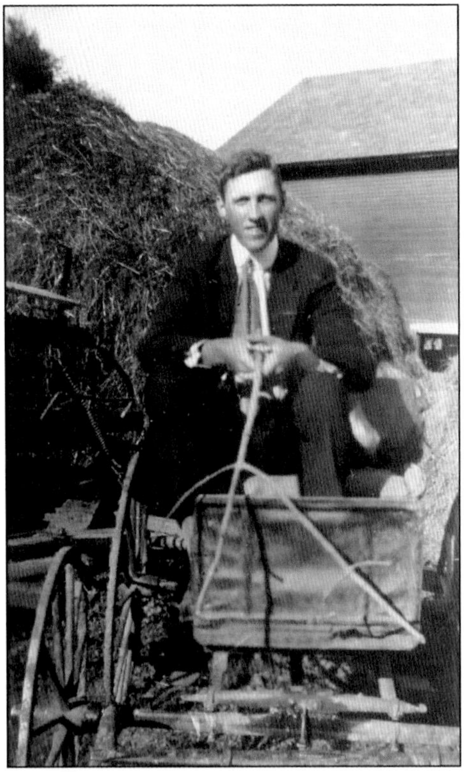

Orville Cooper sits on the pony cart to have his picture taken. Orville Cooper married Fern Chapman, the daughter of Elam and Lizzie Chapman, in February 1928. (Courtesy Marvin Cooper.)

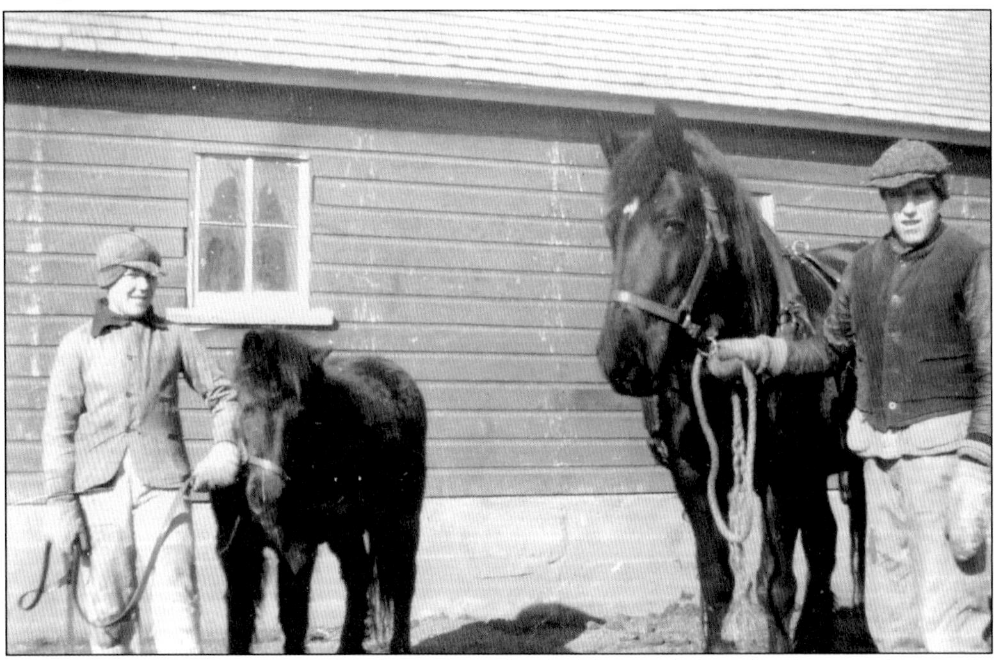

Marvin Cooper is standing at left holding the colt, while his uncle Orville Chapman has a tight hold on the mama horse. The Chapman and Cooper families farmed across the road from each other. The Chapman farm was in Sioux County, and the Orville Cooper farm was in Plymouth County. (Courtesy Marvin Cooper.)

BIBLIOGRAPHY

Central Telephone Company. *Central Telephone Directory for Le Mars, Iowa*. LaCrosse, Wisconsin: 1955.

Downing, Dr. Wendell L. *History of Wasmer Post No. 241*. Le Mars, Iowa: *Le Mars Globe Post*, 1945.

Larson, Arthur. *Le Mars—The Story of a Prairie Town*. Le Mars, Iowa: *Le Mars Daily Sentinel*, 1969.

Second Annual Directory of Plymouth County, Iowa. Le Mars, Iowa: The *Le Mars Post*, 1897.

Taylor, Karen, Joyce Thorson, and Lois Helseth. *Our Life 1882-1982 Akron, Iowa*. Akron and Le Mars, Iowa: *Akron Register-Tribune* and *Le Mars Daily Sentinel*, 1982.

Walsh, James. *Black Loam of Iowa*. Lake Mills, Iowa: 1963.